Labor essays 2001

for the people: reclaiming our government

reclaiming our
government

Labor essays 2001

Edited by Dennis Glover and Glenn Patmore
Series Editor: Gary Jungwirth

First published in 2000 by
Pluto Press Australia Pty Ltd
Locked Bag 199, Annandale, NSW 2038
in association with the Australian Fabian Society (inc.),
PO Box 2707X, Melbourne, Vic 3001

Cover design by Antart Design

Edited by Lucy Sussex

Index by Neale Towart

Typeset by Chapter 8 Pty Ltd

Printed and bound by Griffin Press Pty Ltd

Australian Cataloguing-in-Publication Data

For the people: labor essays 2001.

  Bibliography.
  Includes index.
  ISBN 1 86403 143 3

  1. Australia — Politics and government — 1990–.
  2. Australia — Economic policy — 1990–.
  3. Australia — Social policy — 1990–. I. Glover, Dennis.
  II. Patmore, G. (Glenn Anthony), 1961–. III. Jungwirth, Gary. (Series:
  Labour essays; 2000)

320.994

contents

list of contributors

John Alford is Associate Professor of Public Sector Management at Melbourne Business School, University of Melbourne, and coeditor of *The Contract State: Public Management and the Kennett Government.*

Mark Considine is Associate Professor of Political Science at the University of Melbourne. His most recent book is *The Enterprise University* (with Simon Marginson), Cambridge University Press, 2000. He was joint winner of the American Society for Public Administration's Marshall E. Dimmock Award in 2000 for his international research on the use of markets and networks in new governance systems.

Eva Cox is a long-term activist, still trying to make the world more civil and still researching why the best intentions so often don't produce good change. She is paid to do this through a senior lectureship in the Faculty of Humanities and Social Science at the University of Technology, Sydney.

Michael Di Francesco is a lecturer in the School of Economics and Political Science at the University of Sydney, where he teaches Australian politics and public sector management, and coordinates the graduate program in Public Policy. He is an editor of *The Drawing Board,* a new on-line review of Australian public affairs.

Lindy Edwards is undertaking a Ph.D in the Graduate Program of Public Policy at the Australian National University. She has previously worked as a policy adviser in the Department of the Prime Minister and Cabinet and as a journalist for the *Sydney Morning Herald.* She is currently completing a book entitled *How to Argue with an Economist: a Beginner's Guide.*

Rhys Edwards is an economic adviser to the Premier of Tasmania. He is a graduate of the University of Tasmania and

Oxford University. He has worked in the public sector and as an academic researcher.

Craig Emerson is the Member for Rankin in the Federal Parliament. He is chair of the Labor Caucus Living Standards and Economic Development Committee. He was an economic adviser to former Prime Minister Bob Hawke and has a Ph.D in economics.

Dennis Glover is a political adviser to the Federal Leader of the ALP, Kim Beazley, and a former university researcher. He has a B.A. (Hons) from Monash University and a Ph.D from the University of Cambridge. He has published articles in numerous academic and political journals.

Katrina Gorjanicyn is lecturer in social policy at RMIT University, City Campus, where she teaches public policy and gender studies.

Series Editor *Gary Jungwirth* is President of the Australian Fabian Society.

Andrew Leigh is a Frank Knox scholar at Harvard University's John F. Kennedy School of Government. He served as a policy adviser to the Labor Shadow Minister for Trade, Senator Peter Cook, from 1998–2000. He is a frequent contributor to *Australian Quarterly* and numerous academic journals and newspapers.

Tony Moore has worked as a documentary film-maker and journalist for the ABC, writing, researching and directing many programs, including 'Nobody's Children', 'The Devil You Know', 'One Australia?', 'Four Corners', 'Foreign Correspondent' and the 'Time Frame' ASIO history special. Tony is currently undertaking a Ph.D on the mapping of Australian bohemia in the History Department of the University of Sydney.

Glenn Patmore is a lecturer in law at the University of Melbourne. He teaches courses in law and democracy and constitutional and administrative law. He has law degrees from Monash and Queens University (Canada). He has published articles in numerous legal and political journals.

Lindsay Tanner is the Federal Labor Member for Melbourne and Shadow Minister for Finance and Consumer Affairs. His latest book was *Open Australia* (Pluto Press 1999).

Lucas Walsh has just completed a Ph.D at Monash University in which he examines the relationship between recent education reform and liberal democracy in Australia.

Sally Young is a Ph.D candidate in the Political Science Department at the University of Melbourne. She is investigating political advertising in Australian federal elections. Sally has seven years' experience working for the Commonwealth Government — most recently as a researcher and writer. She is currently a tutor in the Political Science Department, University of Melbourne.

preface

by the Series Editor of Labor Essays

The Australian Fabian Society publishes *Labor Essays* as part of
our commitment to encouraging debate about the future of
social democracy. This year's edition follows in the tradition
begun by last year's volume but there are some important differences. *New Voices for Social Democracy: Labor Essays
1999–2000* was a survey of the trends and influences in the
future direction of social democracy. The contributors were
drawn from a predominantly younger set of commentators
from the centre-left. Essayists commented on 'The Third
Way', 'stake-holderism', neo-liberalism, internationalism and
post-modernism. In contrast, this year's volume, *For the People:
Government and the Public Sector*, focuses on the more specific
topic of the challenges confronting contemporary Australian
government. These arise from the introduction of new technology, budget cutbacks, outsourcing and globalisation.

Our contributors are emerging and prominent public
intellectuals, policy-makers and expert academics who are
well-placed to comment on the future of public administration. Essayists have been given a free hand to range as widely
or as narrowly as they please, and encouraged to offer bold
critiques and practical solutions. Our authors have written on
a diverse range of important topics. These include rethinking
the relationship between representatives and citizens, reinventing the role of government in terms of taxation and
spending, curbing the excesses of the contract state, meeting
the challenges of providing government services over the
Internet and building a civic community on-line, as well as

xi

enhancing the capacity of political parties and government to produce new and innovative public policy. The result is a challenging and thought-provoking philosophical and practical agenda for reform from the Australian centre-left.

Like *New Voices*, this year's anthology addresses itself to the broad labor movement and to the centre-left in general, including supporters of all non-conservative parties, as well as to the general reader and students of Australian politics.

Our editors are political adviser Dennis Glover and academic Glenn Patmore and I would like to thank our editors for their work in preparing this volume. Once again, the Fabian Society has teamed up with Pluto Press to publish *Labor Essays*. I would like to acknowledge the involvement of Tony Moore and Pluto for their commitment to publishing important political debates. Pluto Press is now the pre-eminent publishing house in Australia for issues concerning social democracy.

Gary Jungwirth
President, Australian Fabian Society
Series Editor of Labor Essays

about the Australian Fabian Society

The Fabian tradition is one of achieving social progress through research and education. Bernard Shaw and Sidney Webb began it in 1883, and generations of Fabians have placed a stamp on every facet of British and Australian society. Gough Whitlam adopted the Fabian approach from the day he entered parliament, and the seminal 1972 Whitlam policy speech was a drawing together of the threads of twenty years of systematic Fabian research and planning. Arthur Calwell before him was always proud to call himself a Fabian, and the tradition has been carried on through Bill Hayden, Bob Hawke, Paul Keating, Kim Beazley, John Bannon, John Cain, Don Dunstan, Neville Wran, Bob Carr and Steve Bracks. British Prime Minister Tony Blair is a Fabian, as were Neil Kinnock, Michael Foot, Harold Wilson, Hugh Gaitskell and Clement Attlee before him. Australia had its first Fabian Society as early as 1895, and 1947 saw the establishment of the Victorian Fabian Society, which became the Australian Fabian Society in 1984. The Australian Fabian Society is the largest Fabian body ever to exist outside Britain itself. It operates nationally, with members in every State and Territory.

The society has no policy beyond that implied in a general commitment to democratic socialism, and it issues its publications as the opinions of their authors and not of the organisation. It does not admit members of parties other than the ALP. Its aim is to promote education and discussion on policies designed to further the goals of democratic socialism.

If you believe that reason, education and ideas should play a larger part in Australian politics, if you care about the quality of the society in which we live and the direction it is taking, and if you share the ethic of democratic socialism, the Australian Fabian Society welcomes you as a member.

Gary Jungwirth
President
Australian Fabian Society
Box 2707X
GPO Melbourne 3000

acknowledgments

We would like to acknowledge the generous support and enthusiasm of the Australian Fabian Society and, in particular, the Series Editor of *Labor Essays*, Mr Gary Jungwirth. Special thanks must be given to Mr Tony Moore at Pluto Press for his inspired assistance.

We also wish to thank Ms Anna Thwaites, who provided research assistance and reviews of the text, and made helpful comments. We are also indebted to Ms Frances Gordon, who provided additional research assistance and comments, and to Ms Rowan McRae, Ms Simona Gory and Ms Fiona Hammond, who proofread the text and read material. Thanks must also be extended to Mr Simon Moglia, who provided administrative support. We are also grateful to the Faculty of Law at the University of Melbourne, which provided research funding to Glenn Patmore.

Dennis Glover and Glenn Patmore
October 2000

introduction

Reclaiming our Government: an introduction
By Dennis Glover and Glenn Patmore

One of the key challenges facing social democracy today is how to make government work for people again. Since the early 1980s, the way governments deliver services to their citizens has been transformed — by privatisation, corporatisation, outsourcing, information technology and globalisation. These processes have also redefined the roles of national and sub-national governments. Australia has not escaped these developments.

Government may arguably have become more efficient as a result of these changes, but has it lost its soul? Has it become just another publicly controlled version of the private sector, motivated by the bottom line, not the public interest? Can government once again be made to work for the people? Can it be re-empowered to combat the new inequalities of the 21st century and ensure that citizenship retains its worth? Protesters in cities such as Seattle, Davos, Melbourne and Geneva — regardless of one's opinion of just how representative they are — have made these the questions for our times. Across the left spectrum opinions vary over whether or not the continuing transformation of government service delivery should be opposed or accepted, but all agree that sovereign governments will have to adopt new approaches to advance the interests of their citizens.

1

In this book a number of prominent and emerging public intellectuals, policy-makers and academic experts put forward ideas about how we can give life to our public institutions and renew our democracy in the face of the changes outlined above. In particular, this book addresses:

How we can put the goal of the 'public interest' back into government service delivery without sacrificing the benefits of recent reforms, such as flexibility, innovation and efficiency.

How we can use information technology to deliver better public services, rebuild communities and restore people's confidence in government.

How we can better coordinate government efforts across national and State portfolios and agencies to tackle complex new forms of social exclusion and create a more equal society.

What criteria should be used for determining which public services are best delivered by governments and which by the private sector, and what are the appropriate levels of public regulation and democratic control?

How the taxation system can be reformed to tackle new challenges, such as how to make Australia a 'Knowledge Nation', and how to encourage industry to become 'family friendly' in an age when many children are being raised in one-parent and two-working-parent families.

How we can rebuild the public's trust in our elected representatives and confidence in the organs of government.

How we can encourage the idea of 'public service' and civic engagement by the Australian people.

In tackling these challenging issues, the book is structured around five themes (or section headings): reshaping government; enhancing representative democracy; the limits of the contract state and managerialism; government and the Internet; and improving the making of public policy. Under these themes, various matters are considered, including taxation and spending, enhancing the relationship between representatives and citizens, tackling the problems of equity and inefficiency caused by the privatisation of government services, and the challenge of reformulating public policy in accordance with the fears and hopes of social democrats.

Reshaping government: taxation and spending

Two of our contributors consider future directions for Labor governments, paying particular attention to spending and taxation.

Craig Emerson considers the future role of the Commonwealth government in the Federation. This potential role is contested, reflecting a philosophical division between the Coalition and the Australian Labor Party. The Coalition's agenda to transform the Commonwealth government would phase out national programs and replace them with State and local government schemes. Under this plan, the national government would play an ever-diminishing role in vital social and economic programs.

Emerson argues that the primary means of achieving this transformation is an alteration of the fiscal balance between the State and Commonwealth governments. Accordingly, Emerson's contention is that by distributing GST revenue to the States, which can then be used to fund State-based schemes, a conservative government will be able to justify its withdrawal of funding from Federal government programs.

He then considers the adverse implications of the Coalition's policies for the social and economic well-being of the Australian community. He notes that Australia is slow in making the transition to the information age because it has failed to invest in education, training, and research and development. Furthermore, the Coalition's declining national investment in education and the adoption of regressive indirect taxes like the GST are widening existing inequalities. He concludes that the Coalition's fiscal federalist approach will have an adverse effect on the States and on national programs.

In contrast, Emerson maintains that Labor is committed to promoting government policies that are necessary to enhance the national interest. This requires an equitable taxation system and increasing national investment in education, and research and development. These policies, he argues, are the necessary ingredients of a productive, egalitarian, cohesive and safe community.

Lindy Edwards also expresses concerns regarding the social and economic well-being of Australian society. She argues that in the late 1990s a gulf emerged between the quality of life of Australians and the health of our economy. This divergence, she contends, is linked to the recent fashion in public policy that treats economic issues and social issues as separate. She believes that, in order to bridge this artificial gap, economists should assess the social costs of economic policy.

Edwards offers as a practical example work hours: the numerous social problems that arise when fewer employees work longer hours for employers. She argues that a viable response is to create a tax structure that reflects the social cost of these employment practices. Accordingly, she advocates a revenue-neutral overhaul of the existing payroll tax system. This would mean that those who employ a small number of people to work long hours would pay a high rate of tax.

While Edwards concludes that payroll tax reform runs against current political culture, she maintains that it could have significant benefits in enhancing the working life of ordinary citizens and thereby begin to address the alienation that citizens feel from their political representatives.

Enhancing representative democracy: representatives and citizens

The role of our political representatives is increasingly being questioned by a disenchanted and ever more cynical public. Numerous contributors, including Lindy Edwards and Sally Young, have noted this trend. Young examines this theme in detail in her provocatively titled chapter: 'Why Australians Hate Politicians: exploring the new public discontent'.

She argues that three groups have fuelled this cynicism: the public, the media and politicians. Each group accuses the other of causing or contributing to this discontent. The decline in public confidence in politicians and government may also be explained by deep structural changes. These include a change in social attitudes and the rise of post-modern values as well as economic factors, such as a decline in living standards and the adverse effects of government and corporate re-structuring.

Young maintains that each group can help to redress this cynicism. She contends that the public should continue to question media representation of politicians, politics and public policy. The media should report on issues rather than making the stock and often false representations of political personalities. Politicians should change their parliamentary behaviour and minimise the use of negative advertising and electoral tactics. Her most obvious and yet most challenging point is that politicians should make good policy and explain it well.

While Young addresses the need to rethink the role of our representatives, numerous other contributors reconsider the role of individuals as citizens. Our authors advance new conceptions of the powers of the citizen. The theme of alienation of citizens from government and from the private sector is also picked up by a number of contributors.

Katrina Gorjanicyn examines feminist theories on what it means to be counted as a full and equal citizen. In general, the feminist project of achieving citizenship rights for Australian women has rested on a perpetuation of the difference between men and women. Incorporation of this difference has provided a means to enhance women's life opportunities, as is seen in equal opportunity and anti-discrimination legislation.

However, feminists' advocacy of citizenship rights for women has also involved some blurring of the demarcation between what have been traditionally regarded as public and private spheres. For instance, the issues of maternity leave and access to child-care services have been put at the forefront of the agenda for policy reform. Gorjanicyn concludes that feminists should develop a model of citizenship which downplays the division between public and private, by being inclusive of women's different interests, and their participation in public and private life. Gorjanicyn's analysis of the implications of this argument for the ways in which public policy can be developed to meet the needs and interests of women is outlined later in this introduction.

Lucas Walsh examines government policy for the enhancement of democratic citizenship. He argues that there is a causal relationship between public education and citizenship for democracy, since education is a vital step in the political socialisation of the citizen. Walsh claims that recent neo-liberal reforms of the Australian education system have brought about a growing disjunction of public education from democratic citizenship. He takes as his case study Civics and Citizenship Education (CCE). Government reforms have favoured economic rationalist policies such as market competition, fees, choice and flexibility in teaching and learning. These have reoriented students away from values of reciprocity and community responsibility towards an atomised form of personal autonomy and self-interest.

Walsh argues that the state should foster the link between public education and democratic citizenship by promoting higher levels of participation and political literacy. The participating democratic citizen ought to have a well-developed sense of civic duty that values community and is mindful of cultural differences. He considers some ways in which CCE could better promote these goals and notes that, ideally, regular learning environments, such as the school and university, should be practical examples of an effective democratic civic community.

Public services — the limits of the contract state and managerialism

From the specific roles of citizen and representative we move to the broader issue of the structure of government. Our authors address from a range of perspectives the current method of providing public services and the possibility of new models for the development of government programs. In considering the future of government programs, neo-liberal policy-makers have been successful in recasting public policy debates in Australia. Their views have had a very significant impact on the form and organisation of government itself.

Governments are no longer seen as the exclusive providers of public services. Accordingly, it is argued that there is a role for markets and community organisations. Essentially, neo-liberal proponents of change envisage a greater role for private bodies in the provision of public services. The privatisation of public services represents the most 'significant...change[s] to the public [service] since the "merit and tenure" innovations more than one hundred years ago' (Considine 2000).

Both sides of politics have come to question the ability of governments to provide public services, with neo-liberals emphasising efficiency and the need for budget cuts and social-democrats focusing more on community expectations and needs as well as the current inadequacy of government provision of services (Hodge 1999). The acceptance, by social-democrats, of some neo-liberal criticisms of the traditional model of public service provision has opened the way for wholesale reform of government service provision in accordance with New Right policies. The question for the centre-left is how to concede the validity of some of the neo-liberal arguments without acceding to the total of their reform agenda. One of the critical challenges for social-democrats is to strengthen the vision of public services. In order to develop the policies and programs that would be required to achieve this transformation, it is necessary to understand the schemes that currently exist.

One of the most significant developments has been the introduction of the contract regime as a recognisable system of governance. Under this regime, public institutions are modelled on forms of corporate governance. Central to this model is the use of the contract, to regulate transactions and thereby enable the coordination and control of public services. Formal agreements are seen as the key way to 'identify tasks, goals and costs' and public programs are provided by the market in public services, made up of the bureaucracy, profit and non-profit organisations (Considine 2000). It is important to appreciate that the contracting model goes beyond simply the contracting out of government services to private providers, as Mark Considine explains.

The contract regime includes some or all of the following elements:

1. Social and political contracts in which governments, key interest groups and major social institutions publicly adopt a common program which includes a defined outcome.

2. Employment contracts with heads of agencies, managers and staff which specify tasks and outcomes.

3. Public agency contracts or purchasing agreements.

4. Organisational contracts with public institutions, firms and non-profit organisations which promise payment for delivery of services to a defined population.

5. How we can use information technology to deliver better public services, rebuild communities and restore people's confidence in government.

6. Client contracts which oblige clients to meet defined obligations in order to qualify for assistance (Considine 2000).

Some social-democrats have found contracting models to be attractive because they see it as being more responsive to clients' interests and as providing them with greater choice. Others have identified financial savings to the public sector resulting from competition, efficiencies and the elimination of excessive costs to government.

Other social-democrats see these reforms as problematic. Some reject the contracting regime outright; others see the need to modify the contractual relationship to increase participation in government decision-making. They advocate the development of new forms of provision of public services. This range of views is reflected in the contributions by Alford, Di Francesco, Considine and Cox. However, it is important to note that what each of our contributors has in common is a belief that it is time to limit the adverse effects of the contract regime as a means of structuring public services.

John Alford contends that conservative governments in Australia and elsewhere have recast the public as 'customers' of public services. This development, he believes, is an inappropriate method for describing the provision of public services for numerous reasons. Firstly, the public sector serves a range of different types of citizens, many of whom cannot simply be described as customers, such as welfare recipients and prisoners. Secondly, categorising citizens as customers is inequitable, since some people are more able to pay than others. Thirdly, the 'customer' model devalues the concept of egalitarian citizenship.

He observes that, if the relationship between government and citizen is reduced to a commercial transaction, it does not adequately encompass 'the specific realities of the public sector'. Alford argues that it is not 'good enough for the left to simply condemn that model, without articulating an alternative conception of the relationship between government organisations and citizens' (Alford, this volume). Therefore he offers a concept based on the citizen as a 'client' of the public sector; which acknowledges that a social exchange takes place between government agencies and their clients. This would include the provision of information, consent, compliance, cooperation or productive effort. This conception is not confined to monetary exchange or requiring recipients to pay for services, and it enhances rather than devalues social-democratic citizenship. He concludes that the client model is the most constructive means of conceiving the provision of public services, because it affirms what is valuable about the public sector, while respecting the private concerns of citizens.

Michael Di Francesco provides a critique of 'contractualism', drawing on the work of Boston to address two related questions: 'What is the meaning of "public interest"?' and 'How useful is it as a criterion for testing the limits of contracting in the state sector?' In answering the first question, Di Francesco explores a number of different possible meanings of the expression 'public interest'. He identifies, as one of the most useful definitions, the idea of the 'public good'. He concludes that the 'public interest' is 'an inescapably political concept'. Its power lies in the force with which it can be used for political argument and persuasion, rather than in its use as a neutral or descriptive concept to guide policymakers. In answering the second question, Di Francesco accepts that, in general, policy advice should be retained as a state function. However, he argues that there is no simple way to determine what other government functions should be retained by the state. Nevertheless, he does contend that the concept of 'public interest' has a central role to play in identifying key state functions.

Di Francesco relies particularly on the generation of 'public value' as a crude measure of public interest. In a similar vein, John Alford explains that public value can only be derived from the provision of public services. According to Alford, public value refers to the way in which everyone benefits from the provision of public services. This is because these services are 'consumed jointly' and not provided merely to certain individuals. The concept of public value includes the provision of law and order (without which the market cannot function), remedies to market failure, equity, defence and environmental protection. In other words, as Di Francesco notes, public value is the output of the 'public production process', an attempt to recognise and capture the 'non-market' worth of state activity. He also argues that the concept of public value involves the idea of political legitimacy. Therefore, the public production process involves political authorisation that is not, in all cases at least, reducible to a contractual relationship.

Di Francesco illustrates this with reference to the Job Network, as an example of the contracting out of government services in a highly competitive market. He argues that, if the production of public value is judged to constitute a significant component of employment services, the further use of contracting should be pursued with caution, since it may represent efforts to abdicate responsibility and evade the obligation to secure political consent.

Mark Considine considers the effects of privatisation on public institutions and the public interest. His central argument is that privatisation has changed the role and structure of government, particularly in relation to the old hierarchical model of bureaucratic control of service delivery. This model imposes accountability on the Minister, the Head of Department and the department that actually provides the services. The new structure of government is based less and less on this model of hierarchical control because of the sale of government assets and the adoption of the corporate model as the archetype for the delivery of public services.

Given these developments, he contends, 'current institutions lack the capacity to act strategically in the public interest' (Considine, this volume). Governments need to build new public institutions in order to support these developments and to create order and fairness. Considine's challenge is to re-imagine the public sphere and build governmental capacity. For that reason, he examines the multi-agency system, which is the form of organisation in which the delivery of services requires cooperation by several public and private agencies. He outlines some of the advantages and disadvantages of adopting such a model for governments and parliaments, as well as for citizens.

Considine then argues that governments must re-institutionalise the public interest by legislating it back into the service loop, and provides examples of where this has occurred in other countries. He proposes a new triangular model of government service provision in which accountability would stretch from the Minister and department as purchaser, to the private provider and the citizen consumer, each with distinct mandates. Citizen consumers would be empowered to provide feedback to government and to challenge service provider decisions through review boards, the courts and the media.

Eva Cox presents a feminist critique of those economic and socialist agendas that focus on paid labour and ownership and that ignore social relationships. Each of these political theories draws a distinction between the public sphere of paid labour and exchange and the private, domestic sphere. This distinction represents the traditional division between male and female realms and hides a multitude of relationships that make society both human and social. Thus, for Cox, it is necessary to put the social back into theorising, which may be achieved by relying on concepts such as trust, altruism, inclusion and civility, that recognise the importance of perception and relationships.

She argues that there is a role for government, the market and the community to contribute to an inclusive society. Government must act in the common interest, offering justice and public services. The market provides autonomous choices and trains individuals to make responsible decisions. The community is needed to affirm relationships and the self by pursuing societal interests and acting as advocate and monitor of other sectors. Cox suggests that real problems for society will occur where two sectors collude against the third.

Therefore, she rejects proposals for the three sectors to be involved in a social coalition or partnership. Under partnership arrangements, the market and community sectors are often able to exert power over government by threats of withdrawing essential services. Conversely, government may exercise too much control over the other sectors, especially where it is the major provider of funds. In other words, government increases its control over other sectors and loses control over its own ability to provide services. Furthermore, if business and the community tender for government contracts, it creates the approach of 'one size ought to fit all'. Indeed, this is also a concern for Considine.

Cox argues that we have a capacity to remedy these problems, while conceding that there is no perceivable endpoint utopia. The basic element which must be present when resolving conflicts between diverse interests is a sufficient level of trust to ensure that we can achieve effective negotiations and solutions. Cox suggests that the process of creating links built on trust will itself generate more trust. Thus, she proposes to use trust as social capital to facilitate connective relationships which will formulate policies for collective action.

While Eva Cox is critical of the contract state, *Tony Moore* considers whether some aspects of new public management can improve service delivery by public sector institutions. He uses the ABC as a case study to test these arguments. His conclusion is that, in the area of arts and the media, old forms of top-down management work against creativity and prevent the ABC from utilising the potential of new digital technologies to reflect the interests of a prospective audience, which is increasingly diverse. Moore argues that greater autonomy for content providers combined with enhanced democratic oversight and appropriate financial management has the potential to make the ABC once again a leading public arts and media institution.

Provision of public services over the Internet

The development of information technology and the Internet has created new ways of delivering public services. The building of connective relationships requires communication between citizens and government. While face-to-face communication will always be important, the advent of new forms of electronic communication opens up new possibilities to enhance government-citizen relationships. These

technological innovations have generated new demands and
challenges for government and have significant implications
for social equity and economic growth. On-line services may
also have very beneficial outcomes for citizens, as is
explained by our next two contributors, Tanner and
Edwards.

Lindsay Tanner considers the vital issues that have arisen
for government because of increasing access to the Internet.
He notes that the vast bulk of interaction between government and citizens is about services, which are capable of
being moved on-line. Tanner's main argument is that universal Internet access is critical for social equity and economic development. The Government's provision of on-line
services is the key to realising such access, because it has the
capacity to generate very substantial demand. This would
promote investment, thereby stimulating greater economic
growth. Furthermore, moving government services on-line
would also act as an incentive for people to acquire on-line
skills and reduce costs and increase efficiency in the delivery
of those services.

The current Federal Government's use of on-line services is modest and its approach to 'increasing' those services
must be more urgent, meticulous and committed. Nonetheless, Tanner acknowledges that there are numerous obstacles
to delivering government services via the Internet. These
include the current moderate level of Internet connection,
the technological problems and cost of providing on-line
access to rural communities, and the role of limited competition in keeping regional prices too high. Most importantly,
people will need to be enabled to use this new technology,
which raises the difficult issues of lack of resources, skills and
personal motivation. In sum, Tanner observes that increasingly more people are moving on-line, creating vital opportunities for new methods of delivering services, and that the
challenge is to ensure that others are not disadvantaged or
excluded.

Rhys Edwards, who shares similar concerns to Tanner,
proposes the use of the Internet as a practical strategy for
rebuilding rural and regional communities. He notes the
growing sense of divide that exists between urban, regional
and rural communities in Australia. Edwards identifies glob-

alisation as an important contributing factor in the decline of the well-being of country communities and argues that it presents a challenge to policy makers at the State level of government. He presents the response of the Tasmanian Government to this challenge, in particular describing the development of a network of on-line communities, the Tasmanian Communities Online (TCO) project. The TCO project is not merely a government program to provide computers, computer training and access to the Internet for rural communities: it aims to promote social cohesion and rebuild country communities by facilitating on-line communication between them. The significance of the project is that it seeks to link remote communities in Tasmania with each other, as well as to the State Government. In this way a new relationship between the citizen, the community and the State Government can be developed. This, in turn, can enhance the legitimacy of public institutions in Tasmania and provide a model for other rural communities confronting globalisation.

The TCO project may also address two key obstacles to the development of universal on-line access raised earlier by Tanner. Firstly, the project removes the costs to remote rural communities of connecting to the Internet. Secondly, and most importantly, the TCO project is designed to enable people to use the Internet by overcoming problems of lack of facilities, skills and motivation. Thus, it may also provide a program that could be introduced to benefit disadvantaged urban communities.

Lastly, Edwards further develops the notion of connecting the people with their government via the Internet. He distinguishes between two functions of on-line government communications. The concept of government on-line involves making democratic information and services available to citizens — creating an electronic bureaucracy. The concept of civic life on-line involves enabling citizens to voice their views about government and developing advocacy for various groups and interests. Significantly, the TCO project provides a mechanism to move from the model of electronic bureaucracy to that of the civic society. In addition, the civic society model can address the issues of alienation from government and feelings of citizen vulnerability.

Improving the making of public policy

Greater interaction between citizens and government may also have another benefit: more informed input into policy debates. Some of our contributors examine the factors affecting policy development and policy-making among political parties and governments in Australia.

Dennis Glover believes that there has been a decline in popular participation as the means of formulating public policy in political parties. While he still sees popular participation in political parties as important, he argues that there has been a change in the way detailed policies that form the election manifestoes are generally devised. Political parties, he argues, now obtain advice on detailed policies from specialised advisers and policy units. Policy-making for political organisations has become an increasingly complex and professional task. Additionally, the capacity of governments to make public policy was severely reduced during the 1990s, as a result of cutbacks to the public service and the outsourcing of policy advice to private sector consulting firms.

If this decline is to be arrested, and government in Australia to be transformed, then Glover claims that policy development must be revolutionised. The success of this revolution must be judged by the degree to which public interest is placed in the forefront of the development of public policy. He contends that the prerequisites for successfully promoting the public interest are that policy must be evidence-based and practical rather than theoretical. Policy advice must be innovative, consider cross-departmental issues and be drawn from a diverse selection of individuals and groups with policy-making expertise in both the private and government sectors.

Amongst his suggestions for practical measures to enhance policy development, Glover includes a central government policy unit, an Australian on-line policy network, and a strengthening of the role of public policy bodies and centres in universities and the private sector. Overall, Glover explores in general terms the ways in which Australia's public policy capacity has recently been diminished and can be enhanced.

Andrew Leigh offers a more specific analysis, considering the policy dilemmas posed by 'social exclusion'. This is a term that refers to the ways in which members of our society find themselves excluded from fully participating in its processes and enjoying its benefits. He therefore considers the adverse consequences caused by a lack of financial means, unemployment, geographic isolation, poor education, limited social networks and inadequate access to new technologies. Leigh contends that the Federal Government must be bold in tackling social exclusion and advocates the creation of a specialised unit within the Department of Prime Minister and Cabinet dedicated to researching the problem of social exclusion, designing effective solutions, and overseeing their implementation.

It is worth noting that the notion of social exclusion represents a significant development in social democratic politics. This term is sometimes associated with the 'Third Way', a philosophy which seeks to empower individuals by drawing on programs and policies developed by both the left and right of politics. It has been argued that the concept of social exclusion changes the raison d'être of left-of-centre politics, from promoting equality to addressing exclusion or 'mechanisms that act to detach groups of people from the social mainstream' (Giddens 1998, p. 104; Di Francesco, this volume). It remains to be seen whether this term will supplant or supplement the promotion of equality as the catchcry of social democracy. Nonetheless, the proposal for a social exclusion unit certainly is a practical policy for redressing the position of persons who are seriously disadvantaged in Australian society.

In Gorjanicyn's contribution, mentioned earlier, she considers the important area of women's policy development. She points out that governments intent on rolling back the welfare state have severely curtailed women's policy-making machinery and the delivery of services to women. Gorjanicyn argues that it is time for government to rethink the narrow-minded policies that have been created to promote economic rationalism. In re-inventing the area of women's policy she argues that there is a role for 'femocrats', employed for the purpose of representing women's specific interests. Because there are differences between women, it is questionable whether some can effectively represent the interests of all. Therefore, Gorjanicyn contends that women of diverse backgrounds should be employed as government policy-makers and public servants. Furthermore, she contends that policy-makers should also reject the homogenous notion and essentialist category of 'woman'. Rather, they need to recognise and address the multiple forms of subordination experienced by different women.

Summary of recommendations

Reshaping government: taxation and spending

1. That the Commonwealth must retain a commitment to investing in the nation's capacity as a 'Knowledge Nation' through Specific Purpose Payments and not allow this responsibility to devolve to the States now that they are the recipients of the Goods and Services Tax.

2. That policy-makers reform the taxation system to make the social costs of business decisions economically visible. For example, State governments can reform their payroll tax systems to enforce lower rates for employers who employ more people to work fewer hours, and higher rates for employers who employ fewer people to work longer hours.

Enhancing representative democracy: representatives and citizens

3. That political representatives should explain policies in a manner which centres on information and education (rather than emotive sales techniques). For instance, there should be an annual national address in which the Prime Minister outlines the state of the nation.

4. That participation and political literacy be encouraged through enhanced civics and citizenship education programs. In particular, educational institutions must operate in ways that encourage people to regard themselves as participating citizens.

Public services — the limits of the contract state and managerialism

5. That citizens as 'clients' be more actively involved in the design and provision of public services as a means of enhancing satisfaction with and effectiveness of those services. Accordingly, 'work for the dole' schemes should be remodelled to include greater skill acquisition, which is more likely to elicit job-seeking behaviour.

6. To create public value it is necessary to approach with caution the further contracting out of public services such as the Job Network.

7. That the public interest be put back into contracted-out public services by redesigning them to include triangular input from service purchasers, service providers and the community. These could include:
    *   elected user boards
    *   consumer action groups funded through voluntary subscriptions
    *   enhanced local government involvement in deciding which State and national services best suit the needs of the community.

8. Alternatively, that the contracting out of government services should come to an end. To avoid a range of difficult problems, there needs to be a separation of the Government, market and community.

9. That the decline of voluntary organisations be reversed by discovering which aspects of volunteerism resonate most strongly with younger people and promoting those aspects.

10. New forms of democratic accountability, including an enhanced role for the Parliament and wider representation of interests in decision-making structures, should be considered to improve the ability of the ABC to serve the public. That the key objective in relation to both programming and recruitment at the ABC should be to reflect Australia's complex ethnic, class, generational and cultural diversity. That the ABC should also develop

and deliver programs by sourcing material internally and externally from independent film makers and story-tellers and not just from the commercial sector; and also embrace the information age, and the concept of a 'Knowledge Nation'.

Provision of public services over the Internet

11. That the Federal Government undertake a rigorous process of compelling agencies to offer their services on-line as quickly and effectively as possible.

12. That the Federal Government adopt a total commitment to achieving universal on-line access within a given period as a key strategy for delivering social equity, economic growth and government efficiency.

13. That community Internet access centres based on the model of the Tasmanian Communities Online project be created across Australia to connect communities to the global economy, promote social cohesion, build trust in government, facilitate regional economic renewal and educate individuals for citizenship.

New directions for public policy

14. That government create a central policy unit to promote policy innovation, oversee policy development, harness the knowledge and expertise of public policy specialists outside government (through an on-line policy network) and coordinate cross-portfolio policy reform.

15. That the nation's overall public policy capacity be strengthened by:
   - Improving university public policy schools.
   - Encouraging academics to take study leave in public sector think tanks and government.
   - Establishing a Centre for Management and Policy Studies within the public service to promote a balanced public service policy culture.

- Encouraging more academic publishing in the area of public policy, through the establishment of more public policy journals linked to university departments, and by recognising, for university funding purposes, contributions to public debate by academics on television, radio and the Internet and in newspapers and magazines.

16. That an Australian social exclusion unit be established to research the problem of social exclusion, design effective solutions and oversee their implementation.

17. That in re-inventing the area of women's policy the role of 'femocrats' should be promoted and the function of women's policy units should be strengthened in national, State and local governments.

chapter **1**

The role of government in 21st century Australia
By Craig Emerson

A fundamental reassessment of the role of government is occurring in Australia. While this issue has been perennial and predates Federation (Hancock 1930), it has been given renewed impetus by profound changes in Federal-State financial relations associated with the introduction of the Goods and Services Tax (GST) on 1 July 2000.

The Coalition agenda involves a complete reshaping of the role of government in Australia, including the roles and responsibilities of the Federal, State and local tiers of government. It is an agenda with which Labor profoundly disagrees, for it would phase out national programs and replace them with State and local government programs. The Federal Government would play an ever-diminishing role in education, health and other vital social programs. The Coalition plan involves the ultimate expression of conservative support for States' rights over national programs.

This chapter examines the role of government in 21st century Australia under the conservative and progressive political philosophies. It begins with the specific circumstances of the allocation of GST revenues and the future of tied grants to the States. In explaining these decisions the analysis is broadened to the philosophical divide between the Coalition and Labor parties on the future role of the Commonwealth Government in the Australian Federation. The Coalition seeks to reduce the role of the Common-wealth in the Federation. Labor is committed to promoting government programs that are necessary to enhance the national interest.

The allocation of GST revenues and the future of tied grants to the States

The introduction of the GST has heralded a dramatic change in Australia's Federal-State financial arrangements. The Coalition Government has allocated all revenue from the GST to the States. At the same time, the Coalition has abolished all untied grants to the States, otherwise known as Financial Assistance Grants (FAGs). These untied grants had no strings attached, while tied grants are conditional upon the States meeting particular requirements of the Federal Government.

Untied grants amounted to more than $17 billion in the year of introduction of the GST. After taking account of the abolition of three State taxes and other financial adjustments, the States as a whole were expected by the Federal Government to be worse off for several years under the GST without top-up payments from the Commonwealth. The Coalition has agreed to make these top-up payments with the stated aim of leaving the States no worse off under the GST.

If the States are to be no better off and no worse off financially under the GST, at least for the first several years, why is the Coalition re-arranging Federal-State financial relations under the GST? The answer lies in the Government's plans for the other Commonwealth payments to the States — the tied grants, known as Specific Purpose Payments (SPPs).

Replacing one form of untied grants to the States (FAGs) with another form (GST) is, on the face of it, little more than an accounting exercise. It has the cosmetic appeal of apparently reducing Commonwealth outlays, so that the Coalition can portray itself as an exponent of smaller government. However, there is a deeper purpose: by allocating all GST revenues to the States, the Coalition is developing a pretext to cut the tied grants to the States over time.

The Coalition's argument would be that the States have what they have long desired — a growth tax. When the States seek increases in tied grants to cover inflation and population growth, they will be greeted with the response from a

Coalition Government that, since the States have a major new growth tax, the Commonwealth no longer has a responsibility to maintain the real per capita value of tied grants. In 1999–2000 the Commonwealth provided tied grants to the States of more than $17 billion (coincidentally the same order of magnitude as the untied grants in that year). The main purposes of these payments are set out in Table 1.

Table 1
Estimated Specific Purpose Payments to the States
1999–2000 ($ million)

Purpose	Amount
Legal Aid	58.3
Schools	4,400.7
Vocational education and training	865.7
Health	6,616.9
Social security and welfare	1,096.7
Commonwealth-State Housing Agreement	763.0
Local government	1,263.3
Other	2,061.6
Total	**17,126.2**

Source: 1999–00 Budget Paper No. 3, Table A3.

At the Special Premiers' Conference in November 1998, which discussed the future of Federal-State relations under the GST, Commonwealth Treasury officials made it plain to their State counterparts that there were no guarantees about the level of tied grants to the States beyond the so-called transition period. The actual wording adopted at the Premiers' Conference and essentially repeated in a subsequent inter-governmental agreement was:

> The Commonwealth will continue to provide Specific Purpose Payments (SPPs) to the States and Territories and has no intention of cutting aggregate SPPs as part of this reform process, which would defeat the objective of the States and Territories being better off under the new arrangements. (Commonwealth Govern-ment 1998, p. 2; Commonwealth Government 1999, p. 2)

In bureaucratic language, the phrase 'has no intention' falls well short of a 'guarantee'. The statement 'has no intention' does not indicate how long this absence of intention will last. Moreover, an undertaking not to cut aggregate SPPs leaves wide open the option of simply holding tied grants constant in nominal terms, allowing their real value to be eroded by inflation and their real value per person to be eroded by population growth. The agreement between the Coalition Government and the States therefore allows the Commonwealth to greatly reduce its funding to the States over time.

Looking at the purposes for which tied grants are paid by the Commonwealth, it is clear that vital social services are at risk under the GST arrangements. These include $6.6 billion for health, more than $5 billion for education, more than $1 billion for social security and welfare and more than $750 million for housing. They can be reduced or removed unilaterally by the Federal Government. Already the Coalition Government has begun reducing tied grants, as confirmed by the Prime Minister when he was asked whether the Government was providing less funding: 'No we're, well we're providing, we're providing less dollars, but because the costs of operating will fall, the real financial position will be the same' (Howard 2000). These decisions were taken unilaterally by the Federal Government.

A former Coalition Leader, Professor John Hewson, who proposed a GST in the early 1990s, has raised the prospect of a Coalition Government removing payments to the States:

> The real question is just how long the intergovernmental agreement will last and how long before the Government breaks another 'core promise'. I don't think it will be too long before the Commonwealth starts to try to claw back some of the GST revenue from the States or to seek other arrangements. (Hewson 2000)

Tied grants to the States would be an easy target for the Expenditure Review Committee of a Coalition Government seeking to finance the other main item on its fiscal agenda — further reductions in income tax for high income earners. Treasurer Costello articulated the Coalition's agenda when he declared himself to be 'an income tax cut man' who would want to the top marginal rate pushed out to be 'multiples of average weekly earnings' (Costello 1999a, p. 1; 1999b). Future election promises of reductions in income tax could be financed by cuts to real per capita tied grants to the States (and by the removal of GST exemptions or increases in the GST rate).

Underlying philosophy on the role of government in Australia

Underlying the future of tied grants to the States is a philosophical divide between the conservative parties and the Australian Labor Party. The Coalition parties in Australia are strong advocates of States' rights and see little merit in national programs. This philosophy is evident in the Coalition's policy approach to issues such as mandatory sentencing, where it has exhibited an unwillingness to assert Commonwealth control.[1] The Coalition invariably opposes Australia's membership of international conventions as a means of exerting Commonwealth influence over legal and land use issues within State boundaries.[2] The decision of the Coalition Government to review Australia's relationships with United Nations committees following a report critical of Australia's approach to mandatory sentencing is one example of the Coalition's attitude to national programs and international conventions.[3]

The economic reform agenda of the 1980s and 1990s focused on deregulating the financial sector, lowering Australia's trade barriers, and microeconomic reforms designed to stimulate competition. This is an old and overwhelmingly successful formula. It provided the foundation for rapid growth in productivity during the 1990s that supported many years of sustained economic growth. It essentially enjoyed bipartisan support.

As Australia enters the 21st century this old economic reform agenda is nearing exhaustion. Yet the Coalition pursues doggedly what it sees as two extra items on the old economic reform agenda — introducing a broad-based indirect tax and further deregulating the labour market. Neither of these is part of the Labor Party's platform. In both cases the social costs are high and the economic benefits questionable at best. Even the most optimistic assessments of the economic benefits of the GST are for an increase in living standards of around $500 million a year after five to ten years (Murphy 1999) — not enough to fund one university. The compliance costs of the GST, estimated at more than $1 billion a year, would more than wipe out these meagre gains. Others estimate a long-term reduction in living standards of about $600 million a year and an even greater reduction after compliance costs are taken into account (Dixon 1999).

Relatively few rigidities remain in the Australian labour market following a period of heavy deregulation of the workforce and a move towards contract employment. The Coalition's desire to pursue a second wave of industrial relations changes appears to be motivated more by an extreme neoliberal ideology than by any genuine desire to increase employment.

While the Coalition persists with its unfinished business it prejudices the pursuit of the new economic reform agenda, which is attuned to the reality that if Australia is to be competitive in the global information age the nation will need to boost greatly its skills base and its research and development effort. This new agenda necessarily involves investing in the nation's future through education, training, and research and development (Beazley 2000a; 2000b).

The United States has shaped the information age and adapted to it, while Australia lags behind. The proportion of the Australian workforce with a post-school qualification is around 25 per cent, while in the United States it is almost 35 per cent (OECD 1998, p. 43).

Australian business expenditure on research and development (BERD) has declined as a proportion of GDP in each year of the Coalition Government, from 0.86 per cent in 1995–96 to just 0.67 per cent in 1998–99. It is well below the OECD average of 1.27 per cent (Beazley and McMullan 2000).

Australia's tardiness in entering the information age, leaving much of the workforce with obsolete skills, is a much more powerful explanation of the substantially higher unemployment rate in this country than arguments about ongoing labour market rigidities. Those who leave school at a young age will not be equipped to participate in the emerging information economy. Already unemployment among early school leavers in Australia is as high as 41 per cent.[4] In the information age, early school leavers who rely for work on manual tasks will be highly vulnerable to unemployment.

The slowness of Australia in making the transition to the information age is the true cost of the Coalition's support for the GST. The Government is spending around $25 billion of the Budget surplus over three years in an attempt to compensate for the GST. Some of this Budget surplus could have and should have been spent on improving high school retention rates and equipping young people with the skills necessary to compete for jobs in the information age.

If Australia continues its slide down the international scale of skills attainment, the nation will become uncompetitive in the global economy. Labor considers the Commonwealth has a vital role in building the nation's skills base as a means of acquiring a competitive advantage for Australia in the information economy. Unless this is done, Australia risks becoming a low-skill, low-wage economy with an ever-widening divide between the relatively few who possess the skills to capitalise on the information age and the many who do not.

Australia has already begun its journey along the pathway of increasing inequality. Earnings disparity widened more sharply in Australia over the twenty-year period from the mid-1970s to the mid-1990s than in any other OECD country, but this was almost fully offset by the progressive income tax system and government transfers to low-income earners. As a result, Australia achieved a fall in poverty, which was: '... concentrated in the second decade when Labor was in power' (Access Economics 1999, p. 11).

These findings have been confirmed by the National Centre for Social and Economic Modelling (NATSEM), which found for the period 1982–1993 that: '...increasing progressivity in the income tax system and particularly in the government cash transfer system fully offset this growing market-based inequality' (NATSEM 1997, p. 1).

Subsequent analysis performed by NATSEM for the *Australian* newspaper for the period 1982 to 1997 reached the same conclusions (NATSEM 2000). So, too, has a report prepared by the Department of the Parliamentary Library (2000).

The disturbing trend towards widening locational inequality has been confirmed by several analyses, including those of Birrell (1999) in relation to Sydney and the NSW coast, Vinson (1999), which examines regional inequality in Victoria and NSW, and the *Australian* (NATSEM 2000).

A concerted effort by the Commonwealth to invest in the nation's future through education and support for research and development requires an acceptance on the part of the beneficiaries of the information age of the need to pay their fair share of taxes. Some of those beneficiaries may be altruistic and consider it to be fair enough that they pay their taxes so that social inequality does not widen. However, those high-wealth individuals who revel in the latest aggressive tax avoidance schemes may need a different motivation. Their safety and that of their families will increasingly be at risk if inequality in Australia continues to widen sharply. A fractured society is an unsafe society. Juveniles who miss out on a decent education and leave school early are more likely to be resentful of society and to lash out at the more fortunate whom they consider have not allowed them to participate in a prosperous society.

Over the past thirty years the incidence of breaking and entering has trebled, much of it related to the illicit drug problem.[5] In just ten years the number of deaths from illicit drug use is estimated to have almost doubled to more than 800 a year (Williams 1997). Social exclusion can also lead to an increasing prevalence of child abuse, itself a major risk factor in criminal behaviour. The odds for future delinquency, adult criminality and arrest for a violent crime are 40 per cent higher for people abused and neglected as children (Widom 1992).

The disadvantage suffered by young people and the poor is being further exacerbated by the Coalition's changes to the taxation system. The taxation system has become far less progressive with the introduction of the GST, reversing the gains made by the Labor Government's income tax base-broadening measures during the 1980s. Under the GST, half of the income tax cuts have gone to the top 20 per cent of income earners. The regressivity of this shift in the tax mix towards indirect taxes has been exacerbated by the replacement with the GST of a wholesale sales tax that was applied at graduated rates and that exempted basic goods and all services.

Further shifts in the tax mix towards regressive indirect taxation can be expected under a Coalition Government that is committed to continued reductions in marginal income tax rates for high-income earners and which has a strong preference for adding all food to the GST base. This poses further dangers for the poor and disadvantaged. Treasurer Costello has repeatedly described the partial exemption of food as a 'nightmare on Main Street' and still wants all food to be taxed by the GST:

> Every time you go for an exemption you get into a complication. I argued this in relation to food. You can recall I was arguing all the way through the tax debate that you should have food included as a good. (Costello 2000)

Any increase in the rate of GST would compound the regressivity of the shift in the tax mix towards consumption and away from a progressive income tax system.

Concluding remarks — the future of governance

The debate in Australia about the role of government in the 21st century is usefully viewed as part of a broader international debate on the future of governance. An OECD report on the outlook for the future of governance observes that redefinition of the role of government is vital. It concludes that:

> In this respect, there is probably a minimal consensus that the first goal of the government is to provide public safety, national security and justice, and that it has basic responsibilities for equality of opportunity. Government's role beyond those requirements needs rethinking. (OECD 1999a, p. 7)

The report goes on to note that the knowledge society will create more demand for knowledge-based skills which are usually acquired through education, but many people do not finish basic education. This will create a 'dual society' that leads to social exclusion (OECD 1999a, p. 7). The OECD observes that one of the most important governance issues in the coming decades will also be one of the oldest: providing education. Unless education is made available equitably in the information age the OECD predicts inequality will continue to widen (OECD 1999b, p. 2).

Yet the conservative agenda of reduced marginal rates of income tax for high-income earners, financed by a broad-based consumption tax, fails to provide for extra national investment in education. According to this line of thinking, the highly skilled in the information age are also highly mobile internationally. They seek tax jurisdictions with relatively low effective marginal rates of income tax on the high incomes they can command. Since these highly skilled individuals are essential to the formation of human capital, and therefore a nation's prosperity in the information age, it is argued that the appropriate tax policy is one which relies more heavily on taxes on consumption and less on income taxes applied at progressive rates.

This agenda has been articulated by Treasurer Costello (1999b), who has lamented the 'brain drain' from Australia which he considers has been exacerbated by higher salaries and lower marginal income tax rates overseas. He believes the top marginal rate of income tax is too high at 47 per cent.

The empirical validity of this line of reasoning has not been established. Pre-tax incomes, synergies with other highly skilled individuals in related fields of endeavour, and lifestyle issues are among the other factors in international locational decisions. The ability of highly skilled individuals in the information age to live in one nation and work in another, through communications technology, is likely to become an increasingly important consideration in their locational decisions.

Assertions that highly skilled individuals move to countries applying low marginal rates of income tax, creating a brain drain from countries that apply progressive income taxes, lend a convenient respectability to those advocating broad-based consumption taxes for their own personal gain.

A declining national investment effort in education and shifts in the tax mix towards regressive indirect taxes are the basic ingredients for widening inequality. This is the conservative agenda. Increasing national investment in education and the educated beneficiaries of the information age paying their fair share of tax to help finance this investment are fundamental to a more egalitarian, more cohesive and safer society. This is the progressive agenda. The philosophical divide has never been deeper.

chapter **2**

Bridging the divide between G.D.P and quality of life

By Lindy Edwards

In the late 1990s a gulf emerged between the quality of life of Australians and the health of our economy. While the economy boomed, large sections of the community reported that their quality of life was deteriorating (Eckersley 1999, p. 4). Many said they felt economic growth was coming at the cost of quality of life (Mackay 1999). In recent years public policy communities have assumed the two move together. Their divergence goes to the core of the divide between the community and its policy-makers.

In this chapter I argue that this growing divide is symptomatic of a deeper problem. The fashion in public policy has been to treat economic issues and social issues as separate rather than intertwined and often competing. The artificial separation has seen economic priorities trample over many social and other quality-of-life concerns. There is an urgent need to re-integrate the two, but the challenge is how. Many of the old tools for linking the economic and social no longer apply in our rapidly changing economic landscape. This chapter explores innovative ways to overcome this divide. Using payroll tax reform as an example, it seeks to explore new ways for government to tap into the community's aspirations.

The gulf between quality of life and economic health

The rift between the economy and the quality of life has arisen through the struggle over how government should relate to the economy. Historically, Australian governments intervened in the economy to channel the nation's wealth into delivering the 'workers' paradise'. Governments stepped in to build the communities Australians wanted to live in. They fostered industries they believed to be desirable, located in the places people wanted them to be. They dictated wage and income distributions, and overhauled the power balance between workers and their employers.

However, in the late 1970s and early 1980s, amidst fears about the sustainability of the Australian economy, the debate shifted. Government intervention started to be assessed in terms of its impact on G.D.P rather than on communities. Latching onto the neo-liberal economic ideas that were fashionable in the 1970s and 1980s, it was decided that the economy needed to be liberated from the 'heavy hand of government'. One of economics' classic rules of thumb was invoked as a tool in this liberation. It is the rule that we should organise the economy as efficiently as possible and then redistribute the wealth to achieve social goals afterwards. 'Apply free market principles, then compensate', became the policy catchcry of the era. The approach entrenched an artificial divide between economic policy and social policy.

While Labor was in government the approach of 'apply free market principles, then compensate' was evident in everything from the National Competition Policy through to the social safety net. The Labor Government pursued market-based reforms and then gave assistance to those caught in the worst of the fallout. While the community has been outraged by wave after wave of reform, and attacked successive governments as 'economic rationalists', policy-makers did not acknowledge adequately the community's complaints about their falling quality of life. They insisted that the problem was that people did not understand economics, and were adamant that their task was to educate people about the wealth the reforms would eventually deliver.

2: bridging the divide   33

The notion of intervening in the market to drive social outcomes has vanished. Try quizzing a member of Federal Labor about protecting people from the excesses of the market. More often than not they leap to talking about the social safety net. Even those on the left of politics speak as if preventing those at the bottom from being ground into garden mulch is the only social policy issue. Broader notions of ensuring that the market provides a foundation for a high quality of life for the whole community are entirely overlooked. It is as if we have ceased to recognise that our jobs, what we do and the hours we work are the core of our lives. The economy is the community. How it operates dictates our social relationships, our lifestyles and our culture. Separating the two is the stuff of abstract intellectual models.

This policy failure has created a gulf between what government takes as the indicator of the national well-being — economic growth — and what the electorate experiences as their quality of life. To overcome the gulf between government and the electorate we need to re-focus policy on fulfilling people's aspirations. The economic and the social need to be re-integrated, in order to create the quality of life that people are yearning for.

Bridging the gap between quality of life and economic health

So we need to get better at re-integrating quality of life and economic policy issues, but how? The neo-liberal economists who have dominated the nation's treasuries and found voice in documents such as the Independent Inquiry into National Competition Policy have argued that government's interventions have come at too great an economic cost. They have claimed that government was too cumbersome and its efforts at harnessing the economy too rigid. Governments, they asserted, could not anticipate the direction of innovation and, during periods of rapid change, would struggle to come up with ways of regulating the market that would not hamper economic development. While the claims may be overstated, they gained enough currency to conclude they had some foundation. The question, then, is how to re-integrate quality of life priorities into economic life at minimum cost.

Well, if you can't beat them join them. If the problem is that the economic and social spheres are being kept artificially separate, and the economic is steamrolling the social, then one answer is to find ways for the social to infiltrate the economic. We can take our lead from the environmental economists. Over the last two decades a lot of work has been done on drawing environmental considerations into mainstream economic calculations (Baumaol and Oates 1988). The environmental economists have won the battle of ideas. They have convinced us all that pumping filth into the air, depleting one-off resources and accumulating mountains of waste are not economically efficient. The costs don't go to the businesses' bottom-line, but they are borne by the society. As a result we have moved to taxing emissions into the air, charging for waste disposal and increasing levies on exhaustible resources. By attributing an economic cost to these environmental costs we have brought the environment into the mainstream of economic debate. Where these measures have been put in place, businesses now have to take the impact on the environment into account when they make their economic decisions. The community's interest and the economic interests are integrated. Instead of simply advancing their own profit margin, businesses must deliver a net gain for society.

We can take the same approach towards re-integrating community well-being and quality of life issues into the economy. We can move to include social costs in business bottom-line decisions. There are a number of quality-of-life issues that are being trampled because they are not registering in business decision-making. By making the social costs economically visible — by putting a price on them — we can make sure businesses are not simply making private profit by eroding the community's quality of life. Business efforts to achieve private profit must in fact have to reap a social gain.

In doing so, we not only bridge the divide between G.D.P and quality of life, we might also chip away at the divide between governments and their communities.

A practical example: the problem of work hours

Let's take a practical example — the problem of work hours. One example of a business practice that is reaping social costs is the growing tendency to work fewer employees for longer hours. While unemployment remains stubbornly high, those with jobs are increasingly labouring under longer work hours. In 1982 full-time employees worked an average of 38.2 hours per week. By 1998 this had ballooned to 41.1 hours. The leap in work hours is equivalent to just over 5 per cent of all the current weekly hours of work. This redistribution of work hours — this work hoarding — is a threat to both equity and quality of life (Campbell 1999).

This trend is straining people's health, and their family relationships, and eroding community involvement — while those that are unemployed can't find jobs. A standard economic argument would be that people enter these arrangements voluntarily, so it must reflect what they want. But that is not necessarily so. There are a number of reasons the full social costs are not reflected in private decisions. Firstly, a lot of these costs are borne by the employee. The employee may not consider they have the bargaining power to properly represent their interests. For example, the 2000 Australian Bureau of Statistics (ABS) study of working hours of wage and salary earners in Queensland found that 62 per cent of people who usually worked unpaid overtime would prefer to work fewer hours. This made up a total of 29 per cent of women and 34 per cent of men. According to the ABS the main reason employees gave for not working fewer hours was that they had 'no control over working hours' (ABS 6344.3).

Secondly, there are costs in this business behaviour that are not borne by either the employer or the employee. Individual lifestyle decisions often affect the community. The costs of increased unemployment and reduced community participation are unlikely to factor in individual decisions. Furthermore, there are also costs that are primarily borne by the individual, but that overflow into community costs. These can include health problems and family breakdown, where the individual's personal trauma draws on community resources or affects the people around them.

A *taxing solution*

One approach to tackling longer work hours is to set up a tax structure that reflects the social cost of these hiring practices.

One option would be a revenue-neutral overhaul of the existing payroll tax. Businesses that employ more people to work fewer hours would pay a lower rate of tax, and those that work a small number of people long hours would pay a higher rate of tax.

The tax approach has a number of benefits over regulatory approaches. It would give businesses and employees flexibility about how they go about work reduction. They could chose whether they wanted to shorten the working day, work fewer days per week or have more annual leave. They could tailor their working hours reduction strategies to the needs of their particular business and their employees' preferred lifestyles. The averaging mechanism would encourage workplaces to allow variability and flexibility in the work practices of their employees. And as the business and the industry change, they could update their approach accordingly. As some businesses will encounter excessive costs to make the changes, they can opt to pay their way, rather than be lumbered with very costly regulation, thus averting some of the highest costs of regulation.

Restructuring payroll tax in this way can be sold either as a carrot or a stick. It can be seen as a penalty applied to businesses that pursue socially undesirable work practices. It can be argued that employers that work their employees long hours are inflicting costs on society. These costs include increased family breakdown, lower health, lower community involvement, diminished social capital, and reduced equity and social cohesion. It can be argued that businesses have obligations beyond making a profit and a return to shareholders. They have an obligation to contribute to the quality of life of their employees and their communities. Those that fail in those obligations should be penalised, and the tax inflicts that penalty.

Alternatively it can be argued that the tax aims to help businesses behave in socially desirable ways. Government recognises that there are costs in employing more people to work fewer hours. There are costs in training, accommodation, administration etc. Giving employers a tax break to pursue a low-work-hours policy can be seen as government giving business a helping hand to do the right thing. The tax will help to protect the competitive position of businesses that undertake work practices for the good of the community. In the best scenario, government may even give those businesses a cost advantage over their competitors. In some instances the tax break will more than cover the costs of employing more people, giving 'community friendly' businesses a head start on their competitors.

Either way, the bottom line is the same. The tax is about forcing businesses to weigh up the true costs and benefits of their work practices. Currently, when businesses weigh up the costs and benefits of their employment practices, they are only weighing up the direct cost and benefits to their business. By putting a price or a cost on the social importance of employment practices, businesses can make decisions that better reflect their impact on the community. In economic terms this is referred to as a 'pigouvian tax'. A pigouvian tax seeks to get business to include costs in their decision-making that are a product of their actions, but which might not otherwise appear on their bottom line (Mankiw, Gans and King, 1999, p. 204).

In the long run the tax would skew the economy towards industries that are more amendable to flexible working arrangements. The tax break would make industries with greater capacity to reduce work hours relatively more profitable than industries that are more rigid in their organisational needs. In a macro-economic analysis this would eventually lead to proportionally more of society's resources being invested in these more profitable and flexible 'high quality of life industries'. This has to be seen as desirable. In an international trading economy, surely it is the obligation of governments to encourage their country to specialise in industries that can provide the most attractive combination of wealth and quality of life to their communities.

Payroll tax — an ideal candidate

Payroll tax is ideal for the task. It is a good tax for tackling business behaviour because it starts with a clean slate. The tax has long since lost its original purpose and is now only a source of revenue. It began as a Commonwealth tax that raised money to fund child endowment payments, but that link with child endowment policies was soon cut and the tax transferred to the States in 1971. The rates were rapidly hiked and the tax became a vital source of State revenue, making up 21 per cent of all State tax revenue in 1995–96 (Gabbitas and Eldridge 1998, p. 82).

The tax works slightly differently in each State. However, in broad terms, each business with a payroll over a minimum threshold pays a flat percentage of their payroll as tax. The threshold effectively acts to exempt small businesses from the tax. In 1999 the rates of the tax varied from state to state between 5 per cent and 9.5 per cent and the minimum thresholds ranged from $450,000 in South Australia to $800,000 in Queensland (Crowe 1999, p. 17). There is also some variation across States as to how the tax is phased in, which results in the different States having quite different effective rates of tax.

In tax policy terms, payroll tax is considered to be a 'good' tax. It is a 'good' because it is fairly economically neutral. The tax is applied broadly across sectors of the economy (with exemptions for the social welfare sector), so it does not significantly change businesses' relative competitiveness and profitability, nor the relative prices of products and consumer purchasing patterns (Ryan 1995; Crowe 1999; Gabbitas and Eldridge 1998).

There have been a number of debates about the tax, such as whether it is a tax on jobs, whether small business should be exempted, and whether the tax disadvantages Australia's exports. However, while the bad press has made the tax politically vexing, the economic analysis of the tax is less damning. Research done by State and Federal Treasuries argue that, as taxes go, the distortion of the economy is minimal and payroll tax is one of the better taxes States have been using (Ryan 1995; Crowe 1999).

From our perspective this makes it a good base. It is starting from a relatively clean slate and there are not too many problems with reforms cutting across or impeding other community priorities.

How would it work?

The tax could be structured so that each business with a payroll in excess of the threshold, say $500,000, would pay a flat proportion of their payroll as tax. The rate would be determined by the average work hours of all permanent employees working in excess of sixteen hours per week. There could be three tax rates. The top rate would apply to businesses with an average work hours in excess of 40 hours per week, the second tier could be 30–40 hours per week and the lowest tax rate would apply to those with average work hours of less than 30 hours per week.

The average work hours could be documented and assessed by one of two methods. First, the average work hours and the means for achieving them could be required to be stipulated in employment agreements. This would have the advantage that, while the actual hours would be difficult to monitor, employers could be kept in line by the usual processes for enforcing agreements. Alternatively, businesses could choose to keep records of their employees' work hours. These records could then be used to calculate the actual averages of hours worked. To keep the administrative costs of the tax to a minimum, businesses should have the choice to opt out of the system. Businesses that decide it costs too much to keep the records could choose to pay the highest tax rate.

The tax-free threshold which exempts small business from the tax should be maintained to facilitate the administration of the tax. Large employers are better placed to handle the administrative burden. They are likely to have electronic payroll systems to record employee work hours. They are also more likely to have formal workplace agreements.

Ideally, the tax would be implemented uniformly across the country. While politically difficult to achieve, uniformity would benefit the community and governments alike. Having the same system across state boundaries mitigates against the current practice of companies playing State governments off against one another for tax exemptions. Governments compete against each other offering sweeteners to companies to encourage them to set up in their State. This practice is undesirable as it effectively transfers wealth from the public coffers to big business. This so-called 'tax competition' will also eventually undermine the tax incentive regime as the exemptions eventually leave the regime with patchy coverage.

The consequences

The payroll tax initiative is focused on improving people's leisure/work balance and their quality of life. European experiments on reducing work hours have found that well-designed policies can reap considerable benefits in this regard (Harcourt 1999; Campbell 1999). However, other aspects of the policy approach are more ambiguous. The key issues that need to be addressed are the policy's impact on employment and income levels.

(i) Employment

The jury is still out on how effective work-sharing initiatives are at reducing unemployment. A number of studies of European experiments in reducing work hours have found that the immediate boost to employment was less than hoped. On the other hand, 1996 French experiments similar to the payroll tax proposal achieved a 'quick and surprising success' (Campbell 1999, p. 11). In the French experiments employers were given discounts on their mandatory social security contributions if they reached workplace agreements that reduced the working week by at least 10 per cent and either increased employment by 10 per cent, or reduced planned redundancies by 10 per cent. By the end of 1997 almost 1,500 agreements had been signed covering about 150,000 workers. Analyses at the time suggested about 20,000 jobs were created and about 15,000 jobs were saved from redundancy (Campbell 1999, p. 12).

At any rate these numbers are relatively small, and reducing work hours should not be seen as a quick fix for unemployment. However, the major benefits are likely to be longer term. A key barrier to work redistribution in Australia is that overtime is concentrated in highly skilled jobs (Harcourt 1999). The excess work could not necessarily be given to the next passing unemployed person. Nonetheless, economic theory would argue this sort of structural mismatch would be resolved in the longer term. In time, the workforce can be 'skilled up' to fill these vacancies. It creates the desirable prospect of a long-term shift to a greater proportion of the workforce in higher-skilled, higher-paying jobs.

(ii) Maintaining income levels

Re-structuring payroll tax should not significantly reduce wealth in the economy. As the proposal is for a revenue-neutral re-structuring of an existing tax, the total tax burden on industry would not change. (Hence, for economists the tax deadweight loss would not change.) Only the incidence and the incentives of the tax would shift. As a result, one would not expect there to be any reduction in economic output.

If there is no reduction in wealth in the economy as a whole, maintaining individual income levels only becomes an issue if the policy is effective at boosting jobs. If the number of people being employed stays the same, businesses' total wage bill will continue to be spread over the same number of people. The change in work hours would be accommodated by developing more efficient work practices, and people would be able to demand the same incomes. However, if the policy does create a significant number of jobs, then businesses' total wage bill will be spread over more people, implying an income drop for some of those already employed.

From the community's perspective this would represent a net gain. The social costs of unemployment and of people working long hours would be slashed through the redistribution of work. From society's perspective it is more desirable to have more people working half-time and having their income being topped up by government, than to have some working full-time and the others being entirely reliant on income support. It reduces the loss of confidence, loss of skills and social isolation associated with long-term unemployment, as well as reducing the social costs of people working long hours. These benefits come on top of a windfall of having to pay less unemployment benefits.

Nonetheless, it does create a political challenge, as those that fear a drop in income would need to be won over. However, there is plenty of scope for innovative policy approaches to solve the problem. Redistributing the gains from sharing the jobs around can be used to turn the policy into a win-win. For example, savings from reduced social welfare benefits could be redirected to increasing the incomes of those on reduced hours. People that experience a drop in income/hours could become eligible to take paid training, where they receive an income top-up from government for upgrading their skills. Such an approach would achieve the dual goals of fostering continuous education and boosting the productivity of the economy while also protecting people from a drop in income.

As a result the costs associated with reforming payroll tax are likely to be minor relative to the potential gains. The reforms would force businesses to take into account the social costs of their work practices, ensuring that business decisions reflect what is in the interests of the whole community, not just their own bottom line. The reform would help to overcome the problem of excessive working hours, assisting working people to enjoy a better quality of life, and may have additional benefits in reducing unemployment.

Conclusion

It is likely that policy proposals such as this will be met with some apprehension, as business would inevitably be resistant. It is some time since governments have made political capital out of stepping into the market to curb business practices in defence of employees. However, the fact that this runs against current political culture should in itself be a subject of some contemplation, particularly as politicians scratch their heads about why Australians report they feel betrayed.

Nonetheless, while business will undoubtedly resist moves to integrate social costs into their bottom line, economists should applaud it. In economic theory efficiency means that society's resources are being used so as to provide the highest possible standard of living for the community. When key factors that contribute to our quality of life are ignored or undervalued, society is being short-changed. The full and proper pricing of social costs would ensure that the economy progresses in a way that enhances the well-being of the whole community.

chapter 3

The contract state and the public interest

By Michael Di Francesco[1]

The neo-liberal agenda of state re-structuring was created as a response to perceived inadequacies with bureaucratic provision of public services. This reform program attained the status of policy orthodoxy in a relatively short period of time, but is now under sustained attack (Painter, M. 1996). The current critique of state re-structuring is broad in its scope, but commonly represents a reaction to the consequences — intended or not — of market-oriented policies, in particular the contracting out of government services. At a general level this criticism is couched in terms of how indiscriminate contracting of state functions is at the expense of the 'public interest', however that term is defined. Proponents of the reform, of course, contend that the market best serves these very same interests. If nothing else, the controversy over state re-structuring illustrates how the public interest retains its position in public policy debate.

This chapter investigates contracting out in the State sector as an attack on the public interest, and seeks to assess the prospects for employing that term as an operational concept for policy-makers. Much of this critique assumes that the process of contractualism has the potential to increase inequality in Australian society, by installing private interests at the helm of what were public services. In examining these claims, this chapter follows the pioneering work of Boston

(1995), which sought to identify the conditions in which the public interest may dictate against the use of contracting out, addressing two important questions: 'What constitutes the public interest?' 'Can the public interest be used as a *criterion* for testing the limits of contracting in the state sector?' The chapter continues the work of Boston, although it goes further in acknowledging that the public interest is an essentially contested concept.

The contract state and its critics

The emergence of the contract state in Australia and other liberal democracies is the latest phase in an ongoing project of *public* institutional re-design. The term 'contract state' refers not only to the increasing use of the 'market' to structure relations between the state and the community, but also the application of formal contract arrangements *within* the state with the intention of replacing bureaucratic provision of public services. Whereas bureaucracy seeks consistency in public services through the 'dead hand' of direct hierarchical oversight, the contract state aims for measurable improvements via the 'hands off' control imposed by formal contracts. Whilst few would disagree that ideological winds of change have fanned this transformation, other factors have had an influence. The onset of fiscal stress in the early-to-mid 1980s elevated both efficiency and control as imperatives for institutional design. Agency theory, which addressed similar concerns in the business world, presented a ready-made solution (Althaus 1997). Political control over self-interested bureaucratic implementation could be secured by using contract to separate these functions. At the same time, opening up public service delivery to competitive pressures was expected to increase the efficiency as well as responsiveness of public services, the latter of which was strongly associated with a 'democratic deficit' between what the state did and what society expected of it (OECD 1997, pp. 7–8). Supporters of this model argue that contracting narrows this deficit, creating a hedge against state capture by special interests — the market is deemed to be a more sensitive gauge of public demands than existing political arrangements, and one less vulnerable to manipulation. Critics, however, fear unrestrained contract may corrode the link between the state and civil society, a connection that for many cannot be captured adequately in an economic exchange. These arguments will be considered later in light of the public interest. For now, three strands of this critique are particularly relevant.

Social capital depletion

The first strand sees the contract state as undermining civil society and the conditions for creating 'social capital', a notion which draws on Robert Putnam's exploration of the mutually reinforcing relationship between the state and social institutions (Putnam 1993; Cox 1995). It refers to those features of social arrangements, such as 'norms of reciprocity and networks of civic engagement', that build cooperation within the community and support the state (Putnam 1993, pp. 167, 170–1). Social capital is derived from other social activities; it 'increases with use and diminishes with disuse' (Putnam 1993, p. 170). As the reach of the contract state increases, and market exchange displaces traditional social arrangements, community investment in social capital also declines.

In the context of community services, Brennan (1998) has argued that many social networks that facilitate cooperation for 'mutual benefit' are being so diminished. To this extent the contract state is also a re-structuring of civil society — political engagement is replaced by market participation and an expectation that people no longer act as citizens with collective interests (Brennan 1998, p. 136). In a like vein, Muetzelfeldt (1994, p. 154) contends that the shift to contract as the basis for exchange *within* the state 'leads to a focus on private rather than public interests, to a narrowing of the scope of political action, and to a limited view of citizenship and people's roles as members of society'. In both cases, the public interest (public provision of community services directed at meeting some conception of equity) is being intentionally replaced by incentives to pursue individual or 'private interest'.

Others contend that depreciated social capital is only one possible outcome of the contract state. In tracing the lin-

eage of contemporary developments in social contract theory, Yeatman (1995, pp. 129–136; 1997, pp. 51–4) suggests
that the economic nature of relationships within the contract state is important, but not because it privileges private
over public interests. Rather it derives from contractualism's
status as a new form of 'governance' that shades the idea of
citizenship of a political community into an exchange relationship founded on 'equality of contractual standing' and
freedom of choice, a situation that is plainly not represented
by social reality (Yeatman 1997, p. 52). As a consequence, if
'new' contractualism is to be continued as a governance
strategy that seeks both efficiency and legitimacy, the state
must meet its 'social responsibility' to minimise inequality in
contractual status.

Third Way theory and practice

A second type of critique can be identified in the emergence
of 'Third Way theory', most closely associated with the rise of
New Labour in the United Kingdom. 'The Third Way' is best
seen as 'praxis' for left-of-centre parties in a period of neoliberal ascendancy, where 'governments enable, not command, and the power of the market is harnessed to serve the
public interest' (Blair 1998, p. 7). This claim, however, is less
political and more of a managerial task directed at 'renewing' social democracy through the strategic appropriation of
'individualism' (Giddens 1998). The Third Way responds to
fundamental economic and social change in advanced western democracies associated with globalisation and the onset
of a post-materialist blurring of the left/right divide in politics. Neo-liberal-inspired market reforms are not the *cause* of
this change, but rather one response chosen. The task facing
social-democrat policy-makers is to trace an alternative interpretation of economic and social change that accords the
state an appropriate role in balancing 'individual and collective responsibilities' (Giddens 1998, pp. 37, 64–8). The raison d'être of left-of-centre politics — promoting equality —
is transformed into the minimisation of exclusion or 'mechanisms that act to detach groups of people from the social
mainstream' (Giddens 1998, p. 104).

This practical policy orientation has attracted consider-able criticism. In a mirroring of the type of debate that accompanied the re-positioning of the Australian Labor Party during the 1980s and 1990s, The Third Way has been dismissed as being at best little more than a marketing exer-cise and at worst 'a one-sided compromise' legitimising the neo-liberal reform agenda (Faux 1999, pp. 74–6; but see Ryan 1999). Policy ideas spring not from a 'substantial moral claim about the nature of society' but rather from 'a socio-logical claim about the novel condition of contemporary society' (Finlayson 1999, p. 271). Whilst the transitional nature of the present economic and social condition is cer-tainly arguable, the social hardship and political disorienta-tion stemming from re-structuring is not. The key question is how the Third Way can inform state responses.

As practised by the Blair Labour Government, The Third Way acknowledges the limitations of the welfare state as an instrument for achieving equality in social outcomes, but rejects the emasculation of the state (and its role in securing social justice) in the face of market provision. Its preference is for a 'social investment state' where government retains strong steering capacities to manage the operation of part-nerships 'while ensuring that the public interest remains paramount' (Giddens 1998, p. 125; see also Blair 1998, p. 15). Whilst this stance reflects a reluctance to reverse the structural reforms of the Conservatives, most notably the internal market of the National Health Service, there has occurred a reining in of the 'contract culture' through the use of area-based partnerships (Painter, C. 1999, p. 105). True to The Third Way's emphasis on equality and inclusion, efforts have been made to 'join up' the delivery of social ser-vices in communities suffering from multiple disadvantages, through the creation of 'partnership forums' embracing state and non-state providers (Painter, C. 1999, pp. 108–11).

As this indicates, The Third Way is not a backdoor to the reinstallation of bureaucracy. Third Way thinking accepts some neo-liberal-inspired structural reforms in the public sec-tor, in particular the role of *plurality* in improving the quality of social service conception and delivery. Plurality, however, need not equate with competition. As with the idea of part-nerships between government, local communities and the private sector, and efforts to renew political participation, plurality can be instituted as collaboration and mutual adjust-ment (Painter, C. 1999, p. 111). This balance between central guidance and local responsiveness is unfortunately difficult to achieve. New Labour, for instance, has retained performance management within a quasi-contractual framework for social partnerships. In these circumstances, how can the state know that the contract and *public* resources (defined broadly to include both authority and finances) are being used in the public interest? In other words, where should the balance be struck in terms of the contractual framework?

Public interest limits

The third strand of criticism tackles the practical policy task of marking out the limits to contracting. Boston (1995) asks whether there any functions which *only* government should carry out. Whilst he acknowledges that in a parliamentary democracy questions going to the appropriate role of the state must be resolved through the political process and hence shaped by the prevailing distribution of political power, the 'integrity, legitimacy and even perhaps the sover-eignty of the state' requires certain functions to remain in public hands (Boston 1995, p. 79). This approach echoes some of the wider concerns expressed above, particularly in terms of the maintenance of social capital and the coherence of the state.

It is now widely recognised that public-sector restructur-ing along managerialist and purchaser-provider lines has sought to 'commodify' government activities so they are assessed in terms of their being able to be bought and sold, rather than as an entitlement of citizens. In other words, markets are 'formed' with the intention of facilitating con-tract. The primary weakness of *indiscriminate* contracting out is that state control over public policy, in terms of both design and delivery, is curtailed significantly (Boston 1995, pp. 96–103). Stepping back from the immediate managerial and political repercussions of contracting strategies, Boston focuses on the larger picture of 'state incapacity'. In doing so he adopts a test developed by the United States General Accounting Office to help identify 'inherently governmental functions'. These refer to:

...a function which is **so intimately related to the public interest** as to mandate administration by government employees. These functions include those activities which require either the exercise of discretion in applying government authority or the use of value judgement in making decisions for the government. (cited in Boston 1995, p. 85, emphasis added)

With respect to the particularly sensitive output of policy advice, Boston suggests that a public interest test be invoked for identifying these functions and that contracting out should not be pursued if it is potentially 'injurious' to these wider interests. Although he demonstrates quite convincingly why policy advice, in general, should be retained as a state function, his analysis sheds little light on how the public interest criterion is applied in *specific* policy circumstances (see Boston 1995, pp. 89ff).

Diagnoses of what ails the contract state, such as Boston's, are commonly understood in terms of how the public interest has been adversely affected, in terms of either declining social capital or increased state incapacity. At the same time, remedies are just as likely to be framed in terms of how the 'power' of the state can be used in conjunction with a contractual framework to further those same interests. Given that interpretations of the public interest can be derived only from the political process, can the concept of the public interest be used to mitigate the adverse consequences of contracting out?

Unpacking the public interest

As with many contested political concepts, rendering the public interest operational for policy-makers was a project at its height during the 1950s and 1960s, although it has a much longer history (Gunn 1989). Even then, however, analysis of the concept was more common than the policy-relevant task of designing institutional criteria for its advancement (Friedrich 1962). This is not to say that the public interest is not applied in other contexts. Judicial review, where an equally vague notion of the public interest is used, is an example that comes readily to hand (see Mulgan 2000, p. 12). But certainly claims to the public interest are inevitably determined through the interplay of interests within the political process. As such it is a concept that can be analysed according to the different forms and functions it serves within that process (Mansbridge 1998, p. 12). Four forms will be discussed here.

The first is to consider the public interest *normatively*, to distinguish this type of interest from private or individual interests. Here, the public interest is an ethical concept or a 'standard of goodness by which political acts can be judged; action in the public interest, therefore, deserves approval *because* it is good' (Cassinelli 1962, pp. 45–6). As a tool for evaluating the conduct of political life, it must be founded on a 'unitary scheme of moral judgements which should guide every individual at a given time and place, although these individuals may be unaware of it' (Held 1970, pp. 135–6). The public interest is thus an absolute value that both government, as the embodiment of the collective, and individuals should always aim to achieve. The continuing problem, of course, lies in revealing the particulars of the 'good life' and discovering the 'right' course of action, as well as reconciling valid claims relating to individual *and* public interests.

A second approach is to consider the public interest as an *outcome* or *objective*. This is usually expressed in aggregate terms, as in the assessment of a policy as being 'good for everyone' or 'good for the majority' (Mansbridge 1998, pp. 9–10). Whilst modern survey methods can provide a crude measure of this outcome, the unresolved practical difficulty remains in aggregating individual values, demands and preferences, or, alternatively, avoiding the 'majority' as a surrogate for the 'public'. Nonetheless, with this usage the public interest need have no normative substance at all.

A common understanding of the public interest is as a *process* or *decision rule* (Mansbridge 1998, pp. 10–11). This procedural meaning treats the public interest as the product of a particular process, for example the democratic process, adherence to due process in administrative decision-making, or, as proponents of contracting contend, free competition within a market setting. The process itself is believed to reveal the public interest. Again the practical difficulty is that there is no rule that meets the requirement of being in the interest of all, since these processes are dependent on the exercise of power, for example through the constraints imposed by structural 'inequality' among those who participate (Held 1970, p. 119).

The concept can also be analysed as a site for contesting the terms of public interest and how it is affected by a specific policy (Mansbridge 1998). In policy debate, this fourth approach means specifying with more precision which public is being affected and what their interests comprise. Barry (1965, p. 190) contends this approach permits the public interest to be defined as 'those interests which people have in common *qua* members of the public', although membership of this public is not fixed. Indeed, because the composition of the public differs according to circumstances we can refer only to the public interest within particular contexts (Barry 1965, p. 192). Therefore, the public interest can be considered as 'the interests that people share with one another in virtue of similar roles or capacities' (Barry 1965, p. 196; see also Goodin 1996, pp. 338–9). In this construction the public interest derives from specific shared public roles. So, as Boston notes (1995, p. 88), one way of giving the concept operational meaning is to identify long-standing roles, such as paying taxes and utilising services like transport, education and health care, and to assign interests to these various publics. This is a useful starting point for trying to separate the possible effects of a specific course of action, although it also confirms that the public interest remains essentially contested. Whilst determining the 'public' in any given situation is certainly contingency-based, associating the different interests with different publics does not overcome the problem of conflict between the way individuals rank the importance of different public roles and the impact of any particular policy. In practice, at an aggregate level at least, we return to the problem of priorities.

Whilst it is not entirely clear that Boston's critique of contracting does apply public interest criteria for a specific identifiable public — in fact, it could be argued that Boston's test is more a criterion of *which* (private) interests stand to gain from contracting out, rather than the costs of contracting out to any *specific* public interest — similar public role approaches can be used to apply a type of 'net benefit' test to policy. The most familiar is the 'public good' argument, which justifies state intervention as balancing interdependence in resource use and incentives for individual opportunism (Hood 1986, pp. 1–15). In those situations where public interests in particular circumstances may overlap and clash, public good tests are routinely used to weigh up the social and economic benefits and costs associated with a course of action. Such a 'balance sheet' approach could be employed to determine the public interest.

A good example is the Howard Government's Job Network. The issue here is whether the use of contracting for labour market services meets a public interest test. The 'unemployed public', especially the long-term unemployed, have specifiable interests in equitable access to effective job referral and labour market training services. On the assumption that, in the absence of financial incentives, the market is unlikely to provide training assistance to this group, some state intervention will be required. The 'tax paying public' have specifiable interests in the sustainability of any state intervention and the accountability of service providers. Given that the case management of unemployed individuals has proven to be the most effective and costly component of these services, how does market-based service delivery serve the public interest in this case? This is not just a question of reconciling conflicting outcomes, but also of choosing the most appropriate means. To this extent it is relevant to the kind of 'social capital' investment arguments referred to earlier. A net benefit approach may, for instance, reason that contract-based services which substitute opportunistic drive for altruistic motives generate excessive costs to the unemployed public that far outweigh the benefits of economic manageability to the taxpaying public. Nonetheless, the normative dimension discussed earlier continues to underpin this type of argument, illustrating the difficulties associated with clarifying the public interest as a guide for (as opposed to a *post hoc* rationalisation of) public policy.

Public interest and public value

Logic tells us there are limits to the fragmentation of the state. Ultimately, however, this insight must rest on some common understanding of the appropriate role of the state. Claims to the public interest will continue to reside in a normative form and rely on the force of political argument. Arguments that pit the contract state against the public interest may have more persuasive effect if they focus less on how contract may wear away civil society and more on how the state contributes to its own well-being. A public interest defence of the state might have a firmer footing if it explicates *what* the state does and *how* it creates public value. In other words, the generation of public value can be seen as a crude measure of the public interest.

The idea of public value as a distinct product of government is a significant development in analyses of the state's role in underwriting the generation of social and economic welfare (Moore 1995; Alford 1993). Public value, as the output of the 'public production process', is an attempt to recognise and capture the 'non-market' worth of state activity. As in the private sector, production processes are used in government to convert resources into goods and services. However, the concept of public value acknowledges that this process cannot be reduced to the purely technical task of management, but rather must take account of its *political* context. The role of the state as a producer must incorporate an 'ongoing process of authorization' whereby the relevance of state activity is demonstrated *and* the consent of the citizenry is re-affirmed (Moore 1995, pp. 43–50). In this respect, public value represents an important corrective to the common assertion that there is no public sector equivalent to private economic value (although see Gregory 1995).

The link between public value and the public interest lies in the former's emphasis on the role of the state in social capital formation and maintenance. There are three crucial aspects of the public production process that mark it as a process of political authorisation which is not, in all cases at least, reducible to a contractual relationship (Alford 1993, pp. 139–142). The first relates to the distinct political resources that state managers are authorised to use, specifically public power (coercion). In terms of political legitimacy, there are real limits attached to the exercise of these resources by non-state agents. The state, however, is expected to use these means to secure what might be termed a 'sustainable political environment', the second crucial aspect. Public managers are obliged to take account of the impact of policies on different publics; that is, they have an obligation to mediate between interests. Because the obligation is derived from the processes underpinning political consent, it is difficult to capture within a contract framework. Further to this, the obligation is not one that is normally expected to be fulfilled by those interests operating within a market.

The third aspect acknowledges the role of the citizenry in *co-production* of public value. Co-production is a recognition that in many cases a significant component of a public service is provided by the recipient — 'public value can not be created or delivered unless the client actively contributes to its production' (Alford 1998, p. 130; Alford 1993, pp. 140–1). Alford provides a number of examples, the most immediate of which is the co-production of mail delivery that each of us engage in when we complete postcode boxes on pre-marked envelopes. In such cases, the state facilitates positive client participation in the production process, and both this management task and client co-production constitute public value. Accordingly, whilst it would be a mistake to view co-production purely in terms of volunteerism, the 'downloading' by government of social welfare responsibilities to an increasingly market-oriented non-profit sector is likely to undermine the integrity of the production process. Since contracting out is commonly pursued in tandem with a decline in state sponsorship, the contract state may be leading the non-profit sector away from its traditional role as a *partner* in producing public value (Shields and Evans 1998, pp. 97–102; see also Blair 1998).

The public production process has no template. As Alford notes, whilst this precludes a 'one best way' for organising the state, it should not necessarily exclude the use of contractual arrangements. The notion of public value helps frame the contract state, because it steers a middle course through contract and hierarchy that maintains and strengthens the chain of political authorisation joining the state and civil society. Indeed, there is no reason why an 'empowering' contract state, as envisaged by Hood (1997, pp. 125–127), could not emerge as a viable model. Under this model, initiatives like the Job Network, which rely so heavily on market competition, might be evaluated in terms of their capacity to *facilitate* co-production and citizen involvement. If the production of public value is judged to constitute a significant component of employment services, the further use of contracting should be pursued with caution, since it may represent efforts to abdicate responsibility and evade the obligation to secure political consent.

Conclusion

The public interest is an intrinsically political tool of public policy, which is both a weakness and a strength. It is a weakness because the term can be misused to protect the pursuit of what are essentially private interests. It is a strength because the concept contains both an unarticulated standard for 'good' behaviour in public life and a malleability that permits its application to changing social and economic circumstances. In both cases the power of the public interest lies principally in the force of political argument and persuasion. Rendering the concept 'neutral and descriptive' (Gunn 1989, p. 208) by converting the public interest to a set of criteria or a 'checklist' is likely to provide little policy leverage. Rather, it has a central role to play in constructing a coherent defence of the state as the underwriter of social and economic welfare.

chapter 4

Rethinking the public: paying attention to citizens *and* clients

By John Alford

Over the last decade or so, conservative governments in Australia and elsewhere have sought to recast the public as 'customers' of public services. They have directed public sector organisations to become more 'customer focused' — to understand more clearly who their customers are, listen to their needs and be more responsive to them, just as private sector firms do (Osborne and Gaebler 1992, pp. 166–194). In response, government agencies have adopted the language of customer service and client focus. They are increasingly undertaking market research, operating call centres and help lines, upgrading client reception and contact, and running promotional campaigns (OECD 1987; Scrivens 1991; Wanna et al 1992, pp. 126–7).

Accompanying these devices have been more fundamental measures to bestow customer-like status on members of the public, such as the introduction of 'user pays' or of vouchers for services. According to the authors of the bible of public sector reform in the 1990s, *Reinventing Government,* such measures are seen as 'putting customers in the driver's seat', by placing resources (i.e. vouchers) in their hands and letting them choose among competing providers (Osborne and Gaebler 1992; Self 1993, pp. 129–41). At the same time, public agencies have been prodded to be more customer responsive, even when they don't have to compete for clients, by the imposition of customer service commitments, such as the Citizen's Charter in the U.K. (Major 1991).

In the main, these developments have prompted animosity from people in the labour movement and left, for several reasons.[1] Firstly, the 'customer' is seen as a private sector notion which is inappropriate to the public sector. It is argued that the public sector is different in nature, and those it serves cannot validly be called customers. A related concern is that it casts the relationship between the government and the public in terms of monetary exchange, which is perceived as contaminating the pursuit of lofty government purposes with crass commercialism.

Secondly, the push for a customer focus has often been taken to mean that people should have to pay for services which were previously entitlements, rather than receive them as a right. This of course is inequitable, because some people are more readily able to pay than others.

Thirdly, it is seen as devaluing citizenship, a notion that has long echoed the egalitarianism of the social democratic tradition. In his famous discourse on citizenship and social class, T. H. Marshall postulated that 'the equality implicit in the concept of citizenship, even though limited in content, undermined the inequality of the class system...' (Marshall 1950/1992, p. 19). Citizenship also echoes the social democratic emphasis on the public domain. As Pollitt puts it:

> It is a concept with a strong connotation of collective rather than individual action ('Fellow citizens!'). Citizens owe duties to and possess rights of the state. All this is alien to an individualist model where the market is the chief focus of transactions and values...(1990, p. 129)

There are, therefore, tenable reasons for people in the labour movement to be sceptical of the notion of the customer in the public sector. In particular, the private sector model of the customer does not adequately encompass factors specific to the public sector. But it is not good enough for the left to simply condemn that model without articulating an alternative conception of the relationship between government organisations and the members of the public with whom they interact in their day-to-day operations, whom I shall call, for want of a better word, 'clients'. The reason is that the clients of government organisations deserve good service, just as much as the paying customers of private companies. Indeed, precisely because the rationale of many government programs is to remedy market failure or affirm equity in one form or another, these clients tend to comprise those people in our society who are poorer, less powerful, or otherwise comparatively disadvantaged, and therefore less able to pay or lobby for good service.

Despite this need, the social-democratic tradition, and public administration more generally, has lacked a systematic conception of how to deal with the individual recipients of services. Until recent decades, the public sector has tended to be unresponsive to clients' needs, giving rise to enduring stereotypes of bewildering red tape, officious administrators, endless queues and drab uniformity of services — stereotypes which, while often overstated and fuelled by ideological axe-grinding, have some basis in reality, as clients in past years of the Department of Social Security, public hospitals, Telstra, motor registration offices or public housing will attest.

Since the 1970s, however, people on the left have generally advocated more responsive public services, with the emphasis on improving the accessibility of services, better consultation with the community, and introducing more flexibility and humanity into program administration. This approach was consistent with core social democratic values such as equity, participation and human rights. But it tended to focus in a fairly undifferentiated way on citizens in general rather than clients in particular. It therefore offered little guidance as to how to adjudicate between the respective claims on public services of the citizenry as a whole and of individual clients.

Just as importantly, its call to public servants to treat citizens better was largely normative, and therefore made an easy target for conservative critics, who compared it to the more hard-edged accountability implicit in the private sector customer model. This view was expressed most pithily by the authors of *Reinventing Government*:

> Most American governments are customer-blind, while McDonald's and Frito-Lay are customer-driven... Why is it this way? Simple. **Most public agencies don't get their**

funds from their customers. Businesses do. If a business pleases its customers, sales increase; if someone else pleases its customers more, sales decline. So businesses in competitive environments learn to pay enormous attention to the customers. (Osborne and Gaebler 1993, p. 167, emphasis in original)

By contrast, a normative appeal to public servants to be more cognisant of clients' needs as 'the right thing to do' would fall on stony ground. Even though the research shows that public servants are generally public-spirited (e.g. Wittmer 1991), they may be constrained by lack of resources and heavy workloads from being responsive to clients' needs.

In this chapter, I offer a more compelling rationale for a client-responsive stance by public sector organisations and their staff, based on an alternative conception of the relationship between government agencies and their clients. In this conception, there *is* an exchange between public sector agencies and clients, but it is broader than that which underlies the private sector model. Because there is an exchange, both governments and public servants have good *practical* and moral reasons to take account of clients' needs. At the same time, this alternative conception is tailored to the specific circumstances of the public sector: it is not confined to monetary exchange; it does not necessarily entail forcing recipients to pay for services; and it enhances rather than devalues citizenship.

The limitations of the private sector customer model

The conservatives' archetypal customer is one engaged in a market exchange with a private firm, in which the customer provides money, to the amount of the purchase price, in return for the goods or services provided by the firm. In this exchange, the customer receives private value, i.e. goods and services consumed individually, for which he or she has a positive preference (if not for the particular supplier).[2] As long as it is profitable to do so, the firm seeks to maximise sales, by increasing the number of customers or getting repeat business.

But although the clients of *some* government organisations, such as Australia Post or public transport agencies, appear to be similar to this private sector archetype, most differ from it in important respects. Firstly, as suggested above, members of the public receive not only private value from government organisations, but also *public* value, which is necessarily 'consumed' jointly. For example, public goods such as defence, environmental protection or flood control cannot benefit any one individual without everyone else benefiting from them as well. Public value includes the provision of law and order (without which the market cannot function), remedies to market failure, and equity (Hughes 1994). It accrues to the citizenry as a whole.

Secondly, many government clients do not pay money directly in return for the service. For example, some disabled people receive accommodation and support services without paying a purchase price for it. Pupils at government schools receive the tuition and basic infrastructure without paying for it. Of course they (or their families) do pay for them through their taxes, but these payments are pooled and reallocated through consolidated revenue, and are not directly related to the specific service they enjoy. The agencies providing these services are not seeking to maximise sales to them as individuals, but instead operate to a budget constraint, and seek to ration services, for example by applying eligibility rules or waiting lists. I will call these clients *beneficiaries*, to distinguish them from paying customers.[3]

Thirdly, some of the people the conservatives might characterise as customers in the public sector do not always have a positive preference for the 'service', but instead are being coerced against their will (Pollitt 1990; Pegnato 1997; Patterson 1998). For example, the Victorian prison service under the Kennett Government listed 'prisoners' at the top of its 'client statement' (Office of Corrections 1994), but it is difficult to imagine that these 'clients' were eager recipients of incarceration services, nor that prisons should encourage repeat business! This issue arises not only for people subject to law enforcement agencies, but also with many others, such as those subject to the requirements of regulatory agencies, or indeed of any government organisation whose work entails obliging people to do things. I will distinguish these people from paying customers and beneficiaries by calling them *obligatees* (Moore 1994, p. 301).

All of this points to a key difference between private and public sector organisations, arising from the different kinds of 'customers' they serve. A private firm deals only with paying customers. But a government organisation deals with at least two types of public simultaneously. It inevitably serves the citizenry as a whole, but in addition it also serves paying customers and/or beneficiaries and/or obligatees, in the terms set out above. Its managers and staff must weigh the contending claims of each of these publics on its time and resources.

Thus, most of the customers of public sector organisations differ from the private sector paying customer, in ways which impair the organisations' incentives to provide good service. Contrary to the *Reinventing Government* model, the agency has no *financial* reason to satisfy customers, since they do not provide it with any funds. The conservative solution to this problem, of course, is to call for public sector clients to be transformed into paying customers, for example by giving them vouchers, so they can act as purchasers in the market (Savas 1977; Osborne and Gaebler 1993). But such measures are only applicable to beneficiaries, not to obligatees. And they do not eliminate the role of beneficiary; all they do is displace it. For instance, if school students were to be given vouchers instead of government-provided education, they would still be beneficiaries — but of the voucher-giving agency rather than the education department.[4]

It is indeed true, therefore, that the private sector customer model is largely blind to the specific realities of the public sector. The seemingly obvious implication is that it has no place in social democratic thinking about the workings of government. But this does not address the need, acknowledged above, for a systematic conception of organisation-client relationships. In particular, it does not match the claim of the private sector model to have a built-in incentive to be responsive to customers, founded on the fact that they exchange revenue for services. Here I offer an outline of such a conception, based on a broader notion of exchange — one disentangled from the assumptions of the private sector market.

Beyond market exchange

Sociologists and anthropologists writing about 'social exchange' have long recognised that exchange processes in human society are not confined to economic transactions between two parties (Levi-Strauss 1949/1969; Blau 1964; Ekeh 1974). Firstly, they can involve a broader set of 'things which can be exchanged' rather than only tangible items such as money or goods and services. For example, people may give each other intangible things which are of symbolic significance, such as having their particular status recognised or enhanced, or which have intrinsic value, such as friendship or respect, or which have moral or normative value, such as affirming fairness.

Secondly, social exchange can involve more than two parties, and more complex forms of reciprocity, sometimes known as 'generalised exchange'. The private market transaction is an example of 'restricted exchange' (Levi-Strauss 1949/1969): it occurs between only two parties, who have a mutually reciprocal relationship. In restricted exchange, the parties adopt a *quid pro quo* mentality, explicitly calculating what each is giving or receiving in the short term. By contrast, generalised exchange involves at least three actors who 'do not benefit each other directly but only indirectly' (Ekeh 1974, p. 48). For example, A may give to B, who gives to C, who closes the circle by giving to A. This set of exchanges does not entail *quid pro quo*, and can involve delayed repayment, but the overall result over time is that all of its participants have both given and received something in a circular process.

Although it is indirect, the giving by each party in generalised exchange is conditional on that of the other parties. Each actor will be more willing to give if he or she perceives that others are doing likewise as part of the circular exchange process. This perception will be heightened if the parties share a common attachment to the group they comprise and its rules and purposes.

How does this rather abstract theory apply to public sector clients? In short, it enables us to recognise that public sector consumers, even when they don't pay *money* for services, may be important suppliers of other things the government organisation needs, such as information, consent, compliance, cooperation or productive effort. To prompt these behaviours, an organisation must offer the client what he or she wants — which may involve more than just money. Consequently, in order to achieve its purposes, the organisation has pressing practical reasons to enhance clients' satisfaction with its services.

Exchange and beneficiaries

We have noted that beneficiaries do not pay money for the services they receive, and consequently government agencies have little financial incentive to pay attention to their needs. However, if we acknowledge that beneficiary-serving agencies are engaged in exchange processes involving more complex sets of values and parties, then organisations may find it in their interest to serve clients as well as possible.

Take the case of welfare recipients. The social security agency pays benefits to recipients not in the expectation that they will give it money in return, but rather to fulfil a mandate endowed upon it by the citizenry, via the political process. In return for the authority and resources it bestows on the agency, the citizenry receives various forms of public value, such as social insurance, reduced street crime, social cohesion, and the affirmation of the civilised nature of the society in which we live.

In return for their benefit cheques, the clients do not reciprocate directly to the social security agency, but indirectly to the community at large, in their myriad acts of 'consent' to the social order and its laws. To the extent that they do so, the citizenry perceives that the welfare department is doing its job properly, and in turn bestows its consent and resources on that department. Thus, the government organisation provides public value to the citizenry in the very act of providing private value to its beneficiary clients. This generalised exchange is diffuse and deferred in nature; the citizenry does not expect to appropriate the public value immediately, nor does it calculate it in precise terms.

This conception sheds light on the debate about moves in recent years to impose 'mutual obligation' on some beneficiaries, such as the unemployed, who are thereby obliged to work in return for welfare payments.[5] Such policies have

been criticised not only because they attach potentially onerous conditions to what were previously seen as entitlements,
but also because they have the effect of 'blaming the victim'
(Goodin 1998). Both sides rest their case on the assumption
that welfare benefits hitherto have been entitlements for
which recipients have no reciprocal obligations — a state of
affairs that the proponents of 'work for benefits' deplore,
and its critics applaud.

However, the social exchange framework shows the limitations of both perspectives. In the first place, there *is* a form
of reciprocity in welfare: the generalised exchange among
beneficiaries, the citizenry and the department. The conservatives, focused as they are on economic exchange, fail to
recognise that benefit recipients contribute in other ways,
which are more diffuse and delayed. The critics, by contrast,
fail to acknowledge its normative validity. The question,
therefore, is not whether beneficiaries have obligations as
well as entitlements; in a generalised exchange, clearly they
do. Rather it is: what should be the terms of that exchange?

Ironically, the conservative solution, of *forcing* people to
'work for the dole', may actually reduce the value received
not only by the beneficiaries but also by the citizenry at large.
Because they value more than money — for example, self-
esteem, a sense of self-determination, and the intrinsic
rewards of working — beneficiaries' inclination to seek work
is only partially affected by the risk of benefits being cut off
(Goodin 1998). A large body of research shows that their job-
seeking efforts are more effectively enhanced by assisting
them to obtain the requisite work experience, skills or qualifications, providing job search training and job referrals, and
even by enhancing their life skills (Hayes and Nutman 1981;
Jahoda 1981; Kelvin and Jarrett 1985; Layard et al 1991).
Funding such programs may be cheaper in the long run
than either continuing to provide only benefits or ceasing
benefits for people not seeking work, thereby reducing them
to begging, homelessness and the associated social costs.
Thus, the issue is not so much whether the beneficiary
should obtain work as what the welfare department should
do to elicit job-seeking behaviour. It would entail understanding the specific needs of each client and seeking to
address them — which is what is meant by 'customer focus'.

Exchange and obligatees

Fitting apparently less comfortably into the notion of exchange is the role of obligatee. Here the 'client' does not receive valued 'goods', but rather what he or she reasonably regards as 'bads'. A prisoner, for example, mainly 'receives' restraint of liberty, and the satisfaction of inmates is not the first objective of the prison. It seems quite wrong in a descriptive sense, therefore, to compare obligatees to customers. However, the fact that many regulatory and enforcement agencies do so (Sparrow 1994) suggests that there may be something useful about the idea. In the broader conception of exchange, the client provides not money but *compliance*— specifically, positive actions consistent with the organisation's requirements — without which it cannot effectively function.

One way for an agency to secure that compliance is to apply coercive powers against those who do not cooperate. The problem with this approach is that if obligatees are wilfully resistant, securing compliance is very costly. For example, it is very difficult to operate a prison unless the prisoners at least acquiesce in its procedures and routines. If they do not, prison management must deploy more prison officers, and install and maintain more elaborate facilities (Wilson 1989, p. 18). A similar argument can be advanced about other agencies whose function is to impose legal obligations. If the obligatees are resistant, creating compliance is costly (Diver 1980; Bardach and Kagan 1982; Grabosky 1995). The challenge, therefore, is to elicit from them some degree of cooperation with the agency.

That cooperation is likely to be forthcoming to the extent that the agency treats the obligatees in a customer-like manner, within the confines of its coercive role (Lipsky 1980, pp. 58–9). This means understanding obligatees' needs and rights and seeking to satisfy them to the extent that the agency can, given its primary responsibility to impose legal obligations. In particular, it means applying, and being seen to apply, its coercive powers as far as possible in a manner that the obligatee regards as fair and just. There is considerable research evidence that most people will comply with legal sanctions, even if doing so personally disadvantages them, so long as they regard the manner in which those sanctions have been applied as fair (Tyler 1990; Ayres and Braithwaite 1992).

There will, of course, always be some proportion of obligatees who are wilfully resistant, and the agency will have to exercise coercive powers against them. In doing so it will not be engaging in exchange, since it is not giving these obligatees anything valuable, but rather diminishing the quality of life they enjoy. The application of coercion therefore falls outside the notion of exchange, properly understood. It is rather the application of fairness in dealings with obligatees that can validly be construed as part of an exchange process, in that to treat people justly and respectfully is to give them something valuable. In return for fairness, the agency receives more willing or at least less grudging (and less costly) compliance.

In the process of engaging in this exchange with obligatees, the prison agency also participates in an exchange with the citizenry. In return for their authority and resources, the agency provides them with public value, such as confinement and rehabilitation of actual offenders, and deterrence of potential ones. They also receive normative value, in the form of affirmation that their prisons exhibit the attributes of a fair and just society.

Exchange and citizens

Critics of the customer metaphor point out that it 'puts citizens in a reactive role where they are limited to liking or disliking services and hoping that the administrators will change delivery if enough customers object' (Schachter 1997, p. 9). Over time, this tends to diminish the legitimacy of and support for government as an institution.

But while this is certainly true of the private sector customer model, the social exchange model suggests another way of looking at the issue. When beneficiaries and obligatees are involved in generalised exchanges, in which they provide cooperation or compliance in return for intrinsic, social and normative values from agencies, they are not simply passive recipients. They are engaging in active behaviours which constitute some of their duties as citizens. They are more likely to do so if they are treated by the government in ways that acknowledge their rights as citizens: with fairness and respect. In this sense, the roles of beneficiary and obligatee are facets of citizenship: they embody some of the rights and obligations of citizens.

Conclusion

The public sector has always loomed large in the social democratic vision of society. It is therefore all the more peculiar that this vision has lacked a coherent view about how that sector should interact with the recipients of its services. Disentangling the useful notion of exchange from the limiting assumptions of private sector transactions offers a way of filling this gap. Adopting a broader conception of the relationship between government organisations affirms what is essentially valuable about the public sector, while respecting the private concerns of those whom it serves.

chapter **5**

Governing diversity: prospects for putting the public back into public service

By Mark Considine

In even the most simple, innocent and routine acts of public organisation we now find a new level of diversity. Standard methods and categories are giving way to forms of public service in which dozens or even hundreds of public and private agencies collude and collide in the production of tax-funded outcomes. This is a realm in which public authority is now just as often to be found in the subtle software of quasi-markets as it is in traditional forms of black-letter law or formal ministerial responsibility.

Large questions of scarcity and solidarity are nowadays linked in smaller decisions to close post offices and open freeways, to merge banks and to appoint chicken tycoons to the boards of government agencies. In a revolutionary transformation of public purpose, the public interest is ever at risk of being expelled from the mandate of the public service, to be replaced only by a courtly reverence for stakeholders. Meanwhile Australia's long-respected tradition of 'interesting experiments in law and administration' (Reeves 1902), seems to have become a tradition of emulation in which *the imaginary firm* dominates thinking about the future of governance. So enamoured are some recent converts to this faith that their more sceptical colleagues have deemed them 'more Catholic than the Pope'.

And no amount of contrived nostalgia for the days when things were less confused can overcome the sense that government may have lost its nerve and surrendered the role of defining the shape of our shared future to a chaos of private interests. Certainly public organisation in its widest sense is passing into the hands of contractors, partnerships and competitors whose commitment to the public interest is something short of uncertain. Of course these observations are a necessary exaggeration. Much of the old order does still remain. But it is precisely the exaggerated qualities of reforms that make them the most powerful drivers of change.

What these challenges impose upon us is the need to plan with greater subtlety and longer vision for the forms of public authority that we wish to see in the next ten to twenty years. Building public, governmental capacity is now an equally urgent task besides resolving immediate policy problems. Such a project will require a re-imagined public sphere. To get there we must try to understand just what privatisation has meant to governance. We also need to understand our actual experience of privatisation as being two related but different things: one concerned with the sale of government assets and the other with organisational processes which involve the adoption of the corporate model as the archetype for the delivery of public services. The first form is represented by the sale of the Commonwealth Bank, the second by the closing of the Commonwealth Employment Service (CES) and its replacement by the Job Network and Centrelink.

This second form of privatisation, called process privatisation, revolutionises the operational side of the public sector. It affects everything from the local school to the method for the sale of tickets to the Olympics. In order to assess some of the important consequences of this second form and to reflect upon ways it might be re-structured to reflect civic virtues and community interests, this chapter will focus upon just two aspects of the new order — the executive level and the citizen level. Given the space available this will be a somewhat abbreviated review designed to identify some key issues and alternatives.

The central assertion of this chapter is that here, as elsewhere, governments need to build quite new public institutions to support this kind of development. They cannot be based upon the kinds of relationships that were typical of first wave measures, where the focus was upon creating a market for the buying and selling of assets.

Asset privatisation

The privatisation of assets has been a favoured policy solution in OECD countries since the 1970s. As Handler (1996, p. 3) points out '[n]ot only in Western Europe and the United States, but also in the Third World, governments are trying to lessen their presence (at least in the economy), unload state enterprises, and rely more on private markets'. But for what problem is this a solution? While some commentators have chosen to connect this trend with the collapse of socialism and the exhaustion of communist regimes, in fact the trend in the West has earlier and more prosaic origins. The 'tax and spend' recipes of the Keynesian post-war boom fell into disfavour in the late 1970s because simultaneous rises in inflation and unemployment left policy-makers with dramatic structural problems. One solution has been a major, worldwide interest in managing public budgets through asset selling (Capling, Considine & Crozier 1998).

The public property sales, lease-backs and leveraged deals of the 1980s and the sale of public utilities in the 1990s focused upon reducing the cost of servicing state debt. This 'first dimension' privatisation was fiscal in origin. Governments sought to reduce their exposure to debt and the costs of re-financing public capital projects by shifting services into the private sector. Often these initiatives were somewhat artificial — the same investment in a public power station was defined as debt, while exactly the same expenditure by a private company could be sold to the public and the markets as an investment.

Enclosed within this first wave was another factor not openly discussed, but which was almost always present. This was the role and cost of labour. Mostly through neglect or mismanagement, but also because of a policy blockage created by the Keynesian model, governments arrived in the 1980s with public sector employment practices which were poor by the standards of the best private firms. Productivity for public employees was generally lower in countries such as

the United Kingdom than for equivalent private sector workers (Foster and Plowden 1996).

A popular ideological stance taken in the U.K., New
Zealand, and by some Australian protagonists, was that
strong unions prevented public sector managers from raising productivity. In other words, the productivity problem
was sheeted home to alleged problems of over-staffing.
Labor governments felt this to be a particular problem
because union pressures could be applied within the party
organisation as well as in the industrial realm. Another
explanation is that there was a significant under-investment
in workforce productivity in the public sector during the
1960s and 1970s (King and Maddock 1996). In particular,
governments and managers failed to take advantage of new
technologies and best practice from overseas.

The concern with asset privatisation was actually linked
both to a budget imperative and to an emerging change in
the social model of public service. An older ideal of using the
public service as a pacesetter for award conditions and rises
in employee entitlements was being replaced by the idea that
public organisations did not return sufficient surplus to
shareholders (citizens) because of fundamental inefficien-
cies in the organisation of labour.

Process privatisation

The 1990s saw the sale of assets complemented by a further
form or 'second dimension' privatisation in which the
process of production inside public organisations was re-
designed according to an imaginary ('behave as if') corporate logic. Framed by the assumptions of a loose collection of
theories known as 'organisational economics', this new
model started from the assumption that the first and most
powerful instinct of all employees, managers and politicians
is the will to cheat. Opportunism by managers and staff
could only be reduced by creating powerful competitive
pressures that would enable the power of the purchaser to
overwhelm the influence of rent-seeking producers. In particular, this set of assumptions and theories asserted that
political systems were among the easiest of all systems to rort
because there were no shareholders to put pressure on man-

agers. In response, government reformers in the past ten years have sought to mimic the conditions under which firms operate. Almost all of these innovations in the processes of government and public service rely upon the assumption that organisations are no more than a 'chain of contracts' in which a purchaser seeks to devise the right incentive system to achieve whatever he or she wants.

This model has now become the dominant method for managing services outside the normal or traditional bureau-cratic system, *but still within the public domain.* Government remains directly involved in policy-making, and in commit-ments to service delivery, but it separates these from the act of implementation. Those responsible for implementation need no longer be public servants, and they need no longer answer directly to any government for their day-to-day activities. How-ever the services being managed continue to be largely funded by taxpayers, and in this sense they remain public services. In some cases this arm's-length relationship is further attenuated by the existence of public and private competitors who act within a quasi-market. It is 'quasi' because people are not pay-ing directly from their pockets and there is still a great deal of legislation and regulation in place to determine who gets what. Even here, however, the main feature of the quasi-market is that the end consumer is not the client. The real consumer is the purchaser, that is, the government of the day or its agent.

This second dimension is far more complex than the sim-ple logic of asset privatisation and anti-unionism. It includes a variety of intersecting techniques such as:

Output-based budgets (where programs are funded according to the 'production' of specific outputs).

Contracting out (where a public service is performed by a private agency as part of a short-term agreement).

Purchaser–provider splits (where the government's own role is divided between 'principals' who buy the service under contract, and 'agents' who merely sup-ply what is ordered).

External regulation (where a service is supervised by a public authority other than the department deliv-ering it).

Quasi-markets (where a single public service is handed over to a group of competing contractors).

Multi-agency systems (where the successful delivery of any service requires cooperation by several public and private agencies).

Implications of process privatisation for re-structuring government

It is important to note that there are short-term strategic advantages to executive governments adopting these forms of process privatisation. For example, the state's industrial relations problems are more easily exported to contractors under these conditions. The wages of operators may also be forced down by the creation of predatory forms of tendering. Opportunities to hide mistakes and thus shield ministers from criticism by the use of commercial-in-confidence agreements are seductive. Giving government contracts to business is also good politics and a wonderful new source of patronage. We may lament the fact that ministers might see these as worthy objectives without denying that they will be attractive and even irresistible unless the costs of these buffers and shields are properly identified. And given the many occasions in which ministers will be tempted by this siren song, no simple regulatory device that will tie them to the mast is likely to work for very long. We must therefore accept the existence of this new public sector in which a mixed economy of public and private incentives will be dominant, and then think about the forms of institutional development which will be needed to place civic virtues (tolerance, equality, participation, diversity etc.) on at least the same plane with private incentives and opportunistic behaviours.

Despite the anti-civic stance of these competitive models of delivery, there are in theory at least, some benefits to having multi-agency systems in many areas of public service. Most obviously they allow entry by community interests and smaller organisations which may reflect more diverse cultures and local interests in ways not easily embraced by large organisations. A good example is nursing homes. We might want to champion the cause of greater regulation of this sensitive sector, but not many would favour creating a single national organisation to provide the whole service. Diversity is clearly a means to respecting the different needs of older people and their families, provided of course that they have equal access to a service at a good, reliable standard.

But by saying we expect this mix of diversity and regulation to be achieved without a centralising or bureaucratic form of public organisation we are raising the central question which now dogs all government agencies: how to create order and fairness in the absence of hierarchical control. Governments must create quite new public institutions to support this kind of development. Put simply, these new strategies have replaced the old inflexibility problem with a new level of complexity, allowing one generation of politicians to shift the burden onto a future generation of decision-makers. Asset privatisations did not presume any detailed operational knowledge of services being sold on the part of central agencies and consultants. The whole point was to be rid of the burden and then let the regulator worry about the consequences. Moreover the efficiency of these privatisations could more easily be assessed using conventional estimates of the value of assets, thereby opening such measures to some minimal level of public and parliamentary scrutiny. The new revolution in organisational processes is fundamentally different. Private agents become implicated in longer-term relationships and the nature of interactions between key officials, contractors and clients imposes far higher levels of risk and uncertainty than before. Government stays involved but has less control. It does not release itself from risk, it actually increases the hazards to itself and the citizens.

Consequently these arrangements threaten more minute but significant levels of policy corruption and the further enfeeblement of our representative institutions than did the sale of assets. On the positive side, they also offer far greater opportunities for communities to intervene and make services responsive to their own interests. The new architecture of diversity cannot be easily erected on top of the old bureaucratic foundations because bureaucracies have currently lost their credibility in operational management. And they cannot combine a role as purchaser and a role as provider without risk of terminal contradiction. In a nutshell, my argument is that current institutions lack the capacity to act strategically in the public interest. We need a new round of institution-building, of equal ingenuity to the golden age of post-war reconstruction, including: a major investment in shared information technology; new collaborative training regimes; new institutions of accountability; and nationwide experiments in citizen/consumer empowerment.

New institutions of accountability

For the century between 1860 and 1960, American and Westminster political systems used a common strategy to promote efficiency, honesty and accountability in the bureaucracy. They sought to establish a career service in which merit would govern appointments and promotions. They established rights for employees and clients to take action against unfair action by bureaucrats. And they used both ministerial responsibility and legislative accountability to make certain that due process was observed. By this latter means the modern era established a form of bureaucratic independence which did not significantly compromise the democratic right of legislators to oversee the expenditure of taxpayers' funds, or act to limit the use of the state's coercive powers (Spann 1973; Craig 1955).

In establishing this regime of rules and direct accountabilities, those who fashioned this modern system were employing a form of institution-building that put the law itself at the centre of public administration. Citizens tested their rights in courts, ministers established their powers through legislation and bureaucrats followed a course established by parliamentary mandate, well-known conventions taught within the career service, and explicit standard procedures enshrined within program guidelines. In the language of the management textbooks, officials and citizens knew an 'outcome' was the right outcome when it had been arrived at through proper processes of open deliberation, due process and the application of rules. The legal basis of this reasoning was best exemplified in the court system where governments and the judicial process identified the rights and obligations of participants rather than specifying a preferred verdict.

One of the advantages of the bureaucratic hierarchical model was that it provided clear lines which flowed from the electorate to the Parliament, to the Minister, to the Departmental Secretary and then to the local official. When reformers break up these established bureaucratic systems and install private processes, they undermine these lines of responsibility. This disturbance occurs in cases where the service has been contracted out to a private provider, but it also occurs in cases where new public authorities are created at arm's-length from direct political responsibility. Efforts to 'fill the gaps' in these relationships have been mired in controversy, indicating that we still have a long way to go in building effective alternatives to direct governmental responsibility. The language of 'steering not rowing' and 'steering from a distance' (Osborne and Gaebler 1993), which suggests a potent role for government which is divorced from its own operational commitments, assumes a clearer separation of functions and responsibilities than is always possible. The distance being anticipated in these efforts to claim a new form of accountability is one in which public officials, without any direct operational control or knowledge, seek to regulate from outside the service delivery system. In place of this creation of tight boundaries and separated agencies, governments need better methods to reintegrate services with existing democratic institutions.

The impact of process privatisation on executive governments

The most challenging elements of the 'steering from a distance' model are those which show the agency chief executive officer (CEO) in direct competition with the secretary of the responsible department. The terms of competition are not always clear, however. For instance, in the Commonwealth's design for Centrelink the responsible departments are represented on the board of an agency which they help run and from which they buy services. Directors are also customers. Elsewhere in the same system the government operates its own contracting agency, Employment National, which tenders to serve Centrelink clients, and answers to the Minister of Finance for its performance but to the Minister for Employment for the conduct of its Centrelink work. No one could accuse the respective heads of these ministries and agencies of having clear lines of accountability. Moreover one can only sympathise with staff, employers, parliamentarians and citizens who evidently find all this a little hard to fathom. And the recent spectacular failure of Employment National's senior management only underlines the weakness of 'steering from a distance' as a model for generating economic returns.

Parliament has a weakened power to review these new forms of privatisation because contractors have in-confidence agreements that may not be revealed to third parties. This renders the service or operational system almost invisible to elected representatives and greatly increases the power of senior bureaucrats. They now make major decisions about the shape of markets, the future of contractors and the distribution of services beyond the formal reach of ministers and MPs. And such systems are not easy to amend. It appears that these private processing systems need to be somewhat closed or self-organised in order to deliver the benefits governments seek. This suggests that new institutions will need to respect the self-organising quality of such new systems and find a way to enter them without destroying their innovative capacity.

One of the most impressive aspects of these multi-agency systems is their promise to take the needs of the consumer seriously and, through service empowerment, to make clients more effective actors within the service delivery circuit or network. Reformers spend considerable effort on improving the speed and effectiveness of service delivery, often by creating new organisations with a strong service culture. Some of this emphasis is obviously no more than a sales pitch and we are right to be sceptical of much of it. However there is more to it: some of the organisations being contracted under these schemes have very strong commitments to moving their clients quickly and effectively to an agreed outcome. Sometimes this is a consequence of competition, as in the telecommunications case where public organisations have become more attentive to customers as a result of the advent of alternative sources of supply. Sometimes this improvement is a consequence of creating new service organisations at lower levels of government, thus allowing new technologies and strategies to emerge.

Welfare contracting in the non-profit sector has demonstrated some of these advantages. Where contractors are rewarded in accordance with the results they achieve, and where these results are based upon valid measures of outcomes, many clients find themselves better off. However this is not true in all cases. And even where it is true, there may be some hidden costs that need to be identified and addressed.

In the cases where clients are not better off we find some common problems. The first we can call the 'shallow service trap'. In this case contractors meet the agreed objectives but skimp on qualities that are not clearly specified in each contract. For example, electricity companies seek to meet price objectives and targets for speed in connecting customers to a service, but their record on long-term maintenance and temporary fault corrections is known to be poor. This latter aspect of the business is costly and they choose to let customers wait longer, or experience a higher number of faults, because this is cheaper than the cost of maintaining an expensive network of field staff on duty 24 hours a day in every locality. In the book which helped drive many of these changes, Osborne and Gaebler (1993) wrote enthusiastically of the parks service which cut its maintenance program back until people complained, and then set their service regime just above the expected level at which citizens would voice their discontent. Obviously such complaint-led action begs the question of which citizens are able to have their voices heard, a point we will return to below.

Another problem with contracted services is that the system of payments based upon per-unit outputs encourages 'creaming' — a process in which profitable and easy clients are streamed into the service, and there is explicit or implicit dumping of difficult cases. Because only the state has a general responsibility to all citizens, it will then be forced to take the difficult cases. This leads to stigma problems for public clients as well as economy of scale problems for the government agency with a duty of care for so-called difficult or hard-to-place clients. A fragmented service may be more profitable for those contractors able to cream, but will be less effective overall than a comprehensive service in which service providers can use technologies and skills to treat a range of clients. Residual services will also provide the state agency with a serious marketing problem if it wishes to compete with private agencies. Suppliers, staff and clients given a choice in new quasi-markets will often choose to avoid a public organisation which has a very high proportion of very disadvantaged or difficult clients for fear that this will be a signal of poor quality.

A final problem with contracted services in the social policy field is what we might term the 'cost plus trap'. In this situation contractors do not have strong economic incentives to invest in the development of their sector beyond the current contract, or the one after that. Lack of a certain role in any service industry which relies on human skill and technique (as compared with machines which can be re-sold) will lead entrepreneurs to purchase already existing skills and methods, rather than to invest and innovate for themselves. Put simply, human skills can too easily be poached by other firms. As a result these contracted services will tend to converge on low-skill methods. Governments and their contracting departments wishing to avoid this tendency will be forced to offer longer-term contracts, or forms of provider registration which restrict entry to a smaller group of approved firms. Both of these strategies open the way for oligopolistic behaviour, price corruption and other threats to the separation of principals and agents.

Used in an uncritical fashion, this 'cost plus' approach also threatens the viability of self-help and community-sector service providers. Typically they are pioneers at the advocacy end of the service delivery system. They are also uniquely placed to motivate and integrate clients who have the most severe problems. In some cases the contracting model has forced a small business framework onto these organisations and reduced the distinctiveness of their contribution. I am not saying that we should support inefficiency or poor leadership or any other error in service delivery, but nor is it healthy to use process privatisation as a means to encourage every service delivery agency to resemble every other.

This would not happen in a normal market because some proportion of consumers will seek out variation and choose diverse service types. It is in this sense that novelty is a precondition for innovation. But in quasi-markets this is far less likely because of the government's central role as the primary customer. Paradoxically this opens the door to greater homogeneity than in many bureaucratic services which have third-sector organisations as partners in service delivery.

Civic empowerment

We may now turn our attention to the predicament for those involved in government. Multi-actor systems are here to stay, as apparently is contracting. Single, monopoly organisations are unlikely again to become the norm in the public sector. Yet the current systems of 'new governance' do not meet minimal standards of coherent accountability. People are confused by the flotilla of craft now tendering for services. Contractors themselves are unclear about their futures. Government officials admit that they must often fill orders with agencies they barely know, performing services they no longer fully comprehend.

It is time for a more open, experimental approach in which governments seek to develop new institutions to reinsert the public interest into these service delivery systems. Since that cannot be achieved by further empowering old-style public bureaucracies, it may be achieved by legislating collective interests back into the service loop. This might best be illustrated with some brief examples:

> In Denmark the government has acknowledged the changed role of citizens in the new system of devolved, contracted services by establishing User Boards in many areas of service delivery. They are made up of elected members of the community, they have their own mandates and the service delivery organisation (school, hospital etc) is required to provide them with information and to consult them on key decisions.

> In a number of U.S. or American states the Nader organisation has campaigned for the right for consumer organisations to collect small membership fees through the regular billing systems of large utilities (power, gas etc). When you pay your bill you may choose to have a few cents per

week diverted to a consumer action group. This group then devotes itself to putting pressure on the power company and the regulator to make sure consumers are heard and to sponsor litigation where consumers are ignored.

In France the national government is experimenting with a system called 'Contract de Ville', in which municipalities sign whole-of-service contracts with all the arms of the national government delivering services to their area. This enables the municipality to make choices about trade-offs, rather than have them imposed, piecemeal, from above. These contracts also allow bureaucrats and politicians at the municipal level to present residents with a more coherent plan for local development.

In the U.S. a number of local communities have recently involved themselves directly in the development of new prisons and correctional facilities, using reduced interest by central government as an opportunity to insert local priorities. Colorado now has an active policy for allowing communities to 'adopt a prison' and encourage rural development. Local communities in Kansas, New Mexico and Florida have also sought new prisons or expanded facilities, mobilising local support for museums, tourist visits and support services.

Early studies of Australian contracting systems point to a clearer specification of responsibilities for staff and a widespread tendency for contracting to result in the establishment of complaints and grievance processes in services where none previously existed.

These examples point to different solutions to the problem of rebuilding institutions. They show the potential for exciting new mechanisms to enhance civic empowerment without surrendering effectiveness or efficiency.

Civic institution building

These examples also point to an important underlying issue that is not always well understood in debates about the involvement of private interests in the organisation of the public sphere. The creation of such arrangements cannot be seen as a simple act of purchase and contract negotiation. The factors that determine whether or not a new organisational environment will work, or become problematic, are deeper than simply engineering an initial tender round, or defining a payments schedule. Process privatisation imposes far greater burdens on existing institutions and upon the need to develop new institutional systems than was the case with earlier waves of asset privatisation.

However, if left to its own devices this incentive-based behaviour will not address civic values and longer-term issues of capacity-building. For example, short-term advantage and aggressive competition may well devalue any kind of serious skill investment. A number of studies indicate that contracted services seek greater levels of part-time employment and casual labour (Donahue 1989; Pack 1991; Ernst et al 1997). This further reduces incentives to invest in people skills. How will this cycle of public de-skilling be arrested? Only by the invention of a training and innovation regime which is larger than the individual organisations and ministries searching for cost cuts. Such institutions of civic participation and training need to be built and supported over the long haul. They require continuous improvement but will not survive perpetual revolution. I do not say that governments are the sole answer to this problem of institution building, but as our best representative of common, or collective, interests they must take a leading role in brokering the peace between otherwise unwilling competitors (Considine 1996).

Without this structured negotiation and investment there can be no lasting innovation, and little public legitimacy for multi-actor systems. Private participation will only be a success when it is combined with methods to raise standards and improve accountability. This cannot be left to individual entrepreneurs. They have neither the rational self-interest nor the investment power in the services sector to shape the future. The paradox of markets for public services is therefore that they need more public involvement, more participation, more institution-building than before. Therefore it becomes a priority to re-institutionalise the public interest. Community groups and their peak bodies must be given statutory roles in the contract negotiation process and in regulatory oversight of the service.

Parliament will require new standing orders and protocols to protect commercial-in-confidence rights while allowing scrutiny by the legislature. While a significant challenge, this is hardly an impossible task, especially when one recognises that the sovereignty of Parliament itself is the price that will be paid if such arrangements are not negotiated. It is up to governments, advocacy groups, employee associations, training institutions and regulators to come together and invest in longer-term commitments to keep standards high and the public interest paramount. To do this while maintaining the advantages of a more flexible system of participation by non-government actors is the major design challenge. Moreover, many of the early experiments with this form of 'steering from a distance' have lacked any systematic evaluation procedures, rendering them less accountable than traditional bureaucracies (Van Horn 1991; Handler 1996). New institutional arrangements need to be based upon the development of different forms of public agency. In place of simple dichotomies between purchaser and provider the process needs to articulate a triangulated linkage of purchaser-provider-consumer, each with an identified mandate. The empowerment of clients and the potential for greater local community involvement in service design is only possible if appropriate structures are devised. The key to this appears to be the development of boards, information networks and review panels that include direct consumer and community representation on a continuing basis. Forms of open election must be used to prevent these dissolving into a new patronage game. It will take time for the public and the media to come to terms with the critical tone of some consumer empowerment. A new level of maturity will be required among our political leaders. But in time a culture of continuous improvement will overtake mere carping if governments show themselves willing to acknowledge problems and share information about solutions. These are complex undertakings. No simple blueprint can be imposed on every service or every area of government. But a period of government-sponsored experimentation is vital if such new institutions are to be developed. This willingness to devise new public roles in keeping with the times was once the hallmark of Australian government. Perhaps it could become so again?

chapter **6**

Putting the social back into socialism...
By Eva Cox

The term socialism has tended to be defined by reference to economic attributes of society, mainly the nationalisation of the means of production and exchange. More recently the word has lost currency but still underpins objections to disappearing public assets and government services, and the rise of neo-liberal market forces as the dominant driver of public policy. What I want to suggest in this chapter is that we explore the possibilities of egalitarian social power and relationships as the basis for fairer societies, with the economic being a subset, not the main cause, of social cohesion or conflict. This would move to theories and praxis of social change which take into account perceptions and feelings and their relationship to 'social capital', as well as the material basis of social relationships. The cultures of social systems are therefore seen as being produced by the multiple relationships between people, both social and economic.

When I started researching my 1995 ABC Boyer Lectures, published as *A Truly Civil Society* (Cox 1995), I was attracted to social capital as a means of putting the social back on political agendas. Like many others, I felt that the dominant paradigms of economic *man*, always driven by self-interest and best served by market forces, failed to describe much of the world we live in. On second thoughts, I also found that even the more egalitarian socialist *man* still focused on change to economic systems for progress. So both major ideological blocs shared similar points of views, as both eschewed the social, but read the processes and outcomes differently.

My critique of market and Marxist *men* springs from my feminism and the recognition that life is more than the public sphere of paid labour and exchange so enforced by the public and private divide between traditional gendered spheres. The assumption of the privacy of family/community hides a multitude of relationships which make us both human and social and operate on gifts, obligations and collectivities to offer care, love, belonging, and other aspects joining us in social groups. Starting from a premise that it is human connections to others that make us both social and able to develop our sense of self, we need to start theorising politics or economics which recognise the value of our social bonds. Unlike the concept deep in the social contract, we were never 'born free' and then coerced or chose to join with others, we started as a tribe and moved more recently to individualism (in some western cultures).

The focus on exchange and ownership, in both old left and right politics, has failed to explain enough of social relationships to be useful in analysing post-industrial societies. Here I feel that the current debates on ethics, social capital, social responsibility, civil society and citizenship offer an interesting package of law, mores and social relationships to be explored.

The key words in these debates are unfamiliar to policy and politics. They include trust, gift, altruism, inclusion and civility, which sound more like a 19th century morals tract than anything modern. The debates deal more with the way we interact and form relationships than the more formal processes of law and economics which have tended to dominate the public sphere. They offer an addendum to materialism that recognises the importance of perception and relationships in establishing the narratives that make us social.

The basic western European texts of social contract presumed we contracted as individuals to make society (e.g. Hobbes 1651; Rousseau 1762). These contracts recognised that man alone would not function and develop into a 'civilised' being or member of such a society. The common descriptions of the processes of industrialisation suggested that the cohesive rural customary communities were being transformed into mass urban societies based on the public sphere of law and exchange (e.g. Toennies 1974; Durkheim 1982). Mauss and others sought to explain the complexities of tribe and gift as economically based and tied to mores and obligations that created benefit (Mauss 1966). The overarching tasks appeared to be contrasting the primitive sets of relationships and mores to the more developed functions of literate and logical societies and suggesting that the change was the result of historical progress. There has been little discussion of what might make 'better' societies in the last couple of decades, with most working from the assumption that wealth growth and distribution is the means of ameliorating problematic aspects of the present system. Both political tendencies presume that there is a direct and singular connection between access to material resources and forms of society. Any other links, exchanges or bonds are dismissed as 'externalities', or relegated to the private sphere. However, the rise of critiques on the enlightenment and the assumptions of progress suggest it is time we revisited aspects of the discarded 'primitive' social organisation and see if we can construct other views of making societies better places for people.

I want to look at some alternate paradigms that we can use to determine criteria for defining the society we may aspire to, or even try and create. I want to explore the possibilities of putting the social back into theorising and practising the formation and retention of more civil societies. By making new frameworks for looking at the world through social standpoints and establishing criteria for diverse and civil interactions in the more fractured and fragile groupings, we can establish processes of social connections that respect diversity and recognise commonalties. In particular, my proposition is to use social capital as the basis for improving the processes of building connective relationships through which institutions and groups can engage with each other, both for collective action, and for productive debates and conflict.

Rational justice and/or the ethic of care

One of the most significant paradigms (which are evidence of productive conflict) is the tension between rational justice and the ethic of care. It is this tension that raises some of the pertinent issues, concerning what kind of societies and communities we may want to create. The basic debate between rational justice and the ethic of care is whether justice, law and reason can deliver the appropriate services to address the diverse needs of people. Feminist philosophers have recognised the complexity of human relationships and expressed doubt about trying to solve all 'needs' through law or economics. In their simplest forms, these issues are about the differences between relationships built on feelings of love and care and those built on reason, logic and probabilities, expressed sometimes in mathematics but more often in rules and law.

The valorising of masculinity in some writers has tended to overlook or minimise the significant sphere of life in families and communities which continues to underpin the more 'rational' or legalistic institutions. The human has needs: to belong, to identify with some emotional bases such as family, tribe, political groups, faith communities and national identities. Belonging is based on feelings of commonalities, blood and beliefs that do not easily succumb to rational argument. The resilience of emotion-driven connections presents interesting contradictions to the assumptions of enlightenment leading to reasoned decision-making.

The assumptions of the superiority and long-term dominance of rationality (masculine) versus feelings (femininity) echo the concepts of primitive and civilised. In my Boyer Lectures. I argued for an alternate view of the civil, harking back to its other meanings of interactions based on respect and not coercion. It seemed to me that the social systems that tied us together carried the apparently contradictory aspects of emotion and reason. Often, too much reason may result in tangles of unfeeling, legalistic forms of interaction, and too much emotion in forms of dominance, control and infantilisation of large sections of the population. Neither should be offered unfettered.

Both these aspects can be seen in debates between feminisms of the importance, or otherwise, of using the language of public exchanges to describe the household/community/care nexus. Some of the debates more recently on unpaid work have attempted to create pricing structures equating the market value. Some feminists have adopted these positions as ways of redressing gender inequalities, as if using masculine related 'values' meant their tasks were taken seriously by men. Statistics that reveal the biggest industry in Australia is preparing the evening meal may make household work seem very important.

However, in this process it is possible that there has been a loss of the particular aspects of care that make for different and equally important relationships. Feelings and emotions such as love, care and trust are hard to quantify yet obvious in either presence or absence. Meals prepared with pleasure in gift, love and care for different tastes are more pleasurable than those done mechanically to recipes. Peta Bowden (1997) sees caring as both ethical and an expression of ontological relationships that surpass logical and utilitarian relationships. She teases out the ways in which mothering, nursing and other forms of care define relationships as being much more than the rational.

In a piece I have written for a publication on citizenship (Cox 2000), I explore the possibilities of recognising that neither care nor reason are adequate as modes of analysis. Too much legislation and regulation to create apparent procedural fairness can create bureaucratic nightmares and pressures to comply. Too much care has often been used as a basis for pressuring women to take on grossly unfair burdens, as there seems no other authority than expectations of obligations. So I suggested that we needed a mix by which justice ensured equity but care ensured that the process was sensitive to difference and respect for individual needs.

The social triangle: state, community and market

I would now like to consider another framework for looking at the world from a social standpoint and creating a more civil society. One contributor in this area is Claus Offe (1998a), a German sociologist who, in a seminar in Sydney, drew a triangle on a white board with one angle denoting the community, one the state, one the market. He explained that we needed judicious mixes of each, so our societies could achieve the balance necessary for both social capital and the democratic political process. Too much of any one becomes toxic, and in the examples discussed further below, too much market brings the Mafia, too much government brings Stalinism and too much community brings Bosnia. This model can be related to the differences between care and justice models, with government offering justice and the community offering care. The role of the market can be seen as operating as a third force that distributes the resources by neither passion nor law but by demand, and as such allows the freedom to have diverse tastes and some aspects of choice and autonomy.

In other words, we need governments which are seen as capable of being fair, acting in the common interests, offering justice and public services. We need markets to give us the autonomous choices we want to make, and train us in making responsible decisions. We need community to affirm our identities and relationships, pursuing our particular interests and passions and acting as advocates, participating in civic and political processes. This seems to me to make good sense, as it recognises that no institution or theory can offer all the answers. It assuages my anarchistic concerns about the misuse of power by governments by ensuring there are other sources of power, but meets my commitments to redistribution so we can have fairer and more inclusive societies. There are spaces for activism and rules of engagement so conflict can be seen as part of legitimate political processes, but not to threaten civil order.

The market has too much power in most current dominant models. A wide range of political groupings is constantly undermining the state as government in many areas. Globalisation causes much muttering across the political spectrum about the demise or weakness of the nation state. Most of this appears to be based on the assumption that loss of some controls over economic policy is the end of the modern nation states as we knew them. At the same time, weak or unpopular governance in some of these countries has led to rising nationalisms/fundamentalisms, accompanied by devolution in some areas or threats of civil war in others. This leaves the interesting question of what types of governance would work in a more postindustrial mode.

I suggest that we need to continue to support the state, because the very weakness it may have in economic policy should be taken as an indicator that the state is even more

necessary as promoter of countering effects with social policy. If economic liberalism has created problems for some of
the populace, we need relatively competent and powerful
states to ensure that the rule of law and the continued funding of social programs can limit the damage. Therefore, we
need to reinvent and reclaim the state's capacity to manage
the social environment and allow the development of socially sustainable communities and policies, as well as environmental ones.

We vote for governments and it is their role to offer us
collective, accountable policy-making and spending. We
need to explore what the appropriate levels of collectivity
are. The capacity for linkages with others for mutual benefit
and the concept of the common good runs deep in socialist
history but appears to have been unfairly discarded in the
fall of the command economies.

While there were benefits from state-run enterprises and
the welfare state, there were also limitations. The delivery of
public programs often left much to be desired for a range of
reasons, including the clumsiness of large bureaucracies.
However, there were systems of entitlements and appeals put
in place to ensure that people could claim their rights and
demand fair treatment. Despite its faults, the system delivered many needed services and income support in ways
which were accountable and able to be reformed, albeit slowly. The community sector grew, through both government
funding and its own resources, and often offered innovation
and inclusion. It also modelled better practices and raised
issues for the excluded at the same time as some sections supported the status quo and were coopted by government into
forms of government service devolution.

In some areas, such as indigenous communities, the
state, with its past record of heavy-handedness, is not seen as
the appropriate source of services. However in other areas
there is no evidence that state officers and bureaucracies
were essentially any worse than their private counterparts.
Where the state managed most statutory services and many
support ones as well, staff were often better paid and supported. Services were specified in law, and had standards and
public accountability, and there were sometimes resources
for innovations in the state sector. The present mixing of

roles, with the community sector and religious groups replacing government services, sets up some serious issues of overlapping and conflicting roles.

Offe's social triangle suggests that where two sectors collude against the third this creates real problems for society. By mixing their separate roles, the market and the community lose their special abilities to innovate, to identify diversity, to be free to serve their constituency. Tendering for government contracts by both business and the community creates a 'one size ought to fit all' approach. Businesses 'help' the community groups to become more business-like, while both become arms of government and lose their particular relationships with customers and members. Government then has too much control over the other sectors, particularly the community areas where they are the major providers of funds. The market and community sectors are then often able to wield power over government by threats of withdrawing essential services.

The suggestions given above for a model of the social which involves all sectors as players is very messy. Unlike the governmental claims that the three sectors should be involved in a social coalition (Commonwealth) or partnership, I suggest they be seen as primarily and clearly having different functions which provide critiques and tensions between their roles. This may be a more sophisticated version of thesis, antithesis and synthesis, but it retains within it the concept of institutional differences and the ongoing dialogues and accommodations that probably are part of any complex social organisation. There is no perceivable endpoint utopia but the capacity to ameliorate problems. The objective in this case is to find an appropriate balancing process by which the competing interest groups can manage their differences and agreements without destroying the social fabric.

Environmental and economic concerns become a subset of the social, as it is decisions by people that are the keys to better management of both. If we have a political system which allows for tensions between sectors to be debated and resolved in ways which incorporate social sustainability and the ever-shifting and value-ridden common good, then the major issues will be addressed. If any interest group retains long-term dominance and pursues their interests, we will have serious problems.

The survival of forms of capitalism, and its capacity to coexist with quite serious social democratic constraints, suggests that markets adapt to new circumstances more easily than the state and community. We need to ensure that we retain widespread governance so that the globalised systems will continue to be controllable at whatever level is appropriate — local, regional, national and transnational.

I believe that we no longer can claim any grand theory of everything, so we have to make do with lesser, fallible explanations. We need to make sure we hear the dissenting voices, the diverse views that may add to our ability to make things better, or avoid making it worse. How we do things has to be as important as what we are trying to achieve. So governments, as the rule of law, remain an important part of any future we have, as do the other sectors. The quality of relationships within and between sectors needs to be examined because the current levels of hostility and distrust of various institutions that are often manifested make civil societies very difficult.

Social capital as trust

The third paradigm I want to consider is the use of social capital as trust. The indicator I am suggesting for social capital in this case is the apparent trust levels developed in processes of interaction between individuals and institutions that may reinforce the concept of both situation-specific and more generalised trustworthiness. The basic condition for resolving conflict between diverse interests has to be sufficient levels of trust to ensure that negotiations are effective and any solutions effective. Therefore, social capital lubricates the process, and cannot be owned by anyone or stored for individual advantage.

The term is contested both by definition and politically. The version of social capital I am using is an amalgamation of the bonding and bridging processes. Bonding is what I define as solidarity within groups, and bridging is the developed capacity to relate to others. More strategically problematic is the way that social capital apparently has offered certain political benefits to a range of neo-liberal and concerned conservatives. If translated into offers and imposed values of reciprocity and duty, it apparently justifies cuts to paid services to allow space for more volunteers and concomitant social capital growth.

These and other uses of the ideas, by those seen as the 'right', unfortunately led to most Anglophone leftists rejecting social capital as a conservative idea and failing to explore its possibilities. It has been more popular among Europeans from social democrats and further left. Attacks on social capital by people like Ben Fine (in his discussion of my paper at the UTS conference on globalisation, December 1999) and others tend to judge the concept by its current users, and fail to recognise its possibilities for radical or critical analyses of certain economic views.

Social capital explores the possibility that human behaviour responds to more than materialist stimuli. As some of the right is moving away from the neo-liberal project of expecting the market to deliver, because of its damage to social cohesion, the left must also recognise that relationships to the means of production, or access to financial resources, may be only part of the answer. It is problematic when used to describe cohesion without any normative value base because there are forms of bonding that do not necessarily increase the general well-being of the social fabric because they create further injustice and inequity and reduce generalisable trust.

Mansbridge (1990) sets up the concept of altruistic trust, which she sees as being deliberately prepared to trust others to a higher degree than knowledge may warrant, either to assist them or to intentionally seek public good outcomes. While she does not see trusting on inadequate knowledge or unfounded optimism as praiseworthy per se, she recognises that the spread of trust may act to encourage perceptions of trustworthiness. This she says is causal to trust and not vice versa. She also raises the possibility that our 'tribe' origins may predispose us to trust those we identify as similar, and we have the capacity to bond rapidly with new people we identify with, e.g. indoor cricket teams. So we need optimism.

I am suggesting that the processes of attempting via process reform to create links based on trust will themselves create the social capital needed to move on. Rules are useful as part of such processes, and therefore it is necessary to have governance which is seen as fair to participants. Social capital is therefore in these terms produced in the confluence of care, law and autonomy.

Social capital works best through the potential of relationships to encourage both developing trust and trustworthiness and a willingness to make contacts with others. The experiences people have in developing group cohesion can allow them to learn that strangers and institutions outside the familiar may be worth trusting in defined situations and also offer the confidence that allows for handling or seeking change. It is the interweaving of a multitude of such diverse relationships which strengthens the social fabric.

The basic concepts of democratic processes depend largely on their legitimacy. If a government does what only the majority wants, it may find its country ungovernable. Democracy depends on fairness towards minorities, particularly where a free and active media reports the dissenting opinion. In political systems where there is a high level of systems trust, governance is stable and debates can take place on the rights and wrongs and claims of all. When trust fails, the levels of dissent can become very loud and uncontrollable, and democracy may become too fragile to sustain itself.

So, to be sustainable political systems need to retain trust. They need to convince citizens that they will pursue the common good, i.e. not be captive of any particular interest group. The rise of populism and/or revolts of elites are manifestations of loss of legitimacy, and perceptions that governments favour other interest groups. Therefore, trust in the public sphere, in the roles of governance, is important as a way of retaining government legitimacy as a redistributor. There are also obvious advantages for communities where there are high levels of informal networks and assistance: it can reinforce good relationships and create trust and goodwill. The demand for formal services may be reduced by the informal and the quality of community enhanced if these networks operate equitably and generously. The capacity of areas to work together in crises such as bush fires and floods shows there are capacities in communities which are generally untapped.

Rather than assuming merit in volunteering, I would like to suggest that we see the necessary role of the 'Jeffersonian' citizen, i.e. the involved person, taking their share of respon- sibility for the functioning of the community. The concept of representative democracy has often been interpreted as leav- ing the needs of others to the state, maybe at the expense of civic responsibility, so without replacing paid services with unpaid we may need to examine the idea of being responsi- ble for our neighbours/others. Personal/communal duty comfortably undertaken covers some levels of community interactions both formal and informal, e.g. the unpaid work of voluntary fire services, joining groups running for local council, and offering assistance to neighbours. These sup- ports are seen as core functions and social responsibility, and often not suitable for more formal interventions. These are what some feel have diminished or are only run by older peo- ple. So we need to look at how such roles resonate with a younger group of citizens and maybe recreate them.

The participatory, democratic processes at the local level may increase trust and create better relationships. In fact, the quality of relationships which are created in unpaid work also exist in paid work. Creating a good set of relationships in any workplace is a basis for the satisfactions of work which extend past outputs and pay. There are non-material aspects of working which we tend not to recognise as significant and which may well be undermined by individual 'bargaining', that can destroy workplace trust by confidential contracts.

Social capital qua trust is reduced when inequality is pre- sent. Various surveys have shown that trust correlates with higher levels of equality and government intervention to keep it so. It also correlates with more economic growth and better health outcomes. So it is possible to put a case that social cohesion, respect and trust of others will not function in grossly unequal systems. This may be a good argument for forms of interventions and policies to repair the damage being done by current economic globalisation, which limit the capacities of the state to redistribute economic resources to reduce inequality.

There are interesting debates to be had about whether the state is seen as being there for everyone, or whether social policy, even in some social-democratic states, sees gov- ernment as only providing for the excluded and disadvan- taged. Creating levels of trust in governments as institutions must involve government being seen as fair to all, not just the rich but also not just the poor. It is inequality that is the problem, not poverty, at least in the more developed countries, and the perception of unfairness seems to be the trigger for loss of confidence in political systems.

So in reviewing policies I would suggest that targeting of the public sphere to those in need only is not a trust-building process. The cutting of tax bases reduces the capacities of governments to move, yet distrust of governments seems to go with objections to paying taxes. Compliance with law seems also to relate to trust of the justice system. Reconfiguring a more socially based suite of policies may suggest genuinely alternative options.

Conclusion

There is, therefore, a case for reinstating or putting for the first time an emphasis on the social in left political systems. This requires shifting the ways most people have recently learned to analyse the world and construct the frameworks of governance. If we presume that capitalism offers a dominant mode of discourse by showing its efficiency at creating countable growth of wealth, the left needs to offer alternate debates on what sort of society we want. We need to make the case that there is more than material wealth as the basis for human happiness or the good society.

So, the social for me in this context is developing the sets of relationships and expectations that will make us optimistic about changing the future and enhance our capacity to develop fairness and equity. These are issues of social rather than economic policy. Of course they need to take into account the issues of basic material well-being — enough food, shelter and so on — but to recognise that it is the way that these are seen and interpreted (read) that determines our political and social culture and the way people vote.

Postscript

Trust-building is a relatively new political concept and seen by some as silly when so many players are manifestly untrustworthy. Even raising the concept for discussion has resulted in my being called naïve. There are many who see politics as battles between beliefs, fractions and factions as each group gets the numbers. Into this may be built the arrogance of 'winner takes all', and little recognition that being in power and knowing it all do not coincide. The broad left has been particularly adept at defining as enemies those who deviate from correct thinking. I would suggest that a starting point could be developing political cultures based on solid debates, but not demands of solidarity per se, that could model some trust within the broader left debates and have more chance of finding ways of moving on. Civil societies need to be based on respect for differences, reasonable scepticism and civil debate, rather than deep cynicism, distrust of the Other, and demands for loyalty above all.

chapter 7

Unchaining the ABC

By Tony Moore

Introduction

The current debate about the future of the ABC misses the point. Partisans from right and left are locked in an ideologically driven struggle about old-fashioned models of mass communication, at a time when we need to be considering far-reaching reform aimed at re-invigorating the public media to meet the challenges of a new era of audience and information diversity. On one side we have shrill voices antipathetic to public broadcasting who want to purge the ABC of its supposed left-leaning culture and impose a more commercial approach, typified by chasing ratings, outsourcing, and programming directed at 'mainstream' Australia. On the other side we hear the understandable anger of the ABC's staff and many friends who believe that the reformers risk wrecking a great institution that sets the benchmarks for quality, civilisation and democracy. While often caricatured as 'progressive', the middle-class defenders of 'Auntie' are comfortable in the role of conservatives, championing a status quo that serves their needs very well. But does the ABC meet the needs of all Australians in their differences, across social classes, ever-widening age spans, ethnic difference, geography and diversity of interests? And does the national broadcaster effectively tap the creative and intellectual energy of our moment?

I contend that the ABC has failed to reflect the massive changes that have swept Australia over the last two decades, becoming the captive of narrow class, generational and Anglo-Celtic Australian interests. The problem is a hierarchical management structure that closes the ABC off to cultural change in the broader community and among its own workers. Despite the trend to flatter management and autonomous teams throughout the new economy, the ABC's latest masters seem intent on entrenching this top-down management culture. This chapter considers the real crisis in the ABC in the context of a wider debate about democratising public institutions, and suggests reforms that a future Labor Government should consider if it is serious about a relevant and innovative ABC.

Labor and the reform of public institutions

The ALP needs to rethink our public institutions, to determine how they might better deliver the ends for which they were originally established. The ABC is a case in point. Labor must ask two questions: is the ABC as an institution fulfilling its charter; and, if we are serious about being a knowledge nation, what might be a better vision for public broadcasting in the future? Many younger program-makers who have worked at the ABC were opposed to the creatively stifling Hill/Johns corporation and are now clamouring for changes so that the ABC might better reflect 21st century Australia and draw on the talent of its citizens.[1] When I criticise the ABC, especially television, it is as a friend — someone who sat on the ABC Advisory Council and had the privileges of working in the ABC as a documentary-maker for nine years, and of agitating through my union for internal reform.

While the neo-liberal right, the Coalition, and indeed sections of the Labor Party have run an often dogmatic privatisation agenda, the left side of politics has taken on the role of conservative, fighting a rearguard action to 'conserve' vital public institutions from being sold to shareholders. But in the process we abdicate the reform agenda to people who believe market forces are the universal panacea. While the left correctly saw that there are areas of service and production that are simply unsuitable for market control, their campaign has too often become a sentimental defence of quangos, corporations, boards and commissions that are in fact in dire need of reform. In opposition, the ALP has tended to succumb to nostalgia about public institutions — defending them without questioning whether they are effectively operating in accordance with the objectives of the organisation.

It is because public institutions have often treated their consumers and workers in a shabby fashion — both the CES and Telstra come to mind — that the privatisation rhetoric gets a toehold with the public. Organisations can become bureaucratic and lose sight of their reason for being. A particular group may capture an organisation and use it for sectional ends. The social conditions in which public services were established have undergone rapid change. Reform must be an ongoing process if institutions are to continue to fulfil their charters. Labor, because it cares about public institutions, should be interested in how it can better achieve social democratic goals, such as equity in health, education, justice, information, and creativity for all citizens in our changed times. This is the radical alternative to the crude dualism of market forces or a sentimental clinging to the status quo.

In this chapter I argue that the ABC needs to be revitalised, both in terms of the content of its programs and the processes and structures of its organisation, so that it can better reflect contemporary Australia. I explore the challenge the information age and cultural diversity presents for the ABC, outline its recent history, and offer key democratic standards as a guide for reform.

The information age: future challenges

Thinking about our public institutions has a fine lineage on our side of politics. Pioneers of public service and the welfare state such as Sidney and Beatrice Webb (1897), G. D. H. Cole (1928 and 1935) and William Morris (1896) wrestled with how to balance the interests of producers and consumers at the height of the industrial age. They also asked whether state ownership in itself was enough to best deliver the good society. The challenge for us today is rethinking the public sector from the midst of the information revolution. Industrial age corporations entering a new century have to change the top-down way they have traditionally controlled their assets. The state-funded 'industries' — particularly the ABC — are still operating with out-of-date industrial models and the challenge is to move them away from a control model.

In the case of the ABC, Labor has so far failed to articulate an alternative vision of how public media might operate for a changed Australia, in which diversity is the central fact of life. We are entering the post-broadcast age, where *broadcasting* to mass audiences is being replaced by *narrow*-casting to niche interests. In the post-broadcast world, the coerced majorities of broadcasting fragment. The industrial model with its two standard products, 'high' versus 'low' culture, is already starting to split up.[2] What you now get is cultural multiplicity. Technological developments make narrow-casting, whether digitally, through cable, the airwaves or the Internet, both possible and affordable, but it is the diversity of audiences which is driving the process.

Simultaneously, new technologies reduce the costs of creative production and make obsolete both the factory systems and the corporate hierarchies that characterised television production — both private and public — in the second half of the 20th century. While rightly defending the principle of public broadcasting in the face of the Coalition's attacks, the ALP fails to notice how even under the last Labor government, the ABC was far from living up to a social-democratic vision for public media.

So, from the inside, what did Labor do with the ABC?

Political agendas and the ABC

The ALP in government has often run a warmed-over version of the right's privatisation agenda — either selling off the public's assets outright, or imposing 'managerialism' on public utilities such as the ABC.[3] This is a kind of internal privatisation that combines internalised market forces and costs savings with a top-down re-structure that gives all power to bureaucrats and accountants. Rather than producing lean, mean machines responsive to consumers, the result has been intensification of the old-fashioned civil service hierarchy under the new corporatism, but with the quality of service and public accountability often reduced.

Under Labor, the ABC was subjected to just such a managerial makeover: bureaucracy and central control were strengthened and the organisation's capacity to encourage creativity and reflect a changing Australian society greatly weakened. The growth in bureaucracy and management control over product was disguised by David Hill's energetic maintenance of funding under Labor, which continued sustained levels of Australian programming. Keating's dissatisfaction with Hill's ABC was seen in the *Creative Nation* blueprint for the cultural industries, which directed new funds for innovation to SBS, where the money was less likely to fall victim to bureaucratic inertia.[4] ABC radio, while not immune to managerialism, was exempt from the worst excesses because of the hands-on and immediate nature of its medium. But in television the combination of an old–style public service nomenclature with managerialism's elevation of the accountants produced an infertile hybrid not unlike the Soviet Union in its dying days.

If Hill was an autocrat instilling paranoia, Brian Johns was the well-meaning Gorbachev. Despite the whiff of glasnost on his ascension, Johns proved unable to stave off the massive cuts to ABC funding and political attacks by the Howard Government, which from its inception has alleged anti-Coalition bias and the transmission of material offensive to mainstream Australia. ABC management's response was: an unprecedented downsizing of production staff in tandem with a 'One ABC' re-structure that actually increased the numbers of senior and middle management; intensification of management's control over production; and a conservative programming and commissioning policy that provoked an exodus of younger program-makers away from an orgy of British costume and police drama, high arts and rural escapism.

Johns and Bob Mansfield had a not unreasonable desire to open the ABC's doors to the wider creative community. This had, of course, been happening for years with the independent documentary-makers. With the Coalition in power, this became an ideologically-driven obsession by management to outsource program-making to the big commercial players, who were even less in touch with Australian creativity than the ABC. When the rushed and secret Mansfield inquiry (1997) failed to uphold the allegations of bias or argue for commercialisation, the Coalition contented itself with natural attrition on the board and the end of Johns' term. Now with Jonathan

Shier at the helm, there appears to be an agenda to dumb down ABC TV even further, to make it more like commercial television (Davies 2000). In the words of the late Clement Semmler: 'Heaven forbid that the ABC should ever become involved in a ratings chase — a possibility which is at present alarming dedicated ABC viewers as well as some of its staff'.[5]

Today I'm less concerned about what the Coalition is doing to the ABC than about the long-term structural problems that allows a public asset to be so easily destroyed, and about how the ALP might re-imagine public media.

Benchmarks for Labor

I now outline key standards as a guide to assess a future Labor governments' performance in relation to reform of the ABC:

- Genuine reflection of Australia's cultural diversity — in terms of class, generations, regions, aesthetics, ideas and especially ethnicity in both programming and recruitment. It's noteworthy that this benchmark is already in part reflected in Part 6, 1 (a) of the ABC Charter, which commits the ABC to: 'broadcasting programs that contribute to a sense of national identity and inform and entertain, and reflect the cultural diversity of, the Australian community'.

- Real openness to and support for creativity and innovation, from both in-house staff and from the wider community.

- Training and nurturing of new talent and experimentation in technology and craft skills.

- Accountability of cultural producers to taxpayers who fund it and consume it in their diversity. Measurements should be better than a subjective idea about 'quality' or crude 'bums on seats' (the ratings).

- Recycling and repackaging of ABC-owned content within the community, through the Internet, educational institutions, ABC retail outlets and other vectors so that the ABC and taxpayers realise a true value on investment.

- An internal workplace democracy.

Problems

Diversity

The basic problem with the ABC for a social-democratic party
is that its corporate structure leaves it struggling to be creative
and to respond to the diversity of Australia. The ABC remains
a fairly monocultural, upper-middle-class, Anglo-Celtic institution. This is what John Howard meant when he referred to the
ABC as: 'Our enemies talking to our friends'. As well as con-
travening the ABC Charter, this narrowness stultifies our public culture.[6] The ABC can never be all things to all people, but
it can be the means by which different Australians talk to each
other. At the moment it is the channel through which one section of Australia talks to itself, while a tremendous creative
energy in our community — one that will usually be ignored
by the commercial sector — remains disenfranchised.

In practice, the ABC Charter and those of many other
public cultural bodies is usually ignored for a sectoral appeal
to the Anglo-Celtic upper-middle-class. The problem occurs
when terms like public interest or 'quality' or 'non-commer-
cial' are masks for personal taste, class prejudices or out-
moded aesthetics. Taxpayers and consumers have a right to
say how their cultural dollars are spent. Currently these institutions are run as if they are the property of the managers
who are in fact our servants. It is a far cry from the sort of
cultural democracy that we should be promoting.

Even if many of its stars and managers are fashionably
republican, the ABC remains the great defender of British
culture in Australia and persists in maintaining a colonial
deference to the BBC as the benchmark for quality. More
generally, ABC culture adheres to an old idea of Australian
nationalism, where 'white' Australians speak for the nation,
and migrants and 'ethnic' Australians speak for their own
groups and usually only about migrant and 'multicultural'
issues. The opposing view argues that Australia is now ethni-
cally diverse at its core, and the idea of what is the national
culture is being contested — an unfolding story that ABC
television ignores. This monoculturalism flows in part from
the staff make-up, the result not just of incumbency, but of a
far-from-transparent recruitment process that continues to
favour Anglo-Australians and British immigrants.

The ABC's class bias towards the privately schooled is shared with other private media industries, but the make-up of the commercial sector is not the concern of a social democratic government. The ABC is good at exhibiting working-class individuals and communities as subjects with problems to be diagnosed or eccentricities to be celebrated, but always they are presented as 'the other' to an assumed middle-class audience. As I was told on starting work at the ABC in 1988 on a documentary called 'Nobody's Children': 'Remember mate, you're making films to titillate Pymble'.

In Sydney it is rare for the ABC to consider the audience in the western suburbs where most of the population live. Or, as Mike Carlton reported on taking the job as announcer on 2BL: 'my manager told me to imagine I was talking to my neighbour over the fence in Epping'. I don't recall a member of the production staff or management that lived in outer western Sydney, and anthropological trips 'out there' were generally the subject of snobby jokes.

Ironically, though, the ABC is also losing the younger middle class who live in the inner cities and whose tastes might be described as low brow/high brow. With the exception of Triple J and Radio National, the ABC is too literal, pompous, middle brow and lacking in irony and sense of humour. The ABC has long suffered from a generational constipation that has seen younger program-makers within and outside the organisation either ignored or ghettoised in so-called youth programs, while an aging cohort continue to control 'serious' programs in current affairs, the arts and drama.[7]

Openness and support for creativity and innovation

The *Gangland* thesis has been well debated,[8] but it remains true that the 1960s generation that pioneered current affairs television has been loath to allow subsequent generations to meddle with the formulae or try new aesthetics or ideas (with glorious exceptions like 'Beat Box'). In fact, the same people who invented cheeky, maverick programs (like 'This Day Tonight') have used their second-hand managerial incumbency to enforce their revolutionary experiments as rigid dogma. As a result, shows like 'The Simpsons' now have more to tell us about our changing world than 'Four Corners'.

What I mean is that ABC documentaries and current affairs continue to generalise about simplistic trends learned from 1970s sociology — running down well-worn tracks, when many of us want to explore the interesting tangle of back lanes and clear new trails. This generational myopia extends to the choice of 'talking heads', where television (unlike radio) persists in ignoring the diversity of new commentators who have been educated in our universities over the past twenty years. It's as if the world stopped in 1975.

New talent

The ABC has always played an important role in discovering and fostering new talent, but is hopeless at looking after that talent and allowing it to mature within the organisation's mainstream, which remains enslaved to old ideas of 'quality'. So the problem is not with youth programming, but in allowing a diversity of adult programming. Meanwhile, several generations of talented Australians talk to themselves in e-journals, short films, independent magazines and scholarly publications, or beat a path to other TV stations where younger ideas and aesthetics are appreciated. How is it that the ABC has lost to commercial televison such maverick talent as Mikey Robbins, Jon Saffran, Paul McDermott, Mark Trevorrow, Richard Fiedler and the Working Dog Team, let alone the small army of producers, researchers, editors, journalists, and camera crews that have been downsized into the independent sector?

Reform not easy for Labor

Real engagement with the diversity of our creative community and audiences is not necessarily easy. Everyone supports innovation, but real innovation often offends, angers or leaves one underwhelmed. Similarly with 'quality': one person's quality may make no sense to another person. Perceptions of what constitutes quality may depend on particular cultural literacies which nowadays are not shared by a community criss-crossed by aesthetic and attitudinal divides. This is the real challenge of multi-culturalism and other divergences of opinion based on age and geography that Australia is still to deal with.

The trouble for the left is that the ABC gives most of us what we love: sober, abstract discussion of public affairs;

dramatisations of classic literature; truly intellectual radio programs; the occasional sassy inner-city comedy; and bucolic soaps that buy into our childhood memories. But it is important to think about our fellow citizens who are left cold by this model of broadcasting. Surely it's not post-modern pretentiousness to suggest that we take into account Australians with different tastes, icons, knowledge, humour and dreaming? Public broadcasting has always sought to identify the tastes of the tertiary educated upper-middle class with a universal notion of 'quality'. A diverse society with many different ways of seeing destabilises this once sacrosanct notion, throwing open the parameters to a wider range of ideas, aesthetics, personalities and stories. Labor activists engaged in the debate about the ABC need to be culturally sensitive to the different tastes and positions in the community, and mindful about not enthroning their own tastes as inherently superior.

Agenda for reform

The reform of a public asset like the ABC is too important to be left to the whims of the latest managing director. Perhaps Labor should look to another Dix-style inquiry that invites full public debate? I don't claim to have all the answers but some issues to consider are:

- Why should either the government of the day, or a managing director and an appointed board be able so wilfully to toy with a basic public asset? Surely this is a matter for Parliament or a proper public inquiry where the ABC's stake-holders — the public — can debate the issues? Despite Alan Ashbolt's description of the managing director as a king, he or she is simply administering the ABC in trust for the future. A transparent process of perhaps ten yearly public inquiries should be written into the relevant legislation and the powers of the managing director decisively curbed.

- Flatten management and re-invest in creative and production staff.

- ABC management must stop over-controlling by both senior and middle management. The ABC spends a lot of money making its television boring: chopping, changing, re-cutting, rejecting. Television is not a hospital — no one will die if risks are taken. Radio is again a case in point where the nature of the medium — low tech and immediate — escapes meddling and the results are good.

- Narrow-casting is replacing broadcasting. A guiding principle should be to perceive audience in its diversity. Ethnic diversity is not a side order of tabbouleh salad, but the key unfolding story of contemporary Australia.

- A multi-channel environment presents great oppurtunities. There are five radio networks. ABC TV cannot serve Australia's diversity with only one TV channel. Labor is right to champion the ABC as a player in the multi-channel digital environment.

- Outsourcing needs to be governed by legislated rules and benchmarks and be transparent to the public and parliament. It matters less where and how programs are made than that the public commissioning is spread equitably and those taking the money are accountable.

- Intersection with the outside community is a good thing, but with independent film-makers and storytellers and not just with the commercial sector. These days the cultural energy is in dynamic small to medium-sized production companies: this is where the independent documentaries are made and the youthful explosion in short films, zines and websites has come from. In the information age this growing area of cultural enterprise is re-making the conservative model of a small business.

- The ABC should range outside the television industry as well, employing Australian fiction and non-fiction writers, film-makers, performers, Internet writers and designers.

- ABC Online — the public newspaper Labor always wanted — should be defended at all costs. A Labor government should explore specific grants for Internet projects at ABC Online to ensure that the public sector maintains a creative edge in the medium that may well dominate in this century.

- Meaningful indicators are needed to measure the ABC's success with different audiences rather than executive's instincts or crude ratings designed for advertisers.

- Rather than use ratings as a benchmark for the ABC, it would be far better to use the spread of demographics as a measure of its success or failure. Something for the old, something for women, something for the country, something for Perth. The ABC needs to make its audience research more professional, market test its various audiences, and regularly monitor the impact of its programs on different demographics.

- Likewise the Parliament needs to know what proportion of public funds is directed towards content production and transmission, compared to that proportion siphoned off into management and administration.

- Recruitment — much ABC employment is through a contract system where diversity principles and advertising requirements are ignored in favour of a 'mates' system that limits the talent pool. The so-called 'shadow army' is a privileged group that hampers the ABC's ability to reflect Australia.

- Realise the full value of its content. The ABC spends millions on programs which, once used, wallow in the archive rather than being re-packaged for other uses by the Australian public. While we endure yet another replay of 'Hettie Wainthrop Investigates', many critically acclaimed ABC-produced documentaries have never been repeated. At present the middle-brow criteria employed by ABC Enterprises ensures that only the most obvious material is merchandised, while the smart content sought by the education sector is shelved.

- The new ABC Content Rights unit should implement strategies for recycling and niche- marketing ABC content (including research, interview transcripts and camera tapes) as:

  - Internet sites and study guides targeted at schools and universities

  - videotapes energetically marketed to the education sector

  - books

- articles in a challenging subscriber on-line journal —
  perhaps associated with Radio National and TV history and science.

In addition, the current system of internal accounting is inimical to the reality that teams that work well together create the best television and radio. Bureaucratic convenience and accounting dogma mean that ABC TV employs an assembly-line mentality that gets in the way of creativity. The rigidity of the in-house system has meant that working outside, as an independent, is often the only way to get together an appropriate team. Can the ABC come up with a model that balances autonomy for independent content providers with the budget controls appropriate to the public sector?

Government-sponsored innovation: the 2JJ example

Structural change does matter. With the Whitlam Government's encouragement, ABC Radio embarked on a radical experiment to create a contemporary music station for young people. The station was to give space to overseas and especially Australian music not given airplay by commercial radio locked into top 40 play lists and advertising. The station sought to recognise diversity among young people, and to intersect with the independent music sector. It is now a matter of record that 2JJ was at least midwife to the vibrant Australian music scene of the 1980s and 1990s, and was an agent of cultural renewal for generations of Sydney-siders in the areas of comedy, art and politics. It has since gone national as Triple J, providing Australian youth with a sense of cultural reflection, if not leadership. 2JJ succeeded largely because it was given autonomy from ABC management to do its own thing. What we would now call teams — at the time they were collectives — for a time ran the station almost independently of the ABC, and, while management ultimately re-imposed authority, Triple J retains a measure of freedom within the ABC corporate structure. There is a strong case for similar initiatives — in ABC Online, in television and radio — from an incoming Federal Labor Government.

Our ABC?

Is a board of government appointees the best way to run a public corporation? Are there supplementary ways of involving a diverse community in the decision-making and commissioning process? I was involved in consultation with young people for the ABC National Advisory Council and it at least endorsed the policies then being pushed by some left-field ABC mavericks. How can the current advisory council system — themselves appointed — be democratised and expanded as a public voice within the ABC and a check on the board?

At the time of writing, Jonathan Shier has made some promising noises: encouraging creativity to break through the bureaucracy; bringing an increased audience to the ABC as 'light' consumers rather than playing to a dedicated upper-middle-class club. But he has taken the wrong actions: threatening news and current affairs budgets; trashing 'Lateline', a television program dedicated to in-depth discussion of issues; and employing old-fashioned commercial producers and executives steeped in corporate hierarchy. Rather than proceeding from the bottom up and encouraging program-makers outside and within the ABC to invigorate on-air content, Shier has played corporate war games, shifting generals around his big board, replacing the old commanders with his own loyalists. The craven hierarchical structure that makes the ABC a plaything for whoever sits as managing director is *itself* the problem. Simply changing the people who wield control in a top-heavy corporate hierarchy will not change things, especially when these personalities are 'veterans' of 1970s and 1980s commercial TV — the high watermark of formulaic 'mass taste'.

Kim Beazley's emphasis on the 'Knowledge Nation' makes getting public media right in Labor party policy a priority. While a reform agenda for the ABC may not seem like a vote winner, once the ALP return to government the vandalism of the Howard years will make rebuilding the ABC a national priority. As we rebuild, it is imperative we look forward rather than backwards.

chapter 8

Policy: the new 'hard' politics
By Dennis Glover[1]

Introduction

Former adviser to US President Bill Clinton, Dick Morris, has recently argued persuasively that policy development,[2] not 'spin' or the cultivation of image, is today the most important task of any political candidate or party (Morris 1999, p. xvi). Morris' claim is based on the proposition that voters today are more politically sophisticated than in the past; they now understand the way advertisers try to manipulate them with images and have grown resistant. Instead, voters want to hear what policies each party has to offer and they want to be convinced by argument, not by the endorsement of celebrities or by glib slogans. As Morris puts it: elections are now won by verbs — 'I will do this' — rather than by adjectives — 'I am a better leader' (Morris 1999, p. 32).

If correct, this means that policies and message are now crucial to the electoral success of political parties. The unexpected victory of Victorian Labor in the 1999 state election was in part the result of the effort that the then Opposition Leader Steve Bracks put into transforming Labor's policy and message to meet the new circumstances the party faced (Glover 2000). It seems that one of the best investments a party can make is the development of a positive message and a set of policies to take to the electorate. As in British Prime Minister Tony Blair's New Labour Party, Bill Clinton's New Democrats in the United States and Lionel Jospin's French

Socialist Party, Australian centre-left policy experts need to reassert the dominance they once had. Policy is now the new 'hard politics'.

But obtaining government is only the first step for centre-left policy-makers. Policy development in opposition and in government are different. If we are to make government work for people again and use it to help social democrats remain in government once elected, we will need to wind back the damage done to policy formulation through the neo-liberal economic and management theory excesses of recent years.

As other contributors to this book argue, meeting our traditional social-democratic goals in the 21st century will require a thorough overhaul of the way government operates. Decision-making, administration and program delivery will need to be transformed to cope with a society that is becoming more diverse and with social problems that are becoming correspondingly more complex and difficult to solve. This chapter argues that a key first step in transforming government in Australia will be revolutionising the way policy is created. It also argues that one of the urgent tasks of social democracy at the party, societal and governmental levels is to put the notion of the public interest back into public policy-making. The first issue to be discussed is the decline of public policy-making capacity among political parties and governments. The second section will focus on the requirements for good policy- making, and the third will suggest some practical reforms and innovations for implementing these suggestions.

The decline of public policy capacity

Over the past decade, centre-left policy-making around the globe has changed considerably. New ideas created by high-profile research organisations have had a profound influence on government policy-making, especially in the United States and the United Kingdom. Unfortunately in Australia the situation is less healthy. Despite the best efforts of isolated individuals and organisations, the centre-left's policy culture has declined.

One of the most serious symptoms of this decline is the long-term demise of political parties as policy-making machines. Few political parties today are geared towards producing sophisticated new policy ideas, particularly when that party is in government. This has many causes. The rise of factionalism and machine politics has led to a corresponding decline in the number of idealists willing to join all parties and has led ambitious young joiners to concentrate on 'getting the numbers' to the detriment of policy activism. Another cause is that long periods in government have produced reliance upon well-resourced bureaucracies and professional advisers to produce policy. As well, factors such as declining membership and the increasing ability of voters to influence policy-making more directly (through, for instance, talkback radio, polling and the Internet) make political parties seem less representative of the general community, and make their attempts to impose policies on elected public representatives seem less legitimate. Finally, policy-making has become an increasingly complex and professional task, requiring much specialist knowledge not usually possessed by even the most well-informed party member.

As a result of the relative decline of parties as hands-on policy-makers, the way successful political organisations obtain policy advice has changed. In all parties, policy committees and party conferences are tending increasingly to produce statements of their party's broad philosophical direction. This is particularly the case with the ALP's National Platform, which is devised in platform committees and voted on at the party's biennial or triennial National Conference. However, parliamentary representatives generally devise the detailed policies that form the election manifestoes, and in office, governments are influenced heavily by the work of their internal advisers, the bureaucracy and think tanks. Given the different levels of skill and interest of these groups — party members, advisers, public servants and policy experts — and the fact that their membership overlaps significantly, this is probably a reasonably democratic balance of responsibilities.

Governments as well as political parties have had their policy-making capacity severely reduced over the 1990s as a result of neo-liberal economic and management theory excesses (McAuley 2000a, p. 34). This reduction has happened through a number of ways: cutbacks in the overall number of public servants; the outsourcing of policy advice to private sector consulting firms; the replacement of policy coordinating departments such as the Department of Regional Development; and the ideologically motivated closure, downsizing or consolidation of specialised bureaus, such as the Bureau of Industry Economics and the Secretariat of the Economic Planning Advisory Council. As a result, McAuley (2000a, 2000b) has claimed, our Federal bureaucracy has been 'dumbed down', with the capacity to do little more than implement narrowly conceived policy derived from (ironically) bloated and expensive private sector bureaucracies.

One of the urgent tasks of social democracy at the party, societal and governmental levels is therefore to put the notion of the public interest back into public policy-making. How to do this is the subject of the remainder of this article, including a number of practical solutions listed at the end.

What constitutes good policy today?

One of the first facts we have to confront is that our understanding of the causes of and potential solutions to social problems has become far more complex over the past decade. Experts have provided a more nuanced understanding of these matters:

- Sociologists like Anthony Giddens and others have improved our understanding of the multiple identities and concerns of people of all classes (Giddens 1998; Patmore and Glover 1999).

- Labour market economists are now more aware of the importance of boosting opportunities for individuals and communities through education and training (Reich 1991).

- Social scientists now have a greater appreciation of the spatial concentration of inequality and the complex interrelationships between factors such as education, health, crime and unemployment.

One of the results of this increasing complexity is that good policy-making today must possess a number of new qualities.

First, it must be practical and evidence-based rather than the-oretical, prepared to draw on big ideas in its analysis as well as create small practical solutions to concrete problems. Second, it must be based on wider 'intelligence networks' than in the past. Learning from the recent experience of other centre-left parties, we need to create new connections between govern-ments and policy-makers in our think tanks, universities and the public, private and not-for-profit sectors, including the new social and policy 'entrepreneurs'. These networks need to be international, as well as national, interstate and local. Iron-ically perhaps, this increasing complexity and interrelatedness of social problems and the multiplicity of available solutions and sources of policy advice available requires us to create new central organs of policy overview and coordination. Policy-making must be able to work across departments and govern-ment boundaries to deliver what is being referred to as 'joined-up government'. We need as a matter of urgency to recreate a vital policy-making culture by tapping into sources of ideas and political support outside traditional sources.

Evidence-based policy think tanks

One of the problems to be overcome in establishing new pol-icy organisations and networks in Australia is the enormous and unnecessary gulf in understanding between hard-head-ed practitioners of politics and intellectuals. The blame for this lack of connection lies on both sides. Lloyd (1999) has analysed the recent cooling of relations between academics, public intellectuals and the Blair Government. After initially expressing enthusiasm for the Blair project, a number of high-profile intellectuals have become its critics. The major cause, Lloyd concludes, is not just ideological disagreement (these are inevitable when intellectuals involve themselves in government), but a misunderstanding about the type of pol-icy work that government policy-makers now find useful. While public intellectuals often want to engage politicians in fundamental discussions about the type of society they are trying to create, government policy-makers need policy that contains fewer ideological assumptions about how to solve problems of inequality and more hard-headed analysis and practical ideas based on what will work. In short, policy-makers usually need 'evidence-based research' from academics with the ability to frame practical policy — 'policy entrepreneurs' — rather than philosophical debate from more generalist political theorists (although any government would be foolish to stop listening to academic criticism). A better understanding between government and the academe as to what each other requires could help avoid misunderstandings and unnecessary conflict.

This type of evidence-based research does not, however, come cheaply. Good policy advice requires well-qualified staff and involves high overheads. In the past, the Australian centre-left's resources have been insufficient to meet such needs, apart from a brief period when the Evatt Foundation was well-funded and was able to produce high-class social and economic analysis. Lacking sufficient resources to undertake evidence-based research, Australian left-of-centre think tanks have too often only been able to engage policy-makers at a rather abstract level, insufficient to assist in the design of hard policy. For this reason, most of these think tanks have gone into relative decline over the past decade.

There are many overseas organisations providing this type of evidence-based research.[3] Two in particular provide excellent models for us to consider in Australia — Demos, and the Progressive Policy Institute.

Demos is a U.K.-based think tank, founded in 1993 by former Marxist intellectuals associated with the magazine *Marxism Today*, most prominent of whom were Martin Jacques and Geoff Mulgan. The latter is now head of the Social Exclusion Unit in Tony Blair's Number 10 Policy Unit. The current director of Demos is the education policy researcher Tom Bentley, who toured Australia in 1999, and its researchers include high-profile new economy authors Charles Leadbeater and (the pseudonymous) Perri 6. If Demos has a central idea it is the need to 'think the unthinkable', to move beyond notions of left and right (which it believes belong to the industrial era which has largely passed), to create new understandings of the causes of inequality (such as age and locality), to utilise the potential of 'modernity' — globalisation and rapid technological change — to promote equality, and to revitalise democracy as an end in itself. Demos has had a significant influence on the Blair Government. Many of its major policy prescriptions, including the need to 'rebrand' Britain, adopt a 'holistic' approach to government and tackle new forms of social inequality, have surfaced in the rhetoric of 'cool Britannia', the 'modernising government' project and the establishment of the Social Exclusion Unit. Its latest research projects are typical of its eclectic and small-scale approach to solving social problems. These include looking at the access that the poor have to nutritious food, initiatives to encourage responsible fatherhood, and the learning problems faced by disaffected young people. Core funding from major philanthropic foundations and project funding from private corporations and public bodies provides an annual budget capable of supporting twelve full-time staff and a number of associate staff, as well as a long list of high-quality publications (*Economist* 1997; Denham and Garnett 1998; www.demos.co.uk). Lloyd argues that the success of Demos rests partly on its creation of a new class of 'policy entrepreneurs' with strong links with Tony Blair's Number 10 Policy Unit (Lloyd 1999, p. 24).

The Progressive Policy Institute (P.P.I.) is, in rough terms, the US equivalent of Demos, although as the official think tank of the Democratic Leadership Council it is more directly connected to the Democratic Party than Demos is to New Labour. Founded in 1985 it is the leading source of ideas for the 'New Democrats', and, as such, has had a significant impact on US politics. Like Demos, its success rests on its direct influence over senior policy-makers in Congress, the White House and state administrations, through the quality of its ideas and through the strong advocacy of its leading figures, such as its president and co-founder Al From. In the lead-up to the presidential elections in November 2000, the P.P.I. had its ideas on subjects such as education policy and the new economy adopted by both the Gore and Bush camps. Its ideas are published monthly in its magazines *Blueprint* and *New Democrat* as well as in numerous policy papers (www.dlcppi.org; Baer 2000).

Utilising and strengthening policy networks

In earlier periods of Labor's history, individual academics and think tanks played a key role in the formulation of the great practical programs of Labor governments. In his recent memoirs, the former Chief of Staff to then Opposition Leader Gough Whitlam and later head of the Department of Prime Minister and Cabinet, John Menadue, details the influence a handful of academics brought together by the Fabian Society had on the ALP's 1972 platform (Menadue 1999). The resurrection of the Victorian Branch of the ALP and the election of the Cain Government in 1982 (which, it should not be forgotten, was initially held to be a model of reforming social democracy) was in part due to its harnessing of new policy ideas from across the community through the work of the Labor Resource Centre (Cain 1995, pp. 11, 20, 272).

Unfortunately, Australian universities in general lack a strong public policy tradition, although there are exceptions. The Australian National University was originally set up to assist government in post-war reconstruction and has a history of public policy involvement. A number of schools of government and university-linked institutes have recently emerged, including the Centre for Public Policy at the University of Melbourne, the Social Policy Research Centre at the University of New South Wales and the School of Public Policy at Monash University. One very positive recent addition is the newly created Brisbane Institute at the University of Queensland, which has teamed up with Labor Premier Peter Beattie and Brisbane Mayor Jim Soorley to fulfil the wider public role of boosting Queensland's credentials as a 'smart state'. One of the aims of the institute is to create a broader intellectual climate and help transform Brisbane into what futurist Charles Handy would call 'a buzzy city' that attracts the knowledge workers and investment capital for the new economy (McKew, 2000, p. 48). Despite these improvements there is still a long way to go before Australia reaches the level of interest and excellence in public policy-making that exists in the U.S. and the U.K., where Harvard, Princeton, Stanford, Oxford and the London School of Economics, among many other institutions, have long nurtured expert policy-makers. In these countries, academics often move between the academe and government. Prominent U.S. examples have included Robert Reich, from the Kennedy School of Government at Harvard University, who was appointed President Clinton's Secretary for Labor, and Donna Shalala, former Chancellor of the University of Wisconsin, who was President Clinton's Secretary of State for Health and Social Services. Professor Anthony Giddens, Director of the London School of Economics, is a high-profile adviser to Tony Blair.

Another problem is the poor state of Australian left-of-centre publishing compared to that overseas. In the U.K. there is a wide range of political left-of-centre publications in which ideas can be expressed, including the *New Statesman*, the *Guardian* and *American Prospect*. In the U.S., there are a wide variety of publications, ranging from the intellectual *New York Review of Books* and *Atlantic Monthly* to the policy journals *Prospect* and the *New Republic*. In Australia we have the Catholic *Eureka Street*, the post-modern-leaning *Arena*, the Keynesian *Dissent* (recently reborn under the editorship of *Age* economist Kenneth Davidson) and *AQ*. Of these, none is truly a forum for the discussion of reforming policy ideas (although *AQ* comes closest), focusing instead on journalism and criticism. One promising sign is the emergence of Pluto Press, which is attempting in conjunction with the Fabian Society to promote debate over the future direction of the ALP in its 'Left Book War' series, including this book and its predecessor volumes.

Breaking down the policy 'silos'

Due to the increasing complexity of society, and the increased ability to identify interrelated aspects of social issues, the traditional categories used by governments to address these problems are no longer adequate. This is because many problems and opportunities cut across existing departments and levels of government. One solution is to work across portfolios and levels of government by establishing what are referred to in the U.K. as 'crosscutting' units — policy coordination bodies situated in the Cabinet Office that are overseen by the Number 10 Policy Unit. These bodies not only work to coordinate the work of existing departments, they have the role of developing new ideas and applying gentle pressure from above for change to be implemented by the many departments involved in program delivery

(*Economist* 1999). The Blair Government has established two of these units — the Social Exclusion Unit, which coordinates policies across departments including education, health, housing and transport, and the Performance and Innovation Unit, which aims to encourage more innovation and crosscutting policy work (see Leigh in this volume; www.cabinet-office.gov.uk/innovation/). Four potential Australian crosscutting units are discussed below.

Harness innovation

Innovation has two roles to play for reforming Labor governments. The first is refreshing electoral programs.

One of the ways in which progressive governments often lose their political direction is an over-reliance on bureaucracy to formulate political policy. This over-reliance could be one of the contributing reasons why Labor governments often lose the votes of their traditional supporters over time (Scott 2000, pp. 251–8). As Morris (1999) argues, a professional, apolitical bureaucracy, whilst a key element of good government, is, by definition, concerned with continuity and the administration of existing programs, not innovation. As change is the *raison d'être* of Labor governments, the centre-left needs to consider how it can complement the existing role of the public bureaucracy and encourage greater policy innovation. Some practical suggestions are listed in the final section of this chapter.

The second role for innovation is in the re-designing of government itself. Much work on this has been done overseas, through U.S. Vice-President Al Gore's Reinventing Government project and the recent similar project by the Blair Government, the *Modernising Government White Paper*. These projects seek to re-design government to make it more flexible and efficient, more responsive to new demands being made on government by citizens and better able to utilise new technology, particularly information technology. McAuley (2000a and 2000b) has provided some good criticisms of the 'New Management' ideology that underpins much of these reform attempts, but they do contain many ideas that can be used to strengthen the in-house and across-government policy-making capacity of governments. Some

of the ideas contained in these papers also form part of the
discussion of practical suggestions below.

Some practical ideas

Since Labor was last in office, policy-making has been transformed by a number of factors, particularly the Internet.
Joseph Stiglitz, former Chief Executive of the World Bank
and Chairman of President Clinton's Council of Economic
Advisers, has called upon governments to use the Internet to
improve their policy-making. As Stiglitz has commented:
'Policy-making bureaux in most governments are limited in
size, and are typically overloaded. The new technologies
hold out the promise of drawing upon far wider expertise'
(Stiglitz 2000). Policy-makers in Australia at the State and
Federal levels already conduct lively exchanges with their
counterparts in the U.K., including with Demos, Nexus and
the Number 10 Policy Unit. These types of connections
should continue. Labor needs to reach out further than our
own political parties and existing think tanks to overseas
organisations and to our own community-based organisations, to what are now being referred to as wider 'intelligence networks'. To do this, there are a number of models
we can consider.

Enhance Australia's public policy capacity

Four initiatives to improve Australia's public policy capacity
could be considered:

- Strengthening university public policy schools.

- Encouraging academics to take sabbatical leave in public
  sector think tanks and government.

- Emulating the U.K.'s public service by establishing a Centre for Management and Policy Studies within the service
  to promote a balanced public service policy culture.

- Encouraging more academic to publish in the area of
  public policy through the establishment of more public
  policy journals linked to university departments, and by
  recognising for university funding purposes, contribu-

tions to public debate by academics on television, radio, the Internet and in newspapers and magazines. Currently these unrefereed publications do not attract the points used to determine faculty funding levels. This discourages academics from spending their time contributing to public debates.

Create a central government policy unit

The key first step to putting the public interest back into public policy-making will be central coordination. The successful model we should consider emulating is the Number 10 Policy Unit in the office of British Prime Minister, Tony Blair. This unit was set up after the 1997 election to ensure that policy development across departments remained consistent with Labour's election manifesto and to develop new and innovative ideas from the U.K. and overseas. Under the direction of David Miliband, the sixteen-person unit oversees the two prominent crosscutting Cabinet Office policy bodies — the Social Exclusion Unit and the Performance and Innovations Unit — as well as the U.K. Foresight Programme, which aims to anticipate future social, political, cultural and economic trends through innovative research (*Economist* 1999).

A similar body in Australia would have a number of tasks. It could oversee the work of potential new crosscutting agencies, such as those needed to create a 'Knowledge Nation', tackle social exclusion, create more 'family friendly' workplaces and empower and redevelop regional Australia. It could also liaise with universities, independent research institutions, other governments and the community in general to widen the Government's 'intelligence networks', ideally through a Nexus-type on-line policy forum (see below).

Set up an Australian On-line policy network

As well as facilitating informal contact between policy advisers, the Internet can be utilised in a more structured way to reach out to a wider number of policy experts. The model here was the Nexus on-line think tank, established by acade-

mics at the University of Cambridge in cooperation with the
Number 10 Policy Unit. Nexus' aim was to 'create a space
within which ideas and empirical issues can be debated at
one remove from the immediate electoral and media pressures that face politicians'. Nexus had a two-fold purpose: 'to
develop and extend centre-left thought, and to increase the
profile and quality of public debate'. It operated by arrang-
ing on-line debates between the U.K.'s leading intellectuals,
researchers, political advisers and policy entrepreneurs. Policy areas it debated included health policy, higher education
reform, information and communications technologies, the
changing role of the state, social exclusion and government
accountability.

In 1998 Nexus conducted a prominent public debate on
the philosophical direction of the Blair Government, which
was largely responsible for developing in greater detail than
before the concept of the 'Third Way'. Contributors included: Anthony Giddens; David Marquand, Principal of Mansfield College, Oxford; Julian Le Grand, Professor of Social
Policy at the London School of Economics; and the Directors of the Institute for Public Policy Research and the U.K.
Fabian Society. This debate fleshed out the practical meaning of the Third Way and has had a profound impact on the
direction of the Blair Government, which has flowed on to
Australia, and elsewhere.

Nexus provides a tested model of how intellectuals, academics, social entrepreneurs and policy experts can assist the
development of the public policy of centre-left governments.
It is not necessarily linked to The Third Way, but can be used
to draw out contributions from across the political spectrum.
As stated above, building such a network in Australia can be
one of the key functions of any government policy unit.

Join the Third Way International

Enhanced interaction is also occurring among left-of-centre
government leaders themselves. Since September 1998 a
number of influential social-democratic leaders, including
Tony Blair, Bill Clinton, former Italian Prime Minister Alber-
to D'Assimo, German Chancellor Gerhardt Schroeder and
French Prime Minister Lionel Jospin, have participated in a

series of high-profile summits dubbed the 'Third Way International'. Exchanges of ideas also take place at the ministerial level. A similar type of interaction is now taking place among European Community governments to exchange policy ideas, compare outcomes ('benchmarking') and learn from each other about what works and what doesn't. The idea is to promote 'soft convergence' between the economic, social and education systems of European Community countries. Given that the Hawke and Keating Governments provided some of the inspiration for many of the policies now known as the Third Way, Labor in government should look to participate in these high-level meetings in addition to the ALP's continuing involvement in the Socialist International and the International Labor Organisation.

Practise 'soft convergence' between the States and the Commonwealth

We can do the same at the intra-national level. The Internet provides greater opportunities for Labor governments and oppositions at State and Federal levels to exchange information, copying the 'soft convergence' model of the European Community — sharing ideas that work. There is far too little interaction between policy-makers at the State and Federal levels within Australia. While good ideas tend to circulate around policy-making circles, often this is the result of chance or the result of reading about it in the newspapers. In the recent past, State government has been hampered by the growth of competitive federalism, with State administrations forced into the game of bidding each other down in a never-ending spiral, depleting their taxation bases. Some structured contacts could see the development of a social-democratic alternative based on the European Community's approach of 'soft convergence'. In the U.S. the Democratic Leadership Council has played a similar role by bringing together State and local Democratic Party politicians for an annual two-day conference — dubbed the DLC National Conversation. Internet networks of political advisers, backed up by occasional meetings, would also be an invaluable way of building trust and common interests throughout the Labor Party.

Practise innovation

One of the key qualities that new policy bodies will need is innovation — the identification of new ways to tackle existing problems and future policy opportunities. A commitment to innovation is the hallmark of firms that make up the new economy, and in the 21st century it should be a feature of the centre left and of government as well. There are many components of policy innovation from other governments and the private sector which think tanks and government in Australia should examine. These include locating a public sector policy unit in one of the new economy incubators, such as the purpose-built De Bono Centre in 257 Collins St, and utilising some of the internal ideas generation techniques practised in leading technology firms, including on-line discussion groups utilising the latest software.

Protect intellectual independence

Adopting a strategy based on policy vision requires three notes of caution. First, we need to balance policy-making with commonsense and political judgement and to lean towards practical rather than ideological responses to problems. Second, we need to ensure that the independence and strategic capacity of the public service is protected. And third, that the integrity of academics and public intellectuals is respected and their cooperation is maintained.

In the mid 1990s, the Federal Coalition leader Dr John Hewson sought to win power based almost solely on policy through his Fightback! program. Dr Hewson's folly was not to offer people a vision, but rather to offer an overly detailed and ideologically inspired manifesto that was out of step with the beliefs of the Australian people. His fate alerts us to the need to balance policy-making with commonsense and political judgement and to lean towards practical rather than ideological responses to problems. Like Icarus, in their quest to implement pure policy, politicians and policy-makers must be wary of flying too close to the sun.

As stated earlier, McAuley has warned that one of the pitfalls of 'the New Public Management' theory has been the loss of impartiality, professionalism, continuity and a broader community perspective that was the dominant culture in the older public service and still survives in parts of the present bureaucracy. Any new policy-making structures committed to innovation and to providing new directions run the risk of making this situation worse if adequate care is not taken. New ways of policy-making by governments should not usurp the traditional role of the public service in providing disinterested advice and new public policy ideas, but should be additions to existing structures, to feed in new ideas.

In trying to involve intellectuals in practical policy-making and create 'policy entrepreneurs' we must be careful to retain the integrity of intellectuals as intellectuals. The value to be gained from tapping the ideas of academics and private-, public- and third-sector thinkers will be lost if it is seen merely as an attempt to conscript them into support for a pre-existing program. The task is not to compromise the intellectual integrity of dedicated professionals but to utilise their enthusiasm and expertise to change the world as well as interpret it.

Conclusion

Policy-making is becoming an increasingly complex business. Different types of organisations are suited to different tasks and we need to rethink the relationship between parties and other policy-making groups. The broad philosophical directions proposed by parties should rightfully remain in the hands of the democratic processes of parties themselves. Within this framework there is a place for other types of bodies to contribute to better policy creation. A multiplicity of think tanks, utilising networking techniques, can be a source of innovation and new ideas. Government can be used to draw ideas from the community and work across existing departmental silos to tackle complex problems in new ways. The right in Australia has recognised that changing public policy requires changing the way public policy is created. It is time for progressive parties in Australia to do the same.

chapter **9**

Tackling social exclusion
By Andrew Leigh[1]

At a time when Australia is wealthier than ever, when government spends a greater proportion of that wealth than at any time since World War Two,[2] and when we can draw on more good ideas than ever before, our policy-makers should be bold about tackling social exclusion. The challenge is undoubtedly vast. Rapid technological changes, combined with increased economic openness, have placed new burdens on the most disadvantaged in our society. We should address the problems not only for compassionate reasons, but also because it is in the long-term interest of those who are already socially 'included'. If the stagnation of our national skills base is allowed to continue, the growth of new industries will be impaired. If early-intervention programs are not promoted, crime rates will be higher in later years. And if the benefits of economic openness are not shared, we risk a backlash against globalisation. The serious economic reformers of the first decade of the 21st century will be those who are as innovative about social reform as they were about micro-economic re-structuring in the 1980s and 1990s.

The link between social and economic reform has been recognised by many of the world's progressive governments — in the United States, Britain, France, Germany, Canada, and the Netherlands. Under Labor, Australia developed innovative solutions, such as the Accord, to boost both growth and social cohesion. Yet since its election in 1996 the

Coalition Government has struggled to integrate economic and social reform. This chapter argues that the Federal Government must pay more attention to social exclusion. It advocates the creation of a specialised unit, within the Department of Prime Minister and Cabinet, dedicated to researching the problem of social exclusion, designing effective solutions and overseeing their implementation.

What is social exclusion?

The concept of social exclusion had its genesis in French social policy discourse during the 1970s and 1980s. During the early 1990s it spread to other countries, and by the latter part of the decade had become an established part of the lexicon of the European Union, the Organisation for Economic Cooperation and Development (OECD) and the International Labour Organisation (ILO). In Europe, social exclusion has now become one of the main issues in policy debates (Jones and Smyth 1999, pp. 2–6).

Social exclusion refers to the many ways in which members of our society find themselves excluded from fully participating in its processes and enjoying its benefits. It recognises that disadvantage runs broader than conventional measures of poverty. Not all of those who are poor are socially excluded. Moreover, a lack of economic resources is just one of the conditions that can lead to social exclusion. Others are:

- joblessness or insecure employment
- geographic isolation
- lack of access to transport
- homelessness or sub-standard housing
- vulnerability to crime
- poor education
- inability to communicate in English
- inadequate family support
- limited social networks
- absence of good role models
- lack of access to reasonably priced telephone services
- poor health
- physical or intellectual disabilities.

It is important to consider the many aspects that make some people more disadvantaged than others. Social exclusion recognises that conventional poverty lines have traditionally told only part of the story. Imagine a pair of families — the Nguyens and the De Costas — each with two adults and two children, and receiving $426.36 per week, the amount that currently puts them on the Henderson poverty line.[3] Applying traditional poverty measures, both would be considered equally disadvantaged. Yet the Nguyens may only be poor now because Mrs Nguyen has lost her full-time job the previous month. Living a short distance from the centre of Perth, with a diverse network of family and friends, the household can reasonably expect that their predicament will only be temporary. Their situation contrasts with the De Costas, who are poor because their father has never been able to find permanent work. They live on the outskirts of Lismore. Not having a car, and relying on poor public transport, they are generally restricted to socialising with their near neighbours, with whom both parents have difficulty communicating, since English is their second language.

Broadening the definition of disadvantage allows us to differentiate between transitional poverty and entrenched exclusion. The Nguyens need a short-term safety net, and dynamic assistance to move Mrs Nguyen back into the workforce. But different strategies will be required if the De Costas are not to become further excluded from our society.

Focusing on social exclusion rather than simple poverty also avoids the trap of presuming that all the conditions of disadvantage are mono-causal, and can be solved through a concentration on one policy mechanism, such as raising disposable income. In fact, the processes that cause exclusion are as complex as those that create wealth. This point is best understood by considering four of the key conditions of social exclusion — unemployment, geographic isolation, limited social networks and poor education — as well as some of the new forms of social exclusion that may arise in the future.

Exclusion through unemployment

Unemployment is the key determinant of poverty in Australian society today. Data compiled by Bob Gregory and

Peter Sheehan (1998) show that in 1972–73, 21 per cent of unemployed income units were in poverty, but by 1995–96, the figure had risen to 78 per cent. Duration of unemployment is also closely linked to poverty. While 13 per cent of households where the head was unemployed for less than eight weeks were in poverty, the poverty rate for households where the head was unemployed for over a year was 79 per cent. These statistics are particularly disturbing given the increasing proportion of long-term unemployed people. In 1973, just 5 per cent of unemployed people had been out of work for over a year. Today, the figure is around 30 per cent.

As well as being poor, the long-term unemployed are often disadvantaged in other ways. Half of those who are out of work for over two years cannot read or write (ABS 1997), which poses substantial problems if the long-term unemployed are to be brought into labour market programs. As the OECD has pointed out, 'participants generally require a minimum prior level of skills or competence which many long-term unemployed do not possess' (OECD 1988, p. 55).

The steady shift of unemployed people onto the Disability Support Pension (DSP) has in many cases only exacerbated their exclusion from mainstream society. In the past three years, the number of DSP recipients has grown by 16 per cent, to 577,700 people (Department of Family and Community Services 2000). At this rate, over one million Australians will receive DSP by 2010. Since the DSP benefit is around $20 per week higher than the unemployment benefit, recipients are financially better off.[4] Yet they may often become more excluded, since less emphasis is placed on retraining and finding jobs for DSP recipients than for those who are on the unemployment benefit.

In addition to the long-term unemployed and unemployed people who have been moved onto DSP, social exclusion strategies need to focus on those who are subject to recurrent bouts of unemployment. As a recent report by the Australian Bureau of Statistics pointed out:

> The problem for many of the unemployed is not only that it takes them a considerable period of time to find a job, but that the jobs they find typically last for only a short period, after which they return to the pool of unemployment. (ABS 1999b, p. ix)

High levels of recurrent unemployment have resulted from a number of factors. A sharp rise in the unemployment rate from the mid-1970s onwards, a fall in the rate of full-time employment (particularly for men), lower demand for unskilled labour and the growing phenomenon of contracting out[5] all contributed to greater job instability for many workers. Although the rise of the 'working poor' is not yet a major characteristic of the Australian labour market, the growing group of people who have only a precarious hold on work should be a matter of concern.

Recurrent unemployment is a particular problem because of unemployment's 'scarring' effect. Research from Britain has shown that, after a spell of unemployment, an individual will find it harder to get a job in the future — and the longer the period of unemployment, the greater the scarring effect (Gregg 1999).[6] Certain groups are more vulnerable than others. Workers with minimal work experience or lower levels of education are most at risk of cycling between unemployment and low-paid work. For young workers, low-wage jobs may act as a stepping stone to better careers. But we should be wary of accepting the argument that recurrent unemployment is best solved by lower minimum wages, and the imposition of more onerous conditions on recipients of unemployment benefits. As recent international research has shown, lower minimum wages often drive workers out of the labour market altogether (OECD 1997, p. 10).

Ultimately, assisting those who are socially excluded through unemployment requires the coordination of a number of different strategies. In the long term, early intervention programs appear effective in reducing unemployment (Karoly et al 1998; Danziger and Waldfogel 2000). For those who are unemployed now, tax credits may prove useful in reducing the existing poverty traps. Labour market assistance, with a strong focus on basic skills, can assist in bringing some people into work. For DSP recipients, a thorough analysis of the recent jump in numbers is needed, to assess whether jobs can be found for some DSP recipients. Likewise, more research is warranted on the phenomenon of recurrent unemployment.

In some cases, the dictum that the best option for an unemployed person is to find a job of any sort may be misplaced. In an environment where education is the best determinant of future earnings, there may be instances in which it makes more sense to provide training for someone who has been subject to recurrent unemployment than simply encourage him or her to take up another low-skill, low-pay job.

Geographic exclusion

The locational nature of disadvantage has appeared on the national political radar screen in various guises over the past generation. In the 1970s, the Whitlam Government established the Department of Urban and Regional Development to address the issue, and the Henderson Inquiry (Commission of Inquiry into Poverty 1975) devoted a substantial portion of its report to geographic factors, with a strong emphasis on inner city poverty. During the 1980s, sectoral programs, such as the car plan and the steel plan, focused on the problems faced by declining industrial towns. In the 1990s, the Commonwealth's Social Justice Strategy became spatially aware, with a particular emphasis on those living on the fringes of urban areas. In 1999, substantial swings in rural Victoria not only resulted in the defeat of the Kennett Government, but also a renewed national focus on the problems faced by rural and regional Australia.

In a detailed and wide-ranging chapter on the geographic nature of poverty and disadvantage, Ruth Fincher and Maryann Wulff (1998) list five types of localities where disadvantage tends to be concentrated:

- **Inner city:** In 1975, the Henderson Report concluded that inner city suburbs were characterised by high crime rates, cramped living conditions, traffic noise, pollution and excessive housing costs. A quarter of a century later, two processes have occurred. As Henderson predicted, the gentrification and yuppificiation of the inner city has reduced the proportion of poor people living in these areas, as lower-income neighbourhoods have been pushed further away from the city centre. Yet at the same time the living standards of poor inner city dwellers have fallen. The poor who chose to remain in the inner city have felt the pincer effect of fewer unskilled jobs combined with rising living costs. Others in poverty have been drawn to the inner city, since this is where most public housing and hostels are located, as well as support agencies that provide advice, food and clothing.

- **Urban fringe:** The substantial rise in outer urban poverty rates over recent decades has led to particular emphasis being placed on these areas (Hawke and Howe 1990; Berry et al 1996; Maher 1999, pp. 19–20). Yet some commentators have been more sanguine, arguing that whilst the lowest-income suburbs are now further out from the city core, this is a logical corollary of inner city redevelopment, rather than a reflection of the inherent disadvantages of living on the urban fringe (Raskall 1995). Chris Maher and Robert Stimson, for example, whilst acknowledging the difficulties for outer suburban residents in accessing public transport, hospitals, doctors and shops, contend that these must be matched against the benefits of outer suburban living — cheaper housing, lower congestion and a safer environment (1994, pp. 62–3). Nonetheless, even if this is accepted, outer suburban exclusion remains important. Tackling the geographic basis of social exclusion means not only dealing with the inherent disadvantages of particular locations, but also identifying those places where the worst pockets of poverty are located.

- **Rural areas:** Over the past three decades, the proportion of Australians employed in agriculture has declined from 8 per cent to 5 per cent. Falling world prices, productivity improvements and rising farm sizes have all affected the job opportunities available in the agricultural sector (Garnaut et al 2000, p. 118; Chudleigh 1999; Martin et al 2000). Although the real value of farm production has remained relatively constant,[7] some crops and regions have drastically declined.[8] Moreover, many of the new jobs that have been created require higher skill levels than those that have disappeared.[9] The net effect has been significant increases in unemployment in many country areas. The towns unable to attract new industries[10] have sometimes found themselves in a downward spiral. Skilled workers will often relocate to the cities to find work, whilst a substantial proportion of those moving from urban to rural areas are social security recipients seeking more affordable accommodation (Budge 1996; Garnaut et al 2000). The net result is a country-to-city brain drain. Accompanying this is the closure of many government services in regional Australia. For example, in just three years, Moe, a town in rural Victoria, lost offices for the State Electricity Commission, the Water Board, Gippsland Water, the Department of Social Security, the Department of Conservation and Natural Resources, the Department of Planning, Medicare and the local council (People Together Project 1996, p. 13).

- **Declining industrial towns:** The drop in manufacturing employment from 24 per cent in 1970 to 12 per cent today has been due in large part to job-shedding in the textiles, clothing and footwear, and wood, pulp and paper sectors. Older industrial towns — Newcastle, Wollongong, Geelong, Ballarat, the Latrobe Valley, Burnie-Devonport and Whyalla — have been hardest hit. Routine production jobs have been permanently lost, and the new jobs not only require a different set of skills, but are often located in other parts of the country. The result has been chronic and entrenched unemployment in these former manufacturing centres.

- **Emerging coastal welfare regions:** Recently, specific coastal regions — notably the New South Wales North Coast and the Wide Bay/Burnett and Moreton regions of Queensland — have attracted increasing numbers of low-income migrants.[11] Pushed out of urban centres by the lack of unskilled employment and rising housing costs,[12] and attracted to the coast by the promise of a better lifestyle and possible employment in the tourism sector, such migrants are having a substantial effect on the demographics of these regions. So called 'sunbelt migration' — a term more often used to refer to the movement of retirees — may in time result in the regional concentration of families who are excluded from society.

The concept of geographic exclusion does not only apply to these five types of localities. As Mark Latham has pointed out, neighbourhood effects can produce even wider variations. He cites the example of four public housing estates within the Campbelltown local government area, in which the unemployment rate is nearly four times as high as in the surrounding neighbourhood (1998, p. 105). Similarly, Gregory and Sheehan's analysis of collection districts (consisting of around 2000 people) shows that, since the 1970s, the employment/population ratio has remained constant in the richest areas, but dropped markedly in the poorest (1998, p. 123–5).[13]

Apart from the specific programs outlined at the beginning of this section, Australian social policy has tended not to place much emphasis on locational disadvantage. In contrast, it has been central to the British Labour Government's approach to a range of social problems. Particular boroughs (areas containing 150,000–300,000 people) have been designated as Health Action Zones, Employment Zones or Education Action Zones, or nominated for initiatives under the New Deal for Communities or the Sure Start program. At a neighbourhood level, a government-commissioned report has categorised 1370 public housing estates as 'deprived estates' (Price Waterhouse 1997). Prime Minister Tony Blair's Social Exclusion Unit has recognised the concentration of deprivation in particular neighbourhoods, and identified a range of solutions which communities have used to address the problem (SEU 1998).

Yet area-based initiatives have their drawbacks. As a report from the London School of Economics' Centre for Analysis of Social Exclusion (Smith 1999) points out:

- the majority of deprived people do not live in the most deprived areas and will be missed by area-targeted programs

- area-targeting is unfair on those areas which are not covered

- area-based approaches may simply displace 'the problem'

- small area data on deprivation are not good enough to back up decisions to target resources to neighbourhoods

- area programs may detract from the need to do more at a national level.

Overall, it is clear that deprivation in Australia — measured in terms of poverty, unemployment, poor health, low education and crime — is significantly higher in particular geographic regions. This can be explained in terms of industrial changes, low investment in deprived areas, high numbers of unskilled workers competing for fewer jobs, poor social networks to assist with finding work, and an absence of affordable transport.

Nonetheless, before establishing programs to deal with locational disadvantage, it is necessary to answer a number of questions. What should the balance be between mainstream and area-based programs? Which regions would benefit most from area-targeted initiatives? If selecting smaller pockets, how best to ensure that the right areas are targeted? How much control should local authorities have over area-specific programs? How can a locational approach be implemented so that it does not infringe the Federal balance enshrined in the Australian Constitution? Only once these complex questions have been addressed should locally-based strategies be put into practice.

Exclusion through limited social networks

During the 1990s, a burgeoning literature on trust and social capital (Putnam 1993, 1995 and 1996; Etzioni 1993; Fukuyama 1996; Seligman 1997) led a number of academics to focus on the differences between the social networks of the wealthy and of the poor, and how these networks affect life chances. Research in the United Kingdom and the United States has shown that the networks of working-class people are not only smaller, they are also less diverse than those of the middle class. Peter Hall (1997) argues that working-class patterns of sociability tend to revolve around kin and friends, all of whom are relatively connected with one another. By contrast, those in the middle class tend to see twice as many work colleagues outside the workplace, and have a more diverse set of friends, who are often not connected to one another.

From an employment perspective, the most valuable kind of social network is one made up of 'weak ties' to a wide range of people who are unlike oneself (Granovetter 1973; Perri 6 1997; Bentley 1998). Such ties matter for a number of reasons. They provide sources of information about what jobs are available, role models for the difficult process of moving into training or giving up welfare for a low-paid job, and social resources to stay in work once it is found.

Yet unemployed people often lack these sorts of networks. Many long-term unemployed people are cut off from their families (Combes 1998) and only know other unemployed people (Perri 6 1997). William Julius Wilson (1996) describes the way in which prolonged poverty and joblessness in U.S. ghetto neighbourhoods has meant that many of the successful adults who once provided connections outside the ghetto no longer exist. Those who remain lack both networks to find employment and role models to encourage them to follow this path.

While social networks are no substitute for job training, they may be more important than has been previously recognised. For instance, one study on skilled Eastern European workers who migrated to the U.S. found that those who made contact with someone from their community who worked in their field quickly regained their former status, while those who did not languished in low-wage jobs, regardless of retraining (Schneider 1997).

Analysis of the importance of social networks in Australia should result in significantly more emphasis being placed on them as part of an integrated policy approach. Job Clubs, established in the early 1990s, have proven to be effective in helping unemployed people build links to the labour market. Mentoring programs, employment brokers, volunteering schemes and training that helps build networks should all be considered as innovative ways of improving the opportunities available to those who lack appropriate ties.[14]

Educational exclusion

Education levels are a powerful determinant of life chances. Children with low skills are more likely to be unemployed.[15] When they find a job, they are likely to earn less, and have their pay increase at a slower rate (OECD 1997). Poor education is also connected with low political participation, poor general health and depression (Sparkes 1999).

Moreover, there is some evidence that the gap between the educational haves and have-nots is widening. Since 1981, the proportion of students leaving school before year 12 has fallen from 65 per cent to less than 30 per cent. Yet the number of jobs for which early school leavers were qualified fell even faster, so a child dropping out of school in the 1990s was twice as likely to be unemployed as he or she would have been in the 1980s (Ainley, Malley and Lamb 1997). This trend has been predicted to continue over the next decade (Adams and Meagher 1999). Whether a child finishes school is closely correlated with social advantage. Coming from a high socioeconomic background, having parents with post-secondary qualifications and attending a private school all make a student more likely to complete school (Ainley, Malley and Lamb 1997).

The growing importance of education in the labour market creates further problems for those who are not comfortable with what OECD education ministers have called 'lifelong learning' (OECD 1996). Tertiary education programs, training courses, computer learning and informal learning in the workplace all depend on being able to operate comfortably in these diverse settings. As David Istance (1997, p. 29) points out, the person who is socially excluded, and whose educational experience has largely been one of failure, is thus doubly disadvantaged. Others have highlighted the danger that those who are educationally excluded may come to believe that advantaged people deserve to do well because they are more intelligent or more hardworking (Foster and Hawthorne 1998, p. 205).

If we are to eliminate the educational underclass, it is critical to base solutions around the best available research. One recent compilation of British and United States research (Sparkes 1999) has recommended:

- pre-school and early childhood interventions to help poor children[16]
- improving the quality of schools and teachers — leadership, a vision of success, improved physical environment and common expectations about pupil behaviour can substantially raise attainment, particularly for maths and science
- where parents have low literacy levels, boosting the literacy of parents and children together, since parents' educational

levels are important determinants of their children's, and stronger links between home and school helps improve school performance (St John-Brooks 1997)

- improving environmental factors, such as physical illness and bullying
- lower class sizes — contrary to some earlier research, class size appears to make a difference, particularly for disadvantaged pupils.

Yet, disappointingly, Australia's school retention rates have begun to fall again, and classes of over 30 students are now standard in many primary schools (Probert 1999, p. 60). Reducing public investment in education[17] is a false economy. The cost of each year's early school leavers, for example, is a massive $2.6 billion (King 1999, p. 5). More importantly, cutting funding on education risks deepening educational exclusion.

New forms of exclusion

Social exclusion is not a static notion. Whilst some forms of disadvantage will diminish in the future, we should be alert to the risk that others may arise. One possibility is the emergence of a group of people unable to access banking services. During the 1990s, cost-cutting led to the closure of 20–30 per cent of rural and regional bank branches (Hawker 1999) and the imposition of fees for over-the-counter banking services. Technology has played a major role. Whereas a branch transaction costs around $5, an ATM transaction costs $0.70–$1.30 (IBIS 2000, pp. 30–31). The same factors may soon encourage banks to structure their services so as to advantage non-cash dealings. A banking transaction through the Internet, for example, costs between 10 and 20 cents. In future, the advent of smart cards and technologies allowing mobile phones to be linked to banking services will provide flexibility for many, but risk excluding others. As Dave Birch argues, 'young and techno-hip users will eventually tire of subsidising ATMs, armoured cars and night safes for their less well-off brethren' (1997, p. 23).

A related form of exclusion is the so-called 'digital divide' between those who have access to new technologies and those who do not. Computers are rapidly headed in the same direction as telephones and refrigerators — which went from luxuries to essentials in the space of a few decades. Presently, only 48 per cent of households have a computer, and only 41 per cent of Australians have accessed the Internet (ABS 1999a), but both figures are expected to climb rapidly. On present statistics, we can predict who will be left behind. Rates of computer ownership and Internet usage are highest for those who earn the most, work in managerial or professional occupations, live in cities and own more books (ABS 1999a; Meredyth et al 1999, pp. 298–9). The same disparities are emerging in schools. As computers are integrated into the curriculum, schools in rural and low-income areas are falling behind (Meredyth et al 1999, pp. 125–44). Whilst the Clinton administration has launched a major initiative to prevent the creation of a technological underclass (see(:) www.digitaldivide.gov), Australia has been slow to address the issue.

A third possible form of exclusion may be caused by the growing phenomenon of electronic profiling. With the ongoing expansion and interlinkage of databases, companies now have the ability to tightly target their marketing. Moreover, in the areas of credit, insurance, rental services and employment, companies can use these same databases to minimise the risks to which they are exposed (Kruger 1997). The effect may be to consign certain groups of people to a demographic ghetto. More worrying still is the prospect that genetic testing will create another such underclass. Under present legislation, nothing would prevent credit providers, and probably also employers and insurers, from discriminating on the basis of genetic testing (Keays 1999).[18] If we choose not to ban this practice, we will need to consider how to ameliorate its potentially divisive consequences (Perri 6 1998, pp. 88–9).

An Australian Social Exclusion Unit?

If Australian Labor is to make significant inroads into social exclusion, one of the best innovations it could introduce would be to follow the example of the Blair Government and create a Social Exclusion Unit. In 1997, British Labour launched a specialised unit, with responsibility for research-

ing social exclusion, proposing strategies, and assisting with
their implementation.

The Social Exclusion Unit comprises 33 staff, a substantial
increase from its initial twelve. Its members are a mix of civil
servants, drawn from the relevant government departments,
and external appointees. With an annual budget of £1.8 million ($4.7 million), the Unit's role is to report on key areas of
social exclusion. It has no budget for action. Social exclusion
programs are implemented through other government
departments, with the Unit playing a coordinating role. It is
directly responsible to the Prime Minister, but also has a network of Ministers to provide a political sounding-board.

In its two years of operation, the Unit has published five
reports — *Truancy and Social Exclusion* (1998), *Rough Sleeping*
(1998), *Bringing Britain Together: A National Strategy for Neighbourhood Renewal* (1998), *Teenage Pregnancy* (1999) and *Bridging the Gap: New Opportunities for 16–18 Year Olds Not in Education, Employment or Training* (1999). In December 1999, a
review of the Unit by KPMG Consultants found that it had
been a valuable initiative, and should continue until at least
2002 (KPMG 1999). Crucial to its success has been the selection of issues that were of a manageable size, and where
funding was already in place but could be used better. By
focusing on the themes of joined-up government and neigh-
bourhood-level solutions, the Unit quickly projected a clear
vision. It has now begun implementing the strategy for
neighbourhood renewal, through eighteen Policy Action
Teams. Each is headed by a single Minister, and is responsible for putting into effect one element of the strategy (e.g.
jobs, skills, working with the community), drawing not only
upon the Minister's own department, but bringing together
all necessary expertise and resources.

The creation of the Social Exclusion Unit embodies a
number of essential approaches:

- **Holistic governance:** As a recent publication by the
  British think tank Demos pointed out, holistic or 'joined-
  up' governance reflects the fact that 'people's problems
  do not respect borders between disciplines, professions or
  organisations'. The outcomes that matter 'are the products of many departments, agencies and professions, poli-

cies and practices'. Without a joined-up approach, the risks are that agencies will dump problems and costs on one another, conflict in their goals and behave exclusively in dealing with problems (Perri 6 et al 1999, pp. 48–50). For those in need, duplication can cause confusion about which agency to contact when a problem arises. Greater integration of policy-making is a first step towards a more holistic approach to governance.

- **Early intervention:** It has long been known that intervention programs targeting maternal and child health, parenting skills and early education are far more cost-effective than dealing with the problems of crime, unemployment and low social capital in subsequent years.[19] In addition, recent research demonstrates that taxpayers are willing to invest more money into early intervention programs, so long as they can see that the money is being well spent (Danziger and Waldfogel 2000). The notion that our three-year electoral cycle makes it impossible for politicians to commit resources to projects that will not pay off within one or two parliamentary terms is false. An Australian Social Exclusion Unit could play a valuable role in seeking out (and if necessary, initiating) the longitudinal research that is critical to underpin early intervention policies (Bynner 1998).

- **In tune with the community sector:** In its reports, the British Social Exclusion Unit has looked at ways to help government develop better links, and avoid overlaps, with non-governmental organisations. Government should work in tandem with these bodies, channelling funding through them where appropriate, and not sapping their limited resources.

- **Innovative and pragmatic:** Developing optimal solutions to help those at the bottom of society requires us to draw upon Australian and world best practice. An Australian Social Exclusion Unit would draw upon research in Australia and overseas, with the overriding aim of determining 'what works'. Where necessary, the Unit should be willing to propose major reforms. On the other hand, it should not fear the accusation that its proposals are too minor to solve the problem. Social exclusion is a complex phenomenon, and calls for a single overarching solution often reflect a simplistic understanding of the problems. As Christopher Jencks has pointed out, 'If we want to reduce poverty, joblessness, illiteracy, violence or despair, we will surely need to change our institutions and attitudes in hundreds of small ways, not in one big way' (1992, p. 203).

If a Social Exclusion Unit is created, it is vital that it be situated within the Department of Prime Minister and Cabinet (PM&C). Formed in 1971, PM&C is currently made up of ten divisions — the Office of Indigenous Policy, the Office of the Status of Women, the Economic Division, the Industry and Environment Division, the International Division, the Social Policy Division, the Forests and Olympics Division, the Corporate Services Division, the Government Division and the Cabinet Secretariat.

Decisions to assign responsibility over an issue to PM&C have at times been poorly thought through. Matters have been transferred to PM&C because of their public prominence,[20] the Prime Minister's personal interests,[21] or even because a Minister was thought to have performed poorly.[22]

At other times — most notably in the case of gender policy,[23] indigenous policy[24] and multicultural policy[25] — the decision to shift an issue to PM&C was made because of its importance and the need for policy coherence. The argument for doing the same with social exclusion is just as compelling. By establishing a Social Exclusion Unit in the heart of the Federal Government, Labor would recognise, first, that social exclusion is a critically important problem, and, second, that remedying it requires a holistic response.

A Social Exclusion Unit would operate entirely differently from the current Social Policy Division of PM&C. As James Walter has observed, 'for all its centrality, PM&C continues to mediate rather than originate' (1992, p. 45). By contrast, an Australian Social Exclusion Unit would be, in the words of Tony Blair, 'dynamic ... there to solve problems and to achieve results'. Fundamentally, as Blair (1997) points out, 'the job of refashioning welfare and the job of refashioning government are inseparable'.

Conclusion

During the early 1990s, it might have been politically awkward for Labor to take the step of creating a Social Exclusion Unit. When it began its last term, Labor had held Federal office for a decade. Then, a Unit that exposed new social problems could easily have led the public to query why those problems had not been identified and solved years ago. Such a Unit will be most effective if established when Labor first wins office, when it can fearlessly identify the problems and devise appropriate solutions. The chances of a Social Exclusion Unit bringing a fresh approach to social policy and governance are greatest if it is created at the start of a new term in office.

At the outset, this chapter argued that no government can abrogate responsibility for solving social exclusion, given the resources and ideas that are now available. There is another reason to be optimistic. Throughout the 20th century, problems that once seemed insoluble have been dealt with in the space of a few decades. The 1910s, 1920s and 1930s saw significant advances in public health largely eradicate major disease epidemics. During the 1940s and 1950s, large investments in public housing substantially reduced the problem of family homelessness. The 1960s and 1970s witnessed the breakdown of much institutionalised racism against Aboriginals and immigrants — through important changes to our migration and electoral laws, and an amendment to the Constitution. In the late-1980s and 1990s, high inflation was brought under control. Might the next decade be the time when we finally tackle social exclusion?

chapter **10**

Connecting government

By Lindsay Tanner

As access to the Internet expands rapidly, a new set of vital issues is emerging in the realm of government. More and more people are moving on-line, creating opportunities for new methods of delivering services, and the challenge of ensuring that others are not disadvantaged or excluded.

The vast bulk of interaction between government and citizen is about services, not goods. Moving these services on-line offers governments enormous opportunities to reduce costs, improve the speed and quality of services, and empower citizens. More than almost any other kind of organisation, governments have an enormous interest in ensuring that virtually everyone is on-line.

The importance of accelerating access to the Internet is widely recognised. Universal Internet access was a core theme in the presidential campaign of Al Gore. The need for increased access is acknowledged by the industry union, CEPU (CEPU 1999, p. 3), the Federal Government's Bandwidth Inquiry (NBIDP 1999) and many commentators.

Universal access is critical not only for reasons of social equity, but also to stimulate greater economic development. As David Forman observes:

> Bandwidth creates the environment for leading-edge innovation. For the latent creativity of Australians to be fully unleashed in the new competitive environment, as wide a

proportion of the population as possible needs access to the fattest data pipes possible.

Universal high bandwidth connectivity is usually discussed as an equity issue. It could well be that it is a condition of economic survival for any country engaged in the knowledge economy. (Forman 1999)

The current ALP platform acknowledges the importance of on-line access:

Labor supports the right of all Australians to have equitable access to a defined modern and comprehensive standard communications service, including voice telephony and broadband data services...Labor will ensure that the basic infrastructure of the information age, a high speed data network, is in place throughout Australia ... (ALP 2000, pp. 30, 50)

The ALP Platform also states that 'the public sector must be at the leading edge of on-line information provision and transaction processing' (ALP 2000, p. 50). Beneath this rather bland sentence lies a fundamentally important priority: accelerating the growth of government services on-line to increase Internet access and reduce government costs.

A typical government transaction conducted on-line will be cheaper, quicker and more convenient. Instead of physically visiting a specific location, queuing, and filling in forms, a citizen can perform the transaction in minutes from work or home. Transaction costs incurred by the government can be reduced substantially, sometimes dramatically.

Most government bodies in Australia now have some on-line presence. However, the nature of that presence varies considerably. For many it does not extend beyond the provision of information. Some offer forms that can be downloaded, completed and returned by conventional means. A smaller proportion of government sites enable the citizen to conduct a transaction, such as lodging a planning application.

The immense potential for government services on-line to drive the expansion of Internet access is not widely recognised. The National Bandwidth Inquiry notes in passing that 'the Government may also play a key role as a significant user of bandwidth to provide a viable base of demand to encourage greater carrier investment and service provision' (*NBIDP* 1999, p. 17).

In fact, Australia's ability to realise our on-line potential depends heavily on the capacity of governments to drive the information technology revolution by shifting services on-line. The more government transactions are moved on-line, the more demand for Internet access is generated, the more resources for investment in the information economy are freed up, and the more incentives for acquiring on-line skills are generated.

Australian governments should be working harder to move services on-line and ensure that almost all citizens have the capacity to access them. This will create a virtuous circle in which investment generates increasing cost reductions, wider Internet access and on-line skills, and more empowered citizens. Universal Internet access should be a core objective for the Australian Government, with migration of government services on-line a key mechanism for pursuing that objective. However, the Howard Government is not pursuing that goal vigorously enough. In the next part of the chapter, I explain the weaknesses in the current policy of the Federal Government and suggest a preferable approach, drawing especially on the recent experience in Victoria. Lastly, I outline the obstacles to achieving universal access to Internet services.

The state of play

The Howard Government has taken some initiatives directed to shifting government services on-line. In the *Investing for Growth* statement in December 1997, the Government announced a strategy of moving all appropriate services, including government payments, on-line by 2000, to be overseen by the Office of Government Information Technology (OGIT 1998, p. 8). However, on-line service delivery was seen merely as complementing rather than replacing existing physical delivery of services (ANAO 1999, p. 11). Specific legislative initiatives have been enacted, including amendments to the Income Tax Assessment Act and the Customs Act to enable electronic lodgement of returns (ANAO 1999,

p. 40). The Government's Electronic Transactions Act is designed to ensure that electronic transactions carry the same legal status as paper transactions. Individual arms of government have launched specific strategies, such as the National Health Information Management Advisory Council's Health Online project, which aims to improve processing of Medicare claims and health information by more intensive use of on-line resources (NHIMAC 1999). The Business Entry Point is being developed as a site for registration under the tax and corporations law and to provide other government links for businesses. Many of the Government's spending initiatives in communications have some connection with the delivery of government services on-line. The Regional Telecommunications Infrastructure Fund, the Local Government Fund, Building Additional Rural Networks, the Internet Access Fund, Building IT Strengths, and the Intelligent Island project all involve some initiatives calculated to facilitate the expansion of on-line services (DCITA 2000, pp. 3–9). The Government is trialling a Government Information Centre in Launceston, and has allocated $10 million from 1999–00 to 2001–02 to test innovative methods of delivering government services to rural areas via the Internet (MYEFO 1999).

The task of shifting government services on-line is proceeding under the supervision of the re-named Office of Government Online (OGO). According to the Department of Communications, Information Technology and The Arts (DCITA), its role is to provide 'common infrastructure and management arrangements to enable and support electronic services across government' (DCITA 1999, p. 90).

The recent Australian National Audit Office analysis of progress in moving government services on-line indicates that it has been rather modest. The Auditor-General found that by 2001, 52 per cent of surveyed agencies would only have a website containing information about their functions and services, another 25 per cent would enable users to access the agency database, 21 per cent would allow users to enter secure information and engage in transactions with the agency, and only 2 per cent would offer an integrated on-line service involving information sharing with other agencies (ANAO 1999, p. 14). In other words, in 2001 a majority of Federal Government agencies will only have a passive on-line presence.

In April 2000 the Government upgraded its on-line services strategy in its *Government Online — the Commonwealth Government's Strategy* paper (OGO 2000). This proposal did adopt a regime of mandatory reporting of agency progress to OGO, but there is still no Cabinet level involvement in the implementation process as occurs in Victoria. There is also little attempt to develop a partnership with other levels of government to collectively shift all government services on-line.

The Government's strategy to shift services on-line appears to need reinvigoration. The OGO seems to exert little pressure or scrutiny on individual agencies, it does not properly audit their progress, and provides minimal coordination and direction. OGO appears to function as a booster of on-line service delivery, but has little role in organising outcomes. Only the Australian Taxation Office and the Australian Customs Service have made serious progress in generating savings from delivering on-line services, and many agencies only have a website carrying very basic information without any transaction capacity. In essence, the Howard Government seems to recognise the potential for savings and growth arising from on-line service delivery, but is pursuing its objectives in a very leisurely and haphazard manner.

Things are quite different in other jurisdictions. The Victorian Government under both Liberal and Labor administrations has been committed to shifting government transactions on-line as quickly as possible. In a Cabinet submission, former Treasurer Alan Stockdale stated:

> The rationale for Government Online is to revolutionise service by providing 24 hour a day access to government information and transactions from any location, without the necessity for citizens and business to know the structure of government, to lead by example, provide a catalyst for systematic redesign within government, and reduce costs. (Stockdale n.d.)

Stockdale set a target of moving all high-volume public transactions on-line by April 2000, with all transactions and purchasing on-line by December 2001. Multimedia Victoria was entrusted with the task of monitoring compliance by individual agencies and reporting quarterly to Stockdale and

	Project manager appointed	Website (info only) [Note 1]	ESD strategy transaction audit (mid '98)	Tenders on Internet [1] (Dec '98)	Public forms on-line (Dec '98)	Printed info on Internet (high vol) (Dec '98)	All govt publications on Internet (Dec '99)	High-volume transactions on-line (Dec '99)	All govt purchasing electronic (Dec '01)	All transactions on-line (Dec '01)
DPC	○	●	○	●	◗	◗	◗	◗	◗	◗
DTF	◗	●	○	●	◗	◗	◗	○	◗	○
State revenue	●	●	●	●	◗	●	◗	◗	◗	◗
DoI	●	●	●	●	◗	◗	◗	○	○	○
Vic Roads	●	●	◗	●	◗	◗	◗	◗	○	◗
DSD	●	●	●	●	◗	◗	◗	◗	○	◗
DHS	●	●	●	●	◗	◗	◗	○	◗	○
Justice	●	●	●	●	◗	◗	◗	◗	◗	◗
Police	○	●	○	○	○	◗	◗	○	○	○
Education	●	●	○	●	◗	◗	◗	◗	○	◗
DNRE	●	●	●	●	●	◗	◗	◗	◗	◗

● Completed   ◗ Commenced   ○ Not Commenced

Premier Jeff Kennett on progress. The following table illustrates the comprehensive nature of central supervision of the process.

The 'Maxi' system run in collaboration with Multimedia Victoria is now processing 40,000 transactions per month, and growing at 10 per cent per month. Forty per cent of its transactions occur outside office hours. These include vehicle registration, birth, death and marriage certificates, voter enrolment, title searches, payment of rates, water bills and parking fines. The Victorian Government's on-line strategy is supplemented by VicNet, which provides free website assistance to non-profit organisations and delivers Internet services and training to public libraries and rural areas through mobile facilities. As well as moving government services on-line, the Bracks Government is taking steps to ensure that a larger proportion of citizens can access them. Savings are already beginning to flow. EduMail is expected to save $5 million per annum in Education Department printing and distribution costs, and the Department of Natural Resources and Environment is saving $1.3 million annually through electronic procurement (Victorian Government 2000).

Similar developments are occurring in other developed nations. The U.S. Department of Education accepts student assistance applications on-line, and the Internal Revenue Service accepts on-line tax returns and payments. Voter enrolment, car registration, parking fines, planning applications and housing assistance can all be completed on-line in various States. In Arizona it is possible to obtain a divorce on-line (Birdsell and Muzzio 1999, pp. 3–7). Progress is slower in the European Union, but still substantial. Britain aims to have all government services accessible on-line by October 2000 and 90 per cent of routine government procurement conducted on-line by 2000–01, and the EU as a whole aims to have 25 per cent of all government procurement on-line by 2003 (ANAO 1999, p. 21).

Because these developments are at an early stage, data on cost reductions is scarce. Inevitably, substantial reductions only emerge once a large proportion of the total transactions has moved on-line. According to Multimedia Victoria, critical mass is the key. As Internet access and government services on-line increase, savings increase exponentially.

Obstacles to overcome

In order for large savings in the cost of delivering government services to be achieved, there are a number of barriers that must be surmounted. The most obvious of these is the level of Internet connection. According to the latest Australin Bureau of Statistics (ABS) survey, 33 per cent of Australian households had access to the Internet in May 2000, compared with 23 per cent in August 1999. Forty-six per cent of adults accessed the Internet in the preceding year, compared with 41 per cent during the previous year. The percentage of households with personal computers increased from 48 to 54 per cent (ABS 2000, p. 3).

A large number of Australians cannot access the Internet because of insufficient data-carrying capacity in parts of our communication network. Although there is an oversupply of bandwidth on the major trunk routes, for much of regional Australia bandwidth is limited (*NBIDP* 1999). As a result, the range of applications available to many rural households is limited, and the quality of the data service is poor. Over half a million rural customers cannot even achieve the very limited speed of 14.4 kbits per second through the existing network (CEPU 1999, p. 22).

Massive increase in Internet demand has overburdened the copper network, leading to high fault rates and water damage problems related to inadequate maintenance. This problem is seriously exacerbated by the price charged for many high-speed data services, which has inhibited the take-up rate for these services (Nicholas 1999). Integrated Subscriber Digital Network (ISDN) services, the first phase of advanced data services provided, cost $295 for installation, $720 per annum rental, and 41 to 71 cents per 20 minutes of access. In the wake of a 1998 Government decision, Telstra's Universal Service Obligation now requires it to provide ISDN access to 96 per cent of Australians. Some argue that this commitment carries little meaning because it imposes no restraint on prices, and that Telstra has deliberately delayed the introduction of new Digital Subscriber Line (DSL) technology to protect its overpriced ISDN product (Budde 1999; see also Morrison 1999).

Consultants engaged by the National Bandwidth Inquiry advised that bandwidth prices would fall between 30 and 50 per cent by 2004, but that this reduction would occur disproportionately in the major city routes (NBIDP 1999). The inquiry noted that American bandwidth prices are significantly lower than Telstra's but pointed out that the size of the American market is an important factor (NBIDP 1999). It cautioned that this differential may damage Australia's competitive position in the global information economy:

In the longer run, a sustained difference in the price of an important factor of production for e-commerce, such as bandwidth, is likely to have a structural effect on Australia's competitiveness in the emerging information economy. (NBIDP 1999, p. 16)

The level of competition is a critical factor in this equation. The National Bandwidth Inquiry acknowledges the role of limited competition in keeping regional bandwidth prices too high, and cautions that inadequate competition and excessive concentration of ownership may even lead to a need to ration bandwidth in some way (NBIDP 1999).

Fortunately, changing technology is presenting a variety of possible solutions to these problems. The emergence of Asynchronous Digital Subscriber Line (ADSL) as a modification to the copper network offers a major increase in bandwidth, albeit with the constraint that its quality drops beyond about 5 kilometres (Patrick 1999). Telstra is now installing the early stages of ADSL.

Other new technologies offering more bandwidth include Wireless Access Protocol (WAP) mobile phones, Local Multi-point Distribution System (LMDS) wireless networks, and various satellite options (Clark 1999). Australia's existing broadband cable network also offers substantial potential.

There are numerous associated obstacles to the achievement of a lean model of on-line government service delivery. Universal access is not only crucial for generating maximum possible savings, it is also vital to ensuring that a digital divide in using government services does not emerge (Birdsell and Muzzio 1999, p. 1). Not only might citizens who are not on-line find accessing government services less convenient and more time-consuming, they might have to pay more than their on-line counterparts.

Security and privacy are also essential ingredients of any government services on-line strategy (ANAO 1999, p. 12). The Federal Government has established Government Public Key Authority accreditation to ensure that on-line communications can be securely sent and received and privacy protected (ANAO 1999, p. 49). The U.S. Government is pursuing a similar approach (Birdsell and Muzzio 1999, p. 6).

Other issues which must be addressed include software

compatibility between agencies (Birdsell and Muzzio 1999, p. 4), dealing with citizens with literacy problems (Birdsell and Muzzio 1999, p. 3), the impact of cross-subsidies upon pricing and innovation (NBIDP 1999, p. 13) and legislation which imposes obligations to create documentation with no electronic alternative (ANAO 1999, p. 12).

Perhaps most importantly of all, our ability to move government services on-line is constrained by inadequate skills and cultural resistance. Providing access is one thing, but empowering people with the skills and attitudes necessary to use the technology is critical. As Birdsell and Muzzio observe, 'it is not enough to count the number of people with an Internet connection to determine the impact of providing government services on-line' (1999, p. 7). By definition, those who are not already on-line are likely to manifest significant resistance through any combination of lack of skills, lack of money, insufficient motivation and outright hostility.

Cultural and skill factors may also inhibit the speed at which individual agencies move their services on-line. In particular, they may prevent agencies from entirely rethinking their whole service delivery process, and narrow their objectives to an on-line replication of existing physical service delivery.

Lack of appropriate fiscal data is also a major barrier to pursuing savings through delivering services on-line. In many cases the relevant transaction costs of individual agencies cannot be extracted from their overall budgets. Total Centrelink running costs, for example, are around $1.7 billion. The rate at which this would decline as services move on-line could only be guessed at this stage.

What is to be done?

It is clear that the Federal Government should follow the example of Victoria and inject a great deal more urgency into the process of shifting government services on-line. This could include direct overseeing by the central agencies (Prime Minister and Cabinet, Treasury and Finance), mandatory reporting of progress and regular compliance audits, and incentives for early compliance. The Department of Finance should conduct a rigorous assessment of prospective cost savings likely to emerge from shifting services on-line, and model the fiscal impact of various projected take-up rates. A framework for investing savings in expanding on-line access and usage could provide a growing source of public sector funds for investment in on-line expansion.

The Australian Government should commit to the following objectives:

- A rigorous process of compelling agencies to offer their services on-line as quickly and effectively as possible.

- A detailed assessment by the Department of Finance of prospective savings likely to emerge from this process over the medium term.

- Development of a savings-investment framework through which these savings can be directed into appropriate on-line investment which in turn increases the savings to be derived from the continuing process of moving services on-line.

- Active consultation with major companies likely to be pursuing similar strategies, to explore options for partnership approaches.

- Total commitment to achieving universal on-line access within a given period as a key strategy for delivering social equity, economic growth and government efficiency.

- A requirement that all government suppliers can conduct business on-line by a given target date.

By pursuing such a strategy, government can use its own position as a service deliverer to accelerate the growth of on-line access and achieve significant savings in the medium term.

chapter 11

Communities on-line: a practical strategy for rebuilding rural and regional communities

By Rhys Edwards[1]

Regional Australia is doing it tough. This is nothing new to policy-makers in rural and regional communities, including the State politicians of areas like Tasmania.[2] The current debate over economic performance and living standards is also not new. Australia has a long history of pleadings from the bush about the disparity with their rich city cousins. However, for city-bound politicians and policy-makers, particularly on the conservative side, it must seem as though there is a constant rumbling of discontent — the 'insatiable expectations of rural Australians', as John Hewson has put it (Hewson 2000, p. 25).

The results of the 1999 Victorian election have brought rural problems into sharp focus. At the same time that public infrastructure in rural Victoria was in decline and services withdrawn, Melbourne was in the midst of grand private infrastructure projects, world-class entertainment 'events' and of course the Crown Casino. At the election there was a clear move against the Coalition in the bush, based on the perception that the benefits of Coalition policies had gone predominantly to the city.

The debate is not just a reflection of lack of resources for regional Australia. The republic referendum results also split along a regional/urban divide. A clever 'No' campaign preyed on the notion that the proposed model was a 'Politician's Republic', and tapped a chord with voters cynical of political motives and distrustful of politicians. All the top no-voting electorates were in rural areas or provincial cities and among them are some of the poorest populations in Australia. In Tasmania, despite opinion polls predicting a republican victory, it was only the metropolitan electorate of Denison that voted in favour. In the rural electorates of Lyons and Braddon the results were 67.05 per cent and 68.35 per cent against — despite the leaders of all political parties in the State advocating a yes vote.

The Commonwealth Government has reacted to the newly acquired voice of regional Australia by hosting a Regional Australia Summit. While many of the inputs into the Summit were at the leading edge of thinking about regional issues, the 31 pages of proposed strategies flowing from the Summit contain an extraordinary amount of bureaucratic nonsense. For example, one of the key priorities in response to how government may create a climate for economic development is to: 'Establish central leadership and coordination to reduce hierarchical and adversarial approaches and to derive outcome-driven relationships between the three tiers of government and their agencies' (Department of Transport and Regional Services, 1999, p. 4). Unfortunately, there seems to be no recognition that to substantially improve the lot of regional Australia will take both an *understanding* of the problems facing regional communities (which, admittedly, actions like the Regional Australia Summit are intended to facilitate) and *money*.[3]

The 2000–01 Federal Budget contained a package of initiatives for rural Australia but total expenditure was modest in light of other budget pressures, including financial markets wary of loose fiscal policy and the decision to remove the Timor Tax. For example, there was an allocation of $37.1 million for a leadership program for local communities. Contrast this with the European Union's Leader Program, with funding of Euro $1.75 billion out of a total structural adjustment funding package of Euro $196 billion.[4]

John Howard, in a cynical whistlestop tour of regional Australia in March 2000, pledged not to withdraw any further regional Commonwealth services. For Tasmania, and other regional areas, this is shutting the gate after the horse has bolted. Since March 1996, Commonwealth employment in the State has fallen by 28 per cent, a loss of over 2000 full-time jobs.[5]

What Howard, Kennett and others have failed to recognise is that strong (equalising) regional policies are a precondition to strong structural adjustment policies. Drastic measures to meet economic reform objectives can only be implemented successfully if concurrent regional policies soften the blow on a social level and reduce the political fall-out of unpopular actions (Davies 1995, p. 38).

Is there something that can be done to stem the growing sense of division? Is it possible for government to rebuild a sense of trust and define practical policies and roles that re-engage citizens, particularly in rural and regional areas?[6] The challenge for policy-makers is to find solutions that build trust in government, facilitate regional economic renewal, educate individuals for citizenship and provide a role for community organisations. And we need to do this in an environment of great change and complexity brought about by the 'relentless' process of globalisation.

This chapter will briefly examine some of the key concepts associated with the process of globalisation on rural and regional communities and the challenges these present for policy-makers, particularly at the less than national level. In response to these challenges, a specific Tasmanian project is outlined — the development of a network of on-line regional communities. The Tasmanian Communities Online project is then examined in light of how on-line communities might be used to address the issues of rebuilding regional and rural communities and promoting greater engagement between government and its citizens.

The InCat and the Apple Tree: globalisation and regional communities

In his entertaining book on globalisation, *The Lexus and the Olive Tree*, author Thomas Friedman contrasts the high-technology assembly of the Japanese Lexus motor car — a symbol of post-Cold-War dedication to improvement, prosperity

and modernisation — with the olive tree, a symbol of identification and belonging to our home, community, tribe,
nation or religion. The analogous example in the context of
the implications of globalisation in Tasmania might well be
the InCat and the Apple Tree.

InCat is a manufacturer on a global scale, producing
around 40 per cent of the world's large, high-speed catama-
ran ferry transport. The company employs over a thousand
people and has an annual turnover of around $280 million.
InCat's success lies in the innovative design of its product
and the firm's reputation for quality in production. Apple
growing, on the other hand, remains a powerful symbol for
what was once known as the 'Apple Isle'. However, it is also a
symbol of the State's agrarian past — labour-intensive and
low technology, producing a commodity item for sale on the
world markets. The decline of the apple industry led to
decline in a number of Tasmania's rural centres, particularly in the Huon Valley.[7] The Huon Valley and the Meander
Valley, which are both used as examples in this paper, can be
categorised as part of an 'extractive vulnerability' cluster of
Australian   cities   and   towns.   These   are   mainly
agricultural/pastoral-based towns, often where important
rural product processing functions used to be located, that
are now in decline (O'Conner et al 1999, p. 18). Farming
still employs people, but the younger generation are driven
to the cities — and, in the case of Tasmania, to mainland
Australia, in the search for employment.

Given the extent of the discourse on globalisation it is
surprising how often it is asserted but never defined. 'Globalisation is rapidly replacing the "Cold War" as the most
overused and under-specified explanation for a variety of
events in international relations' (Higgott & Reich 1998,
p. 1).[8] This essay does not attempt to provide a definition or
taxonomy of globalisation. However, while it is possible to
disagree with the idea that globalisation provides a deter-
ministic account of the decline in regional areas, common
sense shows that globalisation as a 'process' has a significant
impact on Australia's rural and regional communities. Three
key concepts help to understand this impact — complexity,
vulnerability, identity (Moisi 1999, p. 1). To these concepts, a
fourth factor should be added, which is the growing lack of

trust of 'government' by citizens and voter alienation from government institutions and politics.

At an international geopolitical level, our world is more complex compared with the artificial simplicity of the Cold War. The complexity is most keenly felt in the area of international trade and the interconnectedness of global economic events. This is a view of globalisation as the confluence of economic phenomena — particularly the liberalisation and deregulation of markets, privatisation of state assets, cross-national distribution of production and the integration of capital markets (Higgott and Reich 1998, p. 7). Complexity leads to increasing pressures of competition on domestic and global capital with consequent impacts on stability, increasing size and influence of transnational corporations, and decline in capacity of national economic regulation (Jacobs 1999, p. 2).

When the Asian crisis came, Tasmania braced itself for an economic downturn, yet unexpectedly the downturn was mitigated by growth in new European markets. However, over the past fifteen years, Tasmania's manufacturing base has substantially declined with the lowering of tariff barriers, exposing our relatively high cost of production due to isolation. New industries like call centres have sprung up but the distribution of employment is unequal. Paradoxically, at the same time as technology seemingly lessens the importance of location, the more important location seems to be. The Huon Valley is never going to be a Silicon Valley, no matter how advanced the state of its telecommunications.

Vulnerability stems from two contradictory but coexisting fears — the fear of being absorbed by an artificially homogenous culture versus the fear of being left out in an increasing unequal world (Moisi 1999, p. 3). Inequality and social fragmentation are growing as a result of the increasing divergence of material conditions and life experience. This has occurred because an increasing disparity exists between those with employment and income and those without (Jacobs 1999, p. 2). The globalised world has created winners and losers, and nothing highlights this inequality more than the growing gap between the information rich and the information poor — a particularly important issue for social-democratic parties (Gillard 1999, p. 25).

Furthermore, the more global the world becomes the more vital is the search for identity. The paradoxical partner to globalisation — 'localisation' — has resulted in a proliferation or reassertion of nation states, a renewal of cultural identity and a rediscovered interest in cultural heritage, religious tradition and interesting ideas of community (Puttnam, D. 1999, p. 3). However, at the same time, there is the growing trend towards 'individualisation' — the increasing sense of and desire for personal autonomy and the decline of traditional collective allegiances, including class, place and religion. This is coupled with the expanded importance of consumption as 'identity' and its apparent impression of personal choice and self-determination (Jacobs 1999, p. 2). It follows that the issue of rural identity and the significance of place in assessing rural communities should be one of great interest for policy-makers in Australia.[9]

A fourth factor associated with the concepts of vulnerability and complexity is the lack of trust in government and the increasing alienation from government institutions and politics felt by the public (Jacobs 1999, p. 2). The alienation stems in part from the remoteness of the political decision-making process from voters. Part may also be attributed to the decline of public sector institutions and the growth of private provision of what were once public services. In addition, broken promises and allegations of unethical behaviour in the media contribute to the decline in regard in which politicians are held.

What can governments do, particularly state governments, in this sort of environment? There is little that can be done about the increasing complexity and economic internationalisation, even at the national level.[10] In the Australian Federal system the Commonwealth has significant control over revenue-raising measures, particularly income taxation, but State governments have responsibility for the provision of most of the services (e.g. education and health). Because of this, the capacity of small Australian State governments to address issues of inequality (including inequality of access to the information age), social fragmentation and vulnerability is small.[11]

This does not mean utter helplessness. There are practical projects that can do a great deal for rebuilding a sense of community in regional areas. These projects, developed in partnership with local government and community organisations, can at the same time help governments re-engage with these regional communities. The following section outlines one such project — the development of Tasmanian Communities Online (TCO), a network of linked Online Access Centres (OACs) providing access to the information age for Tasmanian rural and regional communities.

Tasmanian Communities Online

The notion of providing citizens with access to computer facilities is not new. Many governments around Australia and the world are tackling the concept access to the information age. 'How can we tackle the digital divide? By creating community networks or "freeNets"' (Tapscott, 1999 p. ??). The United States Government has developed a program of Community Access Centres (CACs). By providing public access to the Internet, access centres 'will help these groups advance economically, as well as provide them with the technical skills to compete professionally in today's digital economy' (United States Department of Commerce, p. xiv). In another example, the Blair Government in the United Kingdom has recently announced provision of £250 million to establish 700 Information Communication Technology (ICT) Learning Centres in local communities across England.

The development of TCO follows Tasmania's experience with Canadian models of technology access for regional areas. The project was initially funded by Commonwealth money from the part sale of Telstra. It is interesting to note that John Howard, in his Federation speech in 2000, sweetened a foreshadowed bid for the full sale of Telstra with the promise that this money could be used to fund infrastructure and help address the divide between the city and regional areas.

The TCO project involves the development of a network of 60 OACs across Tasmania outside of the main population centres. Each centre contains a minimum of three computers with Internet access, a printer and a scanner. The goal of the TCO project is to provide equitable access to modern technology and the Internet for the Tasmanian community, especially people in rural areas. The centres are designed to increase community participation in and acceptance of new technologies, to reduce isolation (especially among the elderly), to enhance lifelong learning and to promote local business development. Computer networking and telecommunications can reduce the economic and social disadvantages faced by regional Tasmania and allow communities to interact and compete with larger and better-resourced communities both in Australia and overseas.[12]

OACs are community-owned enterprises and each has a local management committee. All centres are staffed by a paid coordinator but rely heavily on volunteers. The centres are mostly located in schools, public libraries or community centres. To date 53 of the proposed 60 centres have opened. Around 166,000 Tasmanians have access to a centre and over 15,000 Tasmanians have registered as users of centres. More than 7000 new email accounts have been opened and over 5000 people have attended Internet and computer training courses. Approximately 1600 micro-businesses have been assisted and over 1200 web pages have been published for small businesses and community organisations.

In Geeveston, in the heart of the apple growing district of the Huon Valley, approximately half the town's population (approximately 700) are registered users and a quarter of the population have attended computer training courses at the centre. The range of activities undertaken in this small centre is extensive and includes: email and Internet use; use by job seekers to prepare résumés and undertake job search; post-secondary school study, including university study; production of a local newspaper; production of flyers and brochures, and mail outs for local community groups; support to local business; web page development and business information gathering.

On-line Access Centres and regional renewal

'Renewal is more than just a question of finding solutions to problems. It is also about delivering hope for the future' (Shearman 1999, p. 12). People want to share in the benefits of the new economy. This is just as true for people in rural and regional areas. 'This means ensuring that people living in poorer areas have access to the new opportunities at the same time as the rest of us' (Shearman 1999, p. 12). Providing access to the new opportunities provided by information technology is a crucial issue.

This notion of equality of opportunity is an important objective of modern political philosophy. It is most cogently expressed in *Inequality Reexamined* by Amartya Sen. The central question is 'equality of what?' Equality of opportunity is a necessary condition for participation in the new society but probably not a sufficient condition. Lindsay Tanner suggests an additional requirement for participation: 'Society has an obligation to ensure that all its members are able to belong, in the fullest sense of the word... The capacity to participate entails a mutual obligation to contribute to the community in some way'.[13] Tanner continues by saying that '[t]ranslating the capacity to participate concept into practical proposals which build social cohesion is not easy' (Tanner 1999, p. 53).

The mechanisms through which civic engagement and social connectedness lead to better social and economic outcomes are complex. The concept of 'social capital', analogous to notions of physical or human capital, is used as a common framework for understanding this phenomenon. Just as physical and human capital enhance individual productivity, so can the notion of social organisation such as networks, norms and social trust facilitate coordination and cooperation for mutual benefit (Putnam, R. 1995, p. 67).[14]

Accordingly, it is important to emphasise that the aim of the TCO project is not merely to provide people in regional and rural communities with access to computers and the Internet. The significance of the TCO project is that it seeks to link remote Tasmanian communities with each other, as well as the rest of the world. The TCO project will assist the rebuilding of rural and regional communities by promoting social cohesion and community.

Anecdotal evidence suggests that OACs are helping build social cohesion or 'community'. For example, the Geeveston OAC, facing financial difficulties and the need to raise money, decided on a fund-raising strategy of producing a calendar of local history in conjunction with the local history circle.[15] The calender was produced using desktop publishing facilities at the OAC. The remarkable achievement was not so much the application of modern technology to capture oral history but the sense of community engendered by the coming together of a large number of the town's aged population. For example, as Wren Fraser, Coordinator of the Geeveston OAC, states:

> [k]nowing who you are, what your history is and how the past can help you through the present and into the future has been the motivation... this calendar will not only open up a window on the past but will help point towards a future we need to plan for if our community is to survive with a strong sense of place.

Community can act as the catalyst that drives regeneration and neighbourhood renewal. Regeneration and community are linked and community-building is as much a part of the regeneration process as tackling unemployment, promoting better access to services and managing anti-social behaviour (Shearman 1999, p. 30). At Meander in Northern Tasmania, the Centre:

> has become a gathering place where new interests in common are developed — a community group web site, a hobby, a chat forum. People who would not otherwise have a place or reason to meet are finding common ground through their involvement in the Centre and the Online world. (Flittner 1999)

Consequently, Online Communities provide a mechanism to regenerate a sense of regional community. Shearman, following the work of Elisabeth Moss Kantor, articulates three key factors in regeneration. The first is *concepts,* that is, ideas, imagination and innovation. Secondly, *competencies* — embodied in skills, knowledge and experience, and lastly *connectedness,* or a link with other places and the ability to look outwards (Shearman 1999, p. 4).

Economic renewal in rural and regional communities requires ideas, imagination and innovation. The development of new business opportunities must come from the development of local ideas. All too often the solution is seen as being delivered 'externally' by a multinational corpora-

tion or by the whim of a remote central government's industry policy. In the last decade it would have been a large-scale
industrial project, for example 'if only we had a pulp mill'.
The more recent version is 'if only we could attract a call centre'. The risk of these 'inward investment' jobs is that they
encourage dependence — a community remains vulnerable
to the economic interdependence between the fortunes of
that company and its external markets. Access to information technology can transform local entrepreneurial ideas
into business realities. OACs are able to help small businesses with web page development and free web page hosting,
facilities for the design and production of advertising mate-
rials, facilities for compiling data bases of customers and suppliers, and training in computer and Internet skills for pro-
prietors and staff. Time will see the development of access to
electronic commerce solutions.

OACs play a key role in addressing competencies. In its
simplest form this is about building confidence and self-
esteem — particularly for young people and the unemployed. OACs and the locally employed coordinator provide
a non-threatening environment for the learning of computer skills. OACs also provide a new pathway back into education and learning. As well as access to educational content
on-line, including formal qualifications, the centres provide
a mechanism for training in the skills identified as important
in the new economy — creativity, content development and
multimedia literacy. Active involvement as volunteers in the
centres themselves also provides opportunities for relevant
and useful work experience. A number of individuals have
used experience gained as volunteers as a springboard to
paid employment.

Being connected has always been important for remote
communities, particularly for island communities. OACs
provide this link, not only to the outside world through
email and Internet chat rooms but also between members of
the same community and between members of one TCO
community to another. For example, members of one OAC
in eastern Tasmania gather once a week to play cards with
interstate and overseas opponents. Websites based around a
local community of interest provide extensive interaction
between citizens. The networked nature of TCO allows com-

munities to share information and experiences across the 53 geographical locations.

Community Access Centres and government legitimacy — 'A wired Agora'

The massive change brought about by globalisation and the resulting confusion in the face of complexity and feelings of vulnerability have led to a decline in public confidence in politicians and our democratic institutions. A recent survey of attitudes to Tasmanian politicians found that over 50 per cent of respondents did not know or were unwilling to name one politician they believed had performed well during the year. Highlighting the lack of knowledge about our representatives was the fact that, of those who did respond, more than a third of the names offered were not even in the Tasmanian Parliament, being either Federal representatives or retired State politicians (*Mercury* 2000, p. 1).

Is it possible that new technology will provide solutions to this vexing problem? The question is answered by Scobbie, who argues that:

> [w]e must seek to engage the majority of citizens and we must dispel the cynicism that is diminishing our political culture and bringing the legitimacy of our government structures, at all levels, into doubt... Technology will play its part, a part only limited by our imagination. (Scobbie 1999, p. 13)

To restore the legitimacy of government, 'mechanisms of continuous feedback' and 'dialogue between government and citizen' are required (Tanner 1999, p. 203). OACs offer one such mechanism for direct communication with government, but more importantly a forum for political dialogue within and between communities.

It is important to distinguish government on-line from building civic life on-line. The concept of government on-line is making democratic information available like never before (Clift 1998, p. 2). It is very rare now in the Australian system of government, particularly at the State and Federal levels, to find departments that do not have a website. However, this form of communication, essentially an 'Electronic Bureau-

cracy', is all one-way and should not be confused with participation or building civic life on-line (Segal 1997, p. 1).

The actions of citizens wanting to voice their views about
government is leading to a large increase in advocacy on-
line. Many groups, including political interest groups and
political parties, are building impressive on-line presences.
Media organisations are also making a large investment to
provide content that will help inform political discussions. As
these other sectors continue to increase their contribution to
democracy on-line, the piece of the puzzle that is missing is
a forum for communication between citizens and from citizens to government.

Clift argues that citizens are fundamentally disconnected
from one another and hyper-connected through various special interest groups. As Internet technology develops and
access grows, what is needed is an on-line interactive public
commons — 'a wired Agora'.[16] Future development of TCO
should build on Clift's notion of the citizen communications
centre:

> Embracing geography as a vital component of the Internet,
> real communities using virtual tools will facilitate public
> communication on issues — starting in our neighbour-
> hoods and local communities and going up to regions and
> states as well as the national level. (Clift 1998, p. 6)

In this way, CACs provide us with a mechanism to move us
from an 'Electronic Bureaucracy Model' to a 'Civic Society
Model' (Segel 1997, p. 1).[17] Furthermore, a Civic Society
Model would address the issues of alienation from government and feelings of citizen vulnerability.

Conclusion

Federal Opposition Leader Kim Beazley, in an address to the
Lawson Institute, stated that '[i]ncreasingly today, regional
development is about skills, communications, technologies,
and educational opportunities. Increasingly in the future,
communications bandwidth will be as important to regional
communities as roads and bridges have been in the past — if
not more so' (Beazley 2000). However, as important as bandwidth is, access to bandwidth by itself is not enough — even

free access. A community needs the 'infrastructure' to develop and that infrastructure needs to include mechanisms that facilitate a sense of geographical community bounded by common interests and held together by 'social glue'. Without the investment in social capital to match the investment in physical capital, any community will not be maximising its return on investment.

The development of regional on-line communities through the provision of OACs is one mechanism to enhance this social glue, as well as addressing issues of access to the information age. TCO is a practical project that has the potential to build trust in government, facilitate regional economic renewal and educate individuals for citizenship. Projects like TCO should be used as a key plank in any strategy for rebuilding rural and regional communities.

chapter **12**

Why Australians hate politicians[1]:
exploring the new public discontent
By Sally Young

Australians are more angry and dissatisfied with politicians than ever before.[2] This might not be so alarming (after all, Australia has a long history of antipathy towards politicians) but for the worrying evidence which suggests that Australians have not only lost confidence in politicians, but also in the political system generally.[3] A new level of cynicism can be readily observed in angry calls to talkback radio and caustic letters to the editor as well as empirically, in surveys, opinion polls and at the ballot box (where voting behaviour is increasingly volatile).[4] While public opinion is never unanimous, the breadth and depth of this new discontent is quite remarkable — it cuts right across the socioeconomic spectrum.[5]

Democracy requires eternal vigilance but there is a difference between healthy scepticism and corrosive cynicism. A sceptic may finally be persuaded by the facts, but the cynic, never. Widespread political cynicism has the potential to diminish political participation and erode the quality of democracy. Central to democracy is the notion of the public interest, which requires trust. As Al Gore states, 'democracy stands or falls on a mutual trust — government's trust of the people and the people's trust of the governments they elect' (Gore 1994, p. 646).

Australia is not alone. The U.S., Canada, the U.K., Italy, Spain, Belgium, the Netherlands, Norway, Sweden, Ireland,

171

Germany and Japan are also experiencing unprecedented discontent with their elected leaders (Nye, Zelikow and King 1997, pp. 1–2; Kingmann and Fuchs 1995). This is part of a broader phenomenon in which trust in *all* institutions is declining. People have not only lost confidence in politicians but also in bank managers, union leaders, lawyers, doctors, teachers and journalists (Brown 1999, p. 15).

In Australia, three main suspects accuse each other of causing the new discontent: the public, the media and politicians. Politicians generally blame the media for fuelling the new cynicism but also point to the public and their unrealistically high expectations of politicians. Journalists blame the politicians — their lack of leadership, policy failures and personal indiscretions. The public, naturally enough, condemns the politicians who have let them down, but also, and somewhat surprisingly, blames the media — as the media is seen to be 'in cahoots' with the politicians. It is appropriate to begin with these three actors in order to uncover what is really driving the new public cynicism, before moving on to canvass some methods for rebuilding trust.

The public

It may seem strange to consider the public a 'suspect' in causing its own cynicism but this is exactly the argument that some politicians and political scientists have made when they claim that Australians expect too much from their politicians. This is not a new argument. W. K. Hancock observed nearly 70 years ago that: 'Australian democracy has come to look upon the state as a vast public utility, whose duty it is to provide the greatest happiness for the greatest number' (cited in Woodward et al 1997, p. 244). More recently, Ian McAllister has argued that politics is an activity that Australians tolerate 'only so long as it is able to deliver the economic rewards necessary to maintain a comfortable standard of living' (Woodward et al 1997, p. 265). According to proponents of this utilitarian view, Australians have 'come to expect' that the government will ensure their jobs and standards of living (Walter 1998, p. 207; Woodward et al 1997, p. 245).[6]

This begs the question: if Australians only tolerate politicians as long as they 'deliver' the appropriate economic 'rewards' (that is, jobs and decent living standards), what happens when politicians are unable to deliver? According to many politicians and political scientists, it is this very issue which is driving the discontent.

To put it simply, the utilitarian expectations of many Australians are not being met. Although the Australian economy is doing well, many Australians are not (Suter 1999, p. 137). Living standards have consistently declined since the post-war boom. Incomes have grown slowly and become less equal (Lawrence 1997, p. 117). Unemployment, youth suicide, crime and poverty are all visible signs of decline. The problem, according to politicians, is that they are no longer capable (if indeed they ever were) of meeting the high expectations of the Australian electorate. In the context of globalisation, governments are less able to 'determine the economic fortunes of their citizens' and, consequently, less able to ensure their jobs and living standards (Lawrence 1997, p. 131).

For several commentators, the decline in confidence in institutions is a direct result of the economic slowdown that occurred in so many countries after the end of the post-World War Two boom (Nye et al 1997). But economic explanations alone are not sufficient. The broadness and depth of the discontent[7] suggests we need an explanation which is not only economic, but also more general, broad and ideological. (After all, trust in *all* institutions has declined.) Robert Inglehart argues that a declining respect for authority is part of a shift in values brought about by changing lifestyles (Inglehart 1997, p. 217). That is, as people's basic survival needs are met, they increasingly focus on achieving a better 'quality of life' and their expectations of governments rise accordingly.

Aside from policy expectations, people also have expectations about the personal qualities, behaviour and ethics of politicians. These expectations can be high indeed, and they can also be contradictory. For example, people want politicians to negotiate and compromise but not to be weak; to be strong but not arrogant; to be smart but not a 'smart alec'! Indeed, studies have confirmed that most of us expect politicians to live up to a far higher standard of ethics and morality than we apply to ourselves.[8]

Reasonable or not, citizens carry with them expectations, however rudimentary, about political institutions.[9] For some people, the political process lives up to their expectations, but for many others there is a discrepancy between what they think Parliament and politicians ought to be like and what they are actually like (Kimball and Patterson 1997, p. 701). Bound up in this gap between promise and performance is the importance of people's *perceptions*. When people assess the performance of politicians, they do so on the basis of *subjective* perceptions and not on any straightforward response to *objective* performance.[10]

This is because there are no straightforward, objective 'performance indicators' which the Australian public can use to gauge the performance of their politicians. For example, there is no annual national address in which the Prime Minister outlines the state of the nation. Such an event could provide a set opportunity for the public to assess political performance. It would, however, have to use concrete and comparable statistics (such as unemployment, interest rates, and measures of the state of health and education) rather than emotive claims about 'achievements'. (Ideally, it would also allow a forum for questioning and debate). There is a dire need for information of this nature that allows more objective assessment of performance. As it stands, however, people's subjective perceptions are heavily influenced by subjective indicators and, as Papadikis notes, 'this suggests the likely influence of two factors on confidence in institutions namely, the changing role of the media and television' (Papadikis 1999).

The media

Michael Wooldridge and Gareth Evans have argued that the media is a primary factor in causing public cynicism (Wooldridge 1998, p. 184; Evans 1998). While politicians are well-known for accusing the media of unfair reporting, in this case, many academics and social commentators have agreed (including in the unequivocally titled article, 'A Generation of Vipers: Journalists and the New Cynicism').[11] Even some journalists admit that media reporting about politics fosters public cynicism (Simons 1999).

In many respects the media is an obvious suspect and not least because a powerful, uncensored media is common to the many countries experiencing public discontent. However, we must approach this notion of media responsibility cautiously because it is disempowering to hold the media solely responsible for somehow 'producing' people's discontent. People are not mindless, empty vessels waiting to be filled with media views. Recent research shows that people actively select and judge from what the media is putting out (Bessant and Watts 1999, p. 367) and that what people bring to the media is often more important in forming their opinions of politicians than what the media actually presents (Weaver 1996, p. 43).

The media is only one influence amongst a suite of factors which influence people's views about politicians (including partisanship, family, school and personal contact with politicians). And yet it *is* principally through the media that voters hear about politics (Forrest and Marks 1999). Few Australians have direct experience of politics. For example, only 2 per cent have ever helped a political candidate or attended a political meeting (McAllister 1998, p. 18). For the majority of Australians, the media remains the primary source of information about politics.

Despite this reliance on the media, many Australians seem to hold the media in as much disrepute as the political system (Brown 1999, p. 15). In a 1991 Saulwick Poll, the same amount of people who had 'not much' confidence in the political system (48.5 per cent), said they also had 'not much' confidence in the media (Saulwick 1991). This reminds us that the new cynicism is a wide phenomenon that is not confined to politics. However, for some people, distrust of the media and politicians goes hand in hand and is part of a perception that the media and politicians are 'in it together'. This mind set was illustrated most starkly in the views of Pauline Hanson's followers, for whom the alliance between the media and mainstream politics was obvious.[12]

The media is often blamed for fuelling public cynicism — but *how* does the media do this? Sometimes the message is quite direct. Coverage of the 1999 Victorian State election included updates about election promises headlined 'pork-barrelling' ('who is promising what') and the coverage included statements that 'between now and election day, Victorian politicians will promise anything to woo your vote…' (*Herald-Sun* 1999, p. 15). Some media are also more directive than others. Talkback radio in particular thrives on discrediting the political system (Adams and Burton 1997). More often than not, however, cynicism is just part and parcel of the way in which the media reports politics.

From an analysis of the print media over 1999, I observed several common media representations of politicians. One of the most endemic is that of the 'professional politician'. Insidiously ambitious, the professional politician will do any-thing to woo your vote and therefore spends much time and money (often taxpayers' money) poring over polls in order to learn what you think and recycle it back to you. In the 'contest' or 'horse-race' view, politics is represented in the media as an adversarial competition in which politicians vie fiercely for power — not for the power to do good but power for its own sake. Related to this is a new media focus on 'political strategy', including campaign tactics and pre-selec-tion contests. Increasingly, the public gets to see more of the 'grubby daily business' of politics, including the tricks and tactics politicians use in order to win votes. They are also see-ing more and more of the 'private lives' of politicians — their families, social lives, habits and peccadilloes.

This media focus on what goes on 'behind the scenes' parallels media reporting in the U.S. But it is not the only factor which seems to represent an 'Americanisation' of Aus-tralian politics. Australian politics has become increasingly 'presidentialised' through an increased media focus on indi-viduals — particularly leaders. Howard is portrayed as the 'face of the GST' just as Pauline Hanson is used to symbolise the debate about race and immigration. As the media focus-es more attention on an individual, it allows far more scope for that individual to disappoint — to 'trip up' under the glare of media scrutiny. It also takes the focus away from par-ties and from policy, leaving the public with an impression that politics is about individuals and conflict between them.

Although there is no evidence that official corruption has risen, scandals increasingly fill the headlines (Patterson 1996, p. 19). Here we can see several sub-variations: 'the cor-rupt politician' who misuses public office in order to line his own pocket, the 'greedy politician' who does not need to be corrupt but just uses the numerous 'perks of office' to rip off the taxpayers, and finally the 'money waster' who continually wastes taxpayers' money on frivolous and silly things. Of all the messages which the media sends, this suggestion that politicians cannot be trusted seems to be the most prevalent and the most accepted.

Some of these representations of politicians have an historical basis. The image of the fat, greedy politician is as old as the profession itself, and the infamous baby-kissing politician was a precursor to the tactics of today's 'professional politician'. However, some of the other representations stem from, or are being enhanced by, broader trends affecting the media. These trends include the globalisation of the media, the concentration of ownership, the growth of media empires, and technology. One of the primary purposes of the new media is to 'sell' (Lawe Davis 1999, p. 53). This has fostered a convergence between politics and entertainment — a focus on politicians as celebrities, the sense of a permanent campaign and a shift to editorial commentary which has seen journalism (particularly political news) become less focused on events and facts and more concentrated on analysis and interpretation. Politicians increasingly have less chance to speak for themselves.

While media reporting does not necessarily 'create' public cynicism, the way the media frames and presents politics flames the fire — it stimulates and heightens cynicism. There are ways in which reporters and editors can minimise this (for example, by focusing less on scandals or on the personal lives of politicians) but outlining any prescriptions opens up an important debate about the media's watchdog role and whether reducing the amount of criticism would also stifle scrutiny. Ideally, it would be possible to improve the quality of political reporting without diminishing necessary scrutiny. Reporters might consider moving beyond the stock standard representations — to show cooperation between politicians as well as competition and by encompassing more positive representations about politicians (their long hours and community involvement, for example). However, in today's new media, any change in the manner of reporting politics will only work if it 'sells' as well as the old reporting style based on conflict and scandal.

Politicians

When the media is accused of being responsible for fuelling public cynicism, journalists often respond by counter-accusing politicians. Reporters, they argue, are merely doing their duty when they report that politicians waste public money and break election promises: it is the politicians and their behaviour which has really put people off (Donovan 1999, p. 13; Reider 1996). For many journalists, media reporting is only a mirror and the real key to public cynicism is the poor quality of our politicians (Grattan 1998; Kelly 1998, p. 21)

Years of travel rorts, credit card misuse, exorbitant superannuation payouts and broken election promises have confirmed to a weary public that politicians really are 'liars, cheats and scumbags'. There is a widely held perception that politicians waste taxpayers' money, have too many perks, do not listen to the public (except at elections or via consultants and polls), are beholden to big business and/or minorities (i.e. take care of everyone except the 'ordinary Australian'), break promises, and only look after themselves. This image has surely been magnified by the media but politicians and their behaviour are still at the crux of it.

There are two main ways politicians have failed to meet public expectations. Firstly, in the *policy* realm, politicians have failed to 'fix' social ills and to ensure jobs and living standards. Secondly, in the *personal* realm, politicians have behaved badly, failing to live up to that prototypical image of MPs as dedicated, hard-working, honest and respected public servants.

Policy failures

In the policy realm, different commentators have agreed that politicians and their policies have caused public anger, but there are vastly different views about *which* politicians and *which* policies have failed. Many on the right, including Tony Abbott and P. P. McGuinness, blame the political correctness and 'pandering to minorities' of the Keating era for people's loss of faith in politicians (Abbott 1998; McGuinness 1998). For those more to the left, people's anger and exclusion is seen to be more the result of economic rationalism, cutbacks and globalisation (e.g. McGregor 1997; Manne 1998).

For some commentators, the Hawke-Keating years are at the root of public cynicism (Pilger 1996, p. 16). But while it is true that attitudes to politicians changed most markedly during this period, this was also the case in many other countries, including the U.S. and Britain. It is therefore unreasonable to place all of the blame for public discontent on an individual like Keating or even on a particular party. It is necessary to instead look more broadly at factors which can help us explain why public confidence in politicians across so many countries declined in the 1980s.

Most significantly, American commentators Bob Edwards and Michael Foley identify three main policy factors — policies which governments in many liberal capitalist democracies across the world introduced during this era, largely in response to globalisation. These are: economic re-structuring; the dismantling of the welfare state; and the devolution of government. Edwards and Foley note that 'ferocious economic restructuring overturned communities and shattered the work lives and expectations of millions over the past 20 years...' (1997, p. 674).

In many countries, the policy prescriptions of economic re-structuring, dismantling of the welfare state and the devolution of government received widespread acceptance. In a two-party system, for example, the policies often received bi-partisan support and were adopted by political parties which had formerly been identified with very disparate views. As a result, political parties became less differentiated. This has been compounded by 'modern' views about political strategy, which seek to downplay ideology in an attempt to appeal to the maximum number of voters. For example, in Australia the major parties have sought to become 'catch-all' parties — deliberately cultivating policies, leaders and strategies which will maximise their popularity with the greatest number of voters. But as the parties increasingly resemble each other in their aim for the 'centre', voters have become increasingly confused about what they stand for. People no longer see any great differences between the major parties and are less inclined to think that their vote matters (Bean et al 1998). 'Whoever you vote for, a politician always wins' sums up the cynicism many Australians now feel.[13]

Personal failings

We cannot discount that public cynicism stems in part from the perceived 'bad behaviour' of politicians. One of the most visible signs of politicians behaving badly is also one of the most common images: that of Parliament at Question Time. Mackay notes that the parliamentary behaviour of Australia's politicians 'is no longer regarded as a joke... it is rapidly approaching the point where parliamentary behaviour is regarded as a national disgrace...' (Mackay 1993, p. 179). Negative political advertising (such as the 'Guilty Party' advertisements used by the Victorian Liberal Party in the 1992 and 1996 Victorian State election campaigns, or the Keating 'Get a job' jibe advertisement used by the federal Liberal Party in the 1996 federal election campaign) also has a detrimental effect on public perceptions of politics. Stephen Ansolabehere and Shanto Iyengar (1995) argue that negative political advertising can even cause voters to become 'repulsed' by the political system.

If Australia's professional politicians follow the lead of American ones (and they often do), they will begin to use personal tactics more and more. Finsberg and Shefter (1999) call this 'post-electoral politics' in which media revelations, parliamentary investigations and judicial proceedings replace elections as the primary tools of political competition. We can already see the beginning of this in the 1997–8 'travel rorts' scandals and the recent attempt by the Federal Liberal Government to commence an investigation into Paul Keating's 1994 piggery deal.

Putting media influence aside, the culture of cynicism towards politicians has a firm basis in real failures and real problems in the way politicians now practise politics. 'Big vision' policies and policies which have been badly explained or debated have alienated and angered many people. Governments seem unable to meet the array of competing social objectives and the needs and expectations of a diverse electorate. Policies such as privatisation have failed to deliver the promised rewards and all politicians have come to seem the same as the policy gaps between parties have narrowed. In the personal realm, politicians seem childish, ill-mannered and even corrupt, and the political tactics which politicians

use are increasingly unseemly. Politicians can begin to remedy this by changing their parliamentary behaviour, minimis-
ing the use of negative political advertising and resisting the
temptation to follow American-style post-electoral politics.
Of course, the simplest remedy is also the most challenging
— politicians can regain public confidence by making good
policy and explaining it well.

Good policy needs to be based on long-term goals and
the national interest. It should be informed by public input
but also explained to the public in a manner centred on
information and education (rather than emotive sales techniques). Political parties might consider providing forums
such as conferences or summits, which allow people to air
issues, examine problems and recommend solutions. New
technology (particularly the Internet) has fantastic potential
to allow direct participation in such forums for those 98 per
cent of Australians who do not attend political meetings. By
using new technology and media, and presenting political
issues in a different manner, it may be also be possible to
reach younger Australians (who traditionally have shown little interest in 'conventional' politics).

Another option is the use of slogans by politicians, such
as 'policies rather than personalities', 'scepticism rather than
cynicism', and 'civilising global capital', Mark Latham's elo-
quent phrase capturing the idea of how politicians can
inform people about their position and opportunities in
relation to globalisation. Australian politicians might also
consider following the lead of the Blair Government to
'promise only what we can deliver and deliver what we
promise'. They could also take responsibility for communi-
cating their achievements, ideas and policies and tell their
own side of the story through the use of direct mediums,
such as talkback radio, e-mail and web pages.

Rebuilding trust

A certain level of mistrust of politicians is a long-standing and
healthy feature of Australian life but we have seen how healthy
scepticism has changed into deep distrust, cynicism and even
anger. What can we conclude about this phenomenon?

Firstly, we can now say conclusively that no single actor (or single factor) is responsible. Several different things are happening at once and the causes of public discontent are multiple and complex. There have been deep structural changes in social and cultural attitudes over the past three decades, including a trend towards the individual, which have undercut the authority of all institutions — not just government and politics. The rise of post-modern values has led to a shift in people's expectations, needs and desires. We also cannot discount the influence of economic factors. For many people, living standards have declined (or just as importantly, are *perceived* to have declined). The economic slowdown, wage compression, globalisation and middle-class lay-offs have hurt a lot of people and have affected general confidence in government and politicians.

Public 'moods' are never static nor universal and this is particularly true today when we are living in a very volatile political culture. While this volatility makes it difficult to 'keep up' with public opinion, we can take hope from new research that indicates the darkest phase of public cynicism in Australia may already have passed. We hope that this is the case and we will return to a more healthy scepticism as opposed to bleak cynicism. However, it is still very important that we understand this social phenomenon, as some of the changes in social and cultural attitudes which accompanied the rise in public cynicism are here to stay. These changes are going to force us to rethink public expectations, to question the role of the media and to ask what we want of politics, politicians and policy. This chapter has hopefully provided a starting point in this process.

chapter 13

Education for democratic citizenship: the importance of civics education in the era of economic rationalism

By Lucas Walsh

Advocates of citizenship democracy have seen education as a vital step in the political socialisation of the subject to citizen.[1] 'Education for democracy', Bobbio writes, 'takes place as an integral part of the operation of democracy in practise' (1987, p. 35). However, our education system is perennially besieged by contentious debates over everything from literacy levels to issues of access and inequity, who should be responsible for education, how it ought to be funded and so on. The latter half of the 20th century is no exception. The expansion of comprehensive schooling following the Wyndham Report in 1957 was met with hostility and suspicion.[2] Ten years later, Philip Coombs (1968) warned of no less than a global educational crisis. A Senate inquiry into *Education for Active Citizenship* at the end of the 1980s advised of a 'crisis which Australians cannot afford to ignore', while the West Review Committee on *Higher Education Financing and Policy* found a critical sense of 'unease' among academics who felt as though education had become 'rudderless in a sea of change' (SCEET 1989, p. vi; West et al 1997, p. 1).

It would therefore be trite for me to write of a 'crisis' in education. Nevertheless, mounting problems in our education system are exacerbated by policy in ways that are neither banal nor clichéd. I refer to the growing corpus of education policy favouring market competition, student-centred learning and the devolution of responsibility for education from the state to its users and commercial interests. This ideology, constructed according to conservative tenets of neo-liberalism, has for well over a decade guided educational reform, intersecting the domains of institutional governance, political socialisation and identity formation. Recent market-based reforms constitute an ideological change in education policy extending across management, curriculum planning and pedagogy. Given its extensive articulation throughout State and Federal policy, the discourse of neo-liberalism is now capable of bringing about a radical political relocation of the student by shaping his or her transition from subject to citizen.

The scope of neo-liberalism's influence along this axis of reform is as profoundly far-reaching as it is pernicious. In shirking responsibility for access and equity, the state evokes a seductive but illusory rhetoric espousing the virtues of self-determination, competitive advantage, flexibility and freedom of choice as the benefits of marketisation. While many school communities and students have benefited from self-management and flexible learning, for those who start from positions of inequity arising, for example, from racial difference or poverty, these reforms reflect a myth of democracy that conceals new modalities of exclusion.

This chapter has three parts: I begin by describing the historical link between public education and democratic citizenship in Australia. My understanding of this relationship is predicated on a broad notion of civics and citizenship education (CCE). Inasmuch as current definitions of citizenship tend to be limited to a formal status associated with legal entitlements, CCE tends to be taught within a confined framework or relegated to the periphery of curricula. Furthermore, when taught in conventional didactic ways, the subject matter is bled of its dynamic, practical and personal significance. Effective CCE emphasises the social dimension of citizenship, especially the educative value of participation in collective decision-making processes. The second part of the discussion illustrates some of the ways by which neo-liberal ideology has influenced education policy to the detriment of CCE. Examples of this emergent discourse are taken from recent policy statements, such as *Literacy for All* (DEETYA 1998) and the West Committee's findings in *Learning for Life: Review of Higher Education Financing and Policy* (West et al 1998a). These statements give insight into the changing relationship between citizen and state, and of central concern is the growing disjunction of public education from democratic citizenship. Finally, I explore some ways in which CCE could be improved to encourage higher levels of political literacy and participation.

Education for democratic citizenship

In this section I first outline the elements of CCE, the entitlements and responsibilities conferred by citizenship, the workings of government and how it can serve citizens, and discuss its objectives in particular, its emphasis on the educative value of participation in a democratic political culture. I then examine the 'marketisation' of education policy and the influence of neo-liberal ideologies on public education.

Citizenship is more than a status; it is an active *expression* of one's membership of a political community (Kymlicka and Norman 1994, p. 352). For this to take place, all citizens must have equal opportunity to exercise their rights and responsibilities. Collective solidarity is therefore central to democratic citizenship, from which every citizen derives a civic ethic in a developmental process that is vital to the education of active, politically literate citizens. The ideal citizen 'not only believes in the concept of democratic society but is willing and able to translate that belief into action' (Civics Expert Group 1994, p. 68).

The need to re-examine CCE is compelling in light of evidence that levels of 'civic deficit', among young people — ignorance, lack of confidence in Australian politics, feelings of personal alienation and powerlessness — have dramatically increased in recent years (Civics Expert Group 1994, pp. 3, 19). The centenary of federation, the question of republican reform, and greater recognition of the status of Aboriginal peoples have renewed government interest in raising public awareness and stimulated discussion of citizenship. The Government has responded with initiatives such as the *Discovering Democracy* CCE program, which seeks to help students to: 'understand the relevance of political and legal systems to everyday life, and develop capacities to participate as informed, reflective and active citizens in their civic community' (Curriculum Corporation 1998).

Professional literature and government policy on CCE over the last decade has tended to adopt a more sophisticated definition of civics and citizenship, one which encompasses more than the traditional view of citizenship as a status defined by the acquisition of legal entitlements (e.g. a passport) and responsibilities (e.g. compulsory voting). Civics education is seen as different from citizenship education. Where civics education is usually school-based and attached to a formal course, citizenship education concentrates on a broader cultivation of political identity and community values (Civics Expert Group 1994, pp. 16, 68). The sum knowledge of CCE amounts to awareness by citizens of their entitlements and responsibilities, the workings of government and how it can serve them. Most importantly, this knowledge includes an appreciation of the dimensions of democracy that stimulate a general willingness among citizens to participate in decisions affecting their association and collective well-being. I think of this as the sociopolitical function of education. Mike Salvaris and I have written elsewhere about the importance of teaching this social dimension of citizenship (Walsh and Salvaris 1998, p. 30).

The most important aspect of the extended notion of CCE is its emphasis on the *educative value of participation itself*. This participatory model encourages students to become actively aware of how they shape their social environment and how their environment shapes them. This may involve attending historical events (e.g. Anzac Day), creating a mock parliament at school or getting involved in a local community activity, which in this digital era extends from the local neighbourhood to the MUDs and MOOs of cyberspace. This holistic approach to CCE draws attention to the learning environments in which it is taught, so that students become aware of how the environments themselves are imbued with a sense of political possibility. The reflexive nature of participation contributes to students' awareness and, it is hoped, leads to a desire to maintain, improve or change one's living conditions.

A holistic perspective of CCE highlights an enduring link between citizenship and education in Australia. Education has the capacity to facilitate the cohesive social integration of students (as political subjects) into a harmonious civic culture (of productive, 'good' citizens). Education contains *implied* political functions. The state has affirmed the strategic role of education in securing 'an essential base' for 'a productive work-force' within a just and cohesive social system (Hughes 1995; McGaw 1996).

Devolving democracy: 'marketisation', internationalisation, individuation

Issues of financing, access and equity have intensified with the tremendous growth of mass education over the last 50 years. The democratic function of education encounters persistent dilemmas of how educational governance ought to negotiate the diverse needs and imperatives of individuals, groups, bureaucracy and economy in responsible, efficient and effective ways.

The Commonwealth White Paper's giving priority to expansion in higher education enrolments confirmed the Government's intention to align outcomes of education with national economic imperatives.[3] The Government then proceeded to de-regulate institutional management and devolve responsibility for educational governance onto individual institutions, teachers and parents.

Devolution of school management is intended to create 'greater autonomy [and] freedom for schools to improve their teaching and learning that they do not have under centralised systems' (DEETYA 1998). In theory, public schools are 'able to develop their own distinctive identity and expertise' so that 'programs, methods of teaching and school organisation will vary to suit students' needs' (DEETYA 1998). Under the Victorian Government's Schools of the Third Millennium initiative, self-managing schools were encouraged to build closer links with local industry and the local community. At the tertiary level, each university also 'has the freedom to specify its own mission and purpose, modes of teaching and research, constitution of the student body and the range of educational programs' (AV-CC 1997).

Economic globalisation has intensified the widespread adoption of neo-liberalism as the ideological basis of educational reform. Neo-liberalism advocates minimal state intervention, emphasising the need for responsiveness to international markets, and preferring market competition in the name of efficiency, innovation and flexibility. New media enhance transnational flows in information, values and ideology, in the process redefining education as a service and cultural commodity (Cunningham et al 1998, p. 7; IMF 1997). Education policy explicitly links global change, new media and democratic citizenship in the burgeoning area of internationalisation. *The Hobart Declaration of Australia's Common and Agreed National Goals for Schooling in the Twenty-First Century*, for example, aspires 'to develop knowledge, skills and values which enable students to participate as active and informed citizens in our democratic Australian society within an international context' (MCEETYA 1998). In seeking to integrate an international/intercultural dimension into the teaching, research and service of an institution, higher education has most visibly responded to 'new knowledge markets' with fee-paying international students (Knight, cited in Back, Davis and Olsen 1996).

Since introducing fees for overseas students at the beginning of the 1980s, higher education has become as 'a major national enterprise'. International education alone is worth $3 billion per year (Patrick 1997, pp. 2–3). Internationalisation has shifted from targeting cross-cultural exchange programs to the lucrative knowledge industry of international education. Redirection of educational purpose 'from aid to trade' in international education is echoed throughout the domestic system. At the end of the millennium, the user-pays principle is now entrenched in extended fee-based courses for domestic and international students in postgraduate and undergraduate courses.

Devolution, de-regulation and privatisation have been important instruments of neo-liberal reform; however, the practical implementation of education policy negotiates a complex dialectic of tradition, power and cultural differences. Teachers must adapt pedagogy to new technology; corporations such as McDonalds and Mitsubishi are now involved in the business of school funding; geopolitical change has given rise to diasporas of international students — these factors all influence policy implementation in overt and covert ways. Consequently, tensions arise emanating from shifts in control over school planning. Some aspects of planning are devolved from the national level to the institutional level (e.g. staff appointments), while many areas formerly left to schools are now determined by national and international agendas (e.g. curriculum). Attempts to centralise sectorial governance, nationalise curricula and implement universal standards of accreditation are coupled with efforts to devolve educational administration and responsibility to individual institutions, teachers and students.

The central problem confronting educational planners is the question of how to balance the developmental needs of the individual against the interests of an increasingly diverse society. A dialectical interplay of government regulation and autonomy is defining spaces and interfaces of formal learning (i.e. schools, websites, distance providers, etc.). This dialectic of control is central to modern democratic citizenship.[4] Where the state traditionally negotiated issues of 'might versus right' with solidaristic groups, current student-centred approaches relocate political responsibility in the reprivatised realm.

Relocating the citizen: student-centred learning

> It is clear that the University is working towards a model where flexible student-centred learning is the essential philosophy underpinning the practice and values of teaching, and permeating the institutional culture. (West et al 1998a)

In order to ensure that schools and graduates are competitive in the international education market, education policy is addressing the need to adopt flexible and dynamic approaches. The pre-eminent target of neo-liberal reform is the student. Whilst being a welcome change from teacher-centred approaches to learning, these policy responses represent a political reconstitution of citizenship away from conventional state regulation. *Commonwealth Literacy Policy*, for example, aspires to the following:

- all students should be given an equal opportunity to learn

- students and parents should have a choice of schools

- schools should have less regulation and greater autonomy

- educational accountability should be increased through assessment and reporting

- schools should focus on students' needs individually in preparation for work and lifelong learning. (DEETYA 1998)

Concepts such as 'choice', 'less regulation', 'autonomy', 'equal opportunity' and 'accountability' reflect the neo-liberal interpretation of citizenship and civic culture within the context of education. However, student-centred approaches foster a very negative, divisive form of self-governance. In closely aligning personal liberty with choice and market power, neo-liberal reform presupposes that all students enter the system on equal terms. Many, of course, do not. Problems of access and equity are exacerbated as the values, practices and environments of education are economically rationalised into education commodities, teaching services, virtual campuses and knowledge industries. The Finn, Carmichael and Mayer reports of the early 1990s prefigured this process of individuation in their orientation towards competition policy (Australian Education Council Review Committee 1991; Employment and Skills Formation Council 1992; Mayer Committee 1992). Competition policy encourages a form of citizenship that forgoes a genuine commitment to collective responsibility.

Education is now defined in relation to the economy in particular, according to vocational criteria and marketability rather than democracy. Devolution of responsibility to levels of institutional management, private provision and local community is justified by neo-liberal doctrine in neoclassical economic terms (Marginson 1997). Individual freedom, competition and entrepreneurialism are the centre of political and economic life (Carey 1995, p. 244). Education is a private good for which individuals should pay, while education institutions are encouraged to compete for funding as a way of increasing efficiency and productivity. This is the context in which the kind of policy described above must be understood. It is worth unpacking these terms a little further.

A flexible learning framework posits students at the centre of educational practice, enabling them to exercise greater choice, mobility and involvement in teaching and learning (Murphy 1998, p. 14). Information and communications technology is central to flexible learning because it offers an interactive and cost-effective means of delivering education beyond traditional classroom settings to geographically and culturally diverse locations. In addition, it provides 'new ways for everyone involved in education to be openly accountable to parents, to communities, and to students' (Ellmore, Olson et al 1993). On-line learning is widely seen as a fast-track and socially progressive means to the global educational market. It also offers students a more direct role in determining content, pace and environment (OLTC 1996).

Under the neo-liberal rubric of institutional self-management, 'full staffing flexibility' has been implemented to enable individual schools a greater say in the appointment of staff. 'Flexible work arrangements' constitute the latest wave of casual work, undermining job security at the expense of quality teaching and research. New learning technology is further recasting the teacher as a knowledge worker whose role is to act as a kind of shopping guide in a global supermarket of ideas.

The neo-liberal appeal to 'flexibility' as a democratic quality has as its corollary a notion of 'choice' as a form of empowerment. As the Wyndham Report pointed out over 40 years ago, choice is important because it is linked to 'both the freedom and responsibility involved in living in a democracy' (Wyndham 1962, pp. 129–132). However, notions of choice invoked in initiatives such as Commonwealth Literacy Policy often mask disturbing implications, because the freedom to choose is as illusory as it is conditional.

The current re-privatisation of education is undermining any semblance of democratic process from public decision-making, in favour of naked consumerism. As John Ralston Saul demonstrates, this corporate approach of contemporary governance undermines the legitimacy of the individual as democratic citizen and education as a public good, producing instead self-interest and denial of the public good

(Saul 1995, p. 2). Devolution of educational governance forces schools to confront additional pressures of competitive individualism and consumerism, which cause pathological side effects in social relations, such as gross class inequality (Pusey 1987, p. 108). As the *Tomorrow Schools* program in New Zealand has shown, devolution only exacerbates problems of access, quality and racial difference (Bruce 1993). Providing choice in the context of market competition is undemocratic because it disadvantages those without the access to cultural capital, money or networks to make informed judgement. In this sense, the current push for self-regulation as a keystone of 'lifelong learning' produces a pernicious type of knowledge based on an instrumental, pragmatic and therefore limited cultural perspective of society (Beck, Giddens and Lasch 1994).

The economics of fatalism

Economic imperatives assumed an unnerving pre-eminence in education policy during the John Dawkins reforms of the late 1980s. The period was a kind of watershed of neo-liberalist reform, during which time the Federal Government targeted education as a key institutional base upon which to restructure the national economy (Dawkins 1988; West et al 1998; SCEET 1989). Dawkins argued that a reorientation of education towards a more flexible, technically proficient and industrially innovative work force was a matter of economic survival (Dawkins 1992, p. 7–11). The West Review continues in this vein to propose market-driven solutions, arguing that 'in a globally competitive environment, Australia will need to get the best possible value from its educational dollar ("more scholar for the dollar", as one Review member expressed it)' (West et al 1997, p. 69). Governments are using economic conditions to justify their education policies, these conditions appearing to be objective social facts sometimes beyond political influence (and therefore the political accountability of responsible government). This enables the state to minimise its responsibility to provide appropriate and educational facilities and to be accountable for learning outcomes.

What makes this strategy so insidious is the manner by which it deflects responsibility for social well-being, away from state and corporate power onto individuals, communities and groups. In allowing institutions to level fees for tertiary study, for example, the government limits access to those of financial means, which effectively denies some citizens their democratic entitlement to pursue lifelong learning. The state has a responsibility to prevent this kind of discrimination rather than foster its implementation; however, now that access to tertiary study is seen to be a matter of competition and wealth, the *obligation* to successfully gain entrance falls directly upon the students themselves (as well as their parents, guardians, sponsors, etc.). In a society increasingly divided between information rich and information poor, the source of marginalisation appears to emanate not from government or responsible agency, but from the marginalised *themselves.*

This distressing social pathology makes an automaton of the citizen. Neo-liberal policy fosters an extreme version of individual responsibility reliant on popular acceptance of governance by self-discipline as an acceptable and appropriate form of democratic citizenship. Social theorist Zygmunt Bauman connects this alienating conception of market-based autonomy to new forms of human domination. Following Bauman's thesis, it becomes clear that democratic entitlements are eroding as individuals come to expect that issues of access, equity, teaching and learning are *purely* a matter of self-discipline (Bauman 1988; 1993, p. 11).

According to Bourdieu, our social world is defined by overt norms and social convention. Whilst overt norms are open to question, social convention is regarded as social reality and therefore remains unquestioned (Bourdieu 1977, pp. 78, 94, 168–69). Education is a key site in which social convention is articulated and reproduced. State and corporate actors 'are able to use the power conferred on them, especially in periods of crisis, by their capacity to put forward a critical definition of the social world, to mobilise the potential strength of the dominated classes...' (Bourdieu 1993, p. 44). Government uses jargon such as '*acceptable* levels of unemployment', 'the recession we *had* to have' and 'the level playing field' in order to persuade citizens to accept draconian reform. In devolving responsibility for education to local communities, schools and individuals, the government relies on subsequent decisions and actions made by those citizens to become accepted over time, forming a culture of competitive self-preservation and civic deficit. Citizens are oriented away from values of reciprocity and community towards an atomised form of personal autonomy. This relocation reduces citizenship to an economic and legal status based on self-regimentation and isolation. Neo-liberal reforms have undermined solidarity, community and the celebration of diversity.

Educating for citizenship

In falling short of expectations, education becomes an unfulfilled promise of democracy. Effective pedagogy should embrace more dynamic perspectives than traditional, didactic, teacher-centred methods of instruction (Print 1996). Vught suggests that team-based rather than individual learning provides a way of addressing cost and access. The integration of information and communications technology into secondary and higher education is transforming educational institutions: for example, by 1997, eleven mega-universities in China, France, India, Indonesia, Iran, Korea, South Africa, Spain, Thailand, Turkey and the U.K. enrolled nearly three million students by distance mode (Vught 1997). This form of education is likely to be more common in Australia and elsewhere.

Such students must have the opportunity to learn about civics and citizenship education, which must encompass *political literacy*, vital to the active experience of democratic citizenship (Walsh and Salvaris 1998, p. 30). Political literacy concerns the knowledge, engagement and attitudes towards the workings of government and democratic institutions (Baker and Baker 1997). The participating democratic citizen ought to have a well-developed sense of civic duty that values community and is mindful of cultural differences. For this to take place in Australia, our current institutional model of democracy must be transformed into a model for social democracy. Thus, the opportunities and environments in which citizens can participate in determining the conditions of their association must be increased. For a healthy social democracy to exist, the sociopolitical function of education must be to nurture, challenge and develop social citizenship in open but inclusive ways. Ideally, regular learning environments, such as the school, should be practical examples of an effective democratic civic community.

Conclusion

The failure in 1999 of the referendum to establish an Australian republic has highlighted the need for more civics education in Australia. It is difficult, however, to make people think of themselves as citizens when their lived experience is based only on their power within economic markets. This is increasingly the experience of people in our schools and universities. Any new civics campaigns must be widened beyond providing information about constitutional matters; they should instead encourage citizens to understand the full political and social dimensions of citizenship. If civics campaigns in our schools and universities are to succeed, they must be based upon more than curriculum alone. Our schools and universities themselves must operate in ways that encourage people to think of themselves as more than mere clients, but as participating citizens.

chapter **14**

Redefining citizenship and public interest: feminist perspectives
By Katrina Gorjanicyn

The parameters of citizenship and public participation have been redrawn substantially by feminists since the 1970s. This has occurred in two ways — through feminists' liaisons with the state as policy-makers and, more recently, through feminist theories of how notions of the public/private dichotomy may be re-fashioned to include new perspectives on what it means to be a full and equal citizen. Feminist action and debate on citizenship are taking shape within a broader political context where there is an emphasis on social and cultural diversity, Do-It-Yourself (DIY) discourse, and economic rationalism. In this chapter I explore how theoretical and practical dimensions of feminism are responding to new political developments and contributing to the elaborate, evolving debate on citizenship and the definition of the public interest. In the first section of the chapter I trace how theoretical debates on women's citizenship have unfolded. I consider the relevance of these debates to Australian women's citizenship status in the second section of the chapter, by analysing the significance of femocracy, whereby feminists work with the state to advance women's status through policy-making.

Debating inclusion and the public interest:
feminist theories of participation
and citizenship

In recent years there has been a burgeoning body of feminist literature that has critiqued citizenship as a gendered concept (Pateman 1988, 1989, 1992; Phillips 1991, 1998; Mouffe 1992; Sullivan and Whitehouse 1996; Arneil 1999). While feminists generally agree that citizenship privileges men, there is debate about what should constitute full citizenship for women. Essentially, feminist debates about citizenship revolve around the roles assigned to women in the public and private spheres and the degree to which these roles enable women to participate as full and equal members of society. It is this nexus between participation and citizenship, as it has been conceived historically, that I now wish to explore in relation to Australian feminism.

The dichotomy between the public and private spheres represents one of the main topics of debate on the issue of women's participation. This duality in conventional liberal political theory, which places women outside the 'rational' sphere of political life, has historical dimensions. The separation of 'public' from 'private', whereby men were public citizens and women were relegated to domestic duties in the private sphere, underpinned the philosophies of the Ancient Greeks. While men were seen to represent reason, rationality, science and culture, women were constructed as suited only for nurturing, caring and domestic responsibilities. The public/private dichotomy continued to be a salient feature of liberal philosophy during the 18th and 19th centuries, albeit in revised form, with the individual now a focal point (Arneil 1999).

Constructions of gender difference that give rise to the distinction between public and private continue to hold currency in contemporary politics, preventing women from participating equally in public life and determining the extent to which the state can regulate civil society. Despite gaining the vote and making significant interventions into public life, women still are not full and active citizens because they continue to be excluded in various ways from key decision-making processes. Nevertheless, feminists have had considerable success in reconfiguring the boundaries of public and private and thus redefining politics.

Feminism's historical development has been described metaphorically as advancing in waves. At the turn of the 20th century first-wave feminists argued that, in order for women to become empowered and achieve equality, they must have direct input into the political world. While first-wave feminists actively pursued female suffrage as the key means of political participation, they did not challenge the role allocated to women as mothers and carers in the private sphere. In fact, they upheld women's involvement in the private sphere. Women's participation in public life was considered to be a means of representing the interests of home-makers and mothers whose experiences were very different to those of men. This adherence to 'maternal feminism' clearly linked notions of citizenship to what first-wave feminists perceived as women's differences from men that placed them in the role of mother and carer of the family (Lake 1995, 1999).

While Australia's involvement in 20th century warfare reinforced gender stereotypes, the absence of men from home opened up opportunities for women to experience public life. Many women gained unprecedented access to the public sphere when during war years they were required to fill men's jobs. While women's new-found activity only served to modify gender relations and did not radically change women's involvement in the public sphere (Van Acker 1999, p. 52), it nonetheless provided them with an unprecedented knowledge of it. This brief engagement was the forerunner of women's involvement with the New Left of the 1960s and the development of second-wave feminism.

With the advent of second-wave feminism, the dichotomy of the 'rational' male public sphere and the 'emotive' female private sphere was critiqued extensively. It was argued widely in feminist literature that women's suitability to occupy the 'natural' realm of the private sphere had been socially and politically constructed (Okin 1978; Elshtain 1981). Incorporating women into public life continued to be considered a priority by many second-wave feminists, to ensure that women had the same access to citizenship rights as men and that women were provided with a public forum to voice their different experiences and policy requirements (Sawer and

Simms 1993). However, first-wave feminists' emphasis on women's difference, which they believed made them suitable for the role of home-maker, was rejected by the second generation of feminists. While the strategy of entering male political institutions did not appeal to or relate to the experiences of all feminists, such as lesbians, women of colour or women living in poverty, the goal of claiming public space through organised marches and demonstrations received widespread support. Therefore, rethinking political space was fundamental to second-wave feminism. Feminists made unprecedented connections between the public and private spheres so that women's 'private' experiences could be politicised. Indeed, one of the most poignant slogans of 1970s feminism was 'the personal is political', which welded what were previously considered to be 'personal' problems, such as domestic violence and childcare, to state action. The reform of political thought concerning the interaction between public and private spheres, which occurred as a result of this political discourse and action, was one of the monumental achievements of second-wave feminism.

Second-wave feminists in Australia developed their own unique brand of activism that involved direct participation in policy-making. The feminist movement formed an alliance with the Australian state, and femocrats were recruited into senior positions within bureaucracy for the specific purpose of formulating feminist policies. At that time many feminist theorists equated full citizenship with participation in the public sphere of government and bureaucracy. However, despite the considerable inroads that Australian women have made into political institutions that give them access to public space and policy-making, this does not guarantee them full and equal citizenship rights. Recently, the notion of what constitutes political participation and citizenship has been of central concern in feminist theory. Do women need to enter the overtly public realm of politics in order to participate as equal citizens? Or is the contribution women make to the private sphere, particularly through motherhood, a sufficient political act in itself to constitute active citizenship? Furthermore, should the dichotomy of public and private be made redundant in order to achieve new outlooks on citizenship?

Several key contemporary feminist debates on citizenship are concerned with the extent to which participation in mainstream political institutions and involvement in the private sphere as mothers provide opportunities for women to be active, full and contributing citizens. However, the extent to which these debates are progressive is doubtful because they perpetuate the public/private dichotomy. Many feminist theorists have fallen into the 'either/or' debate — *either* women enter public life with vigour and seize opportunities to effect political change *or* women redefine motherhood so that it comes to be understood as a political act that constitutes a contribution to the nation. However, Carole Pateman and Chantal Mouffe have provided new ways of thinking about public and private and the relevance of whether women should be treated the same as or differently from men in the debate about equal citizenship.

Maternal or social feminists urge women to break away from existing notions of citizenship that are based on involvement in the public arena. They argue that the public world is defined by men and excludes the experiences and skills of women who function in the domestic sphere. Maternal feminists advocate a new model of citizenship that values women's contributions in the private sphere. They claim that the 'feminine' and 'maternal' should be politicised in order for women to create their own definition of citizenship. According to maternal feminists, private sphere activity takes precedence over political and economic activity and this should be recognised in the criteria of citizenship. Maternal feminists believe that love, care and intimacy arise from the act of mothering and that these qualities should be upheld as the basis of a new form of citizenship which would tame the arrogant, individualist, 'male' values that shape the public world (Elshtain 1981, 1992; Ruddick 1990). The position that maternal feminists take on participation is grounded in the theory that women should be treated as different from men in order to achieve equal citizenship rights. While maternal feminists provide an escape route for women from the confines of a male political order, they run the risk of essentialising women as carers and nurturers and cutting them off from participating in the formulation of public policy that ultimately has a direct bearing on their lives.

The notion of linking mothering to citizenship is rejected by other feminists who argue that women's citizenship should be derived from partaking in the public world. Participation in established, mainstream political institutions is considered to be an appropriate means of ensuring women exercise equal citizenship rights with men. Mary Dietz views citizenship as a separate activity to mothering and domesticity: as an interaction between adults that requires operating with a different set of values than those of intimacy, compassion and care, which are associated with mothering. According to Dietz, mothering is not integral to democratic politics, which she associates with citizenship, because the mother-child relationship is not equal. In the public world, equality, mutual respect and responsibility are the core values that underlie citizenship (Dietz 1985, 1998). However, there is a problem with Dietz's approach because it suggests that women should fit into a political order that was designed to privilege men; it assumes that women should be treated the same as men in order to achieve equal citizenship rights. Yet participating in the dominant model of citizenship does not necessarily mean that women will adhere exclusively to 'masculine' values. It is argued that women can bring their different experiences and views from men into the public arena, which can redirect political debate and public policy. Women are more likely to be better represented in the public world when more women participate in the political process (Phillips 1991, 1995, 1998). This line of argument has been an important consideration for Australian feminists who have made interventions into policy-making by working for the state. The enactment of the Federal Sex Discrimination Act 1984 and the Affirmative Action (Equal Opportunity for Women) Act 1986 have facilitated Australian women's ability to progress in the public world.

Notions of citizenship that are structured around male, rational, liberal imagery of the public sphere have come under scrutiny from feminist theorists who postulate new interpretations of participatory politics. The pioneering and notable contributions to this discourse made by Pateman and Mouffe continue to stimulate feminist debate on citizenship, particularly amongst the new generation who constitute third-wave feminism.

Carole Pateman acknowledges feminists' difficulties in developing criteria for women's citizenship that is separate from patriarchal categories yet does not exclude women from political life (1988, 1989, 1992). She attempts to bridge the divide between maternal feminists, who celebrate women's difference, and feminists who are committed to incorporating women into public life. She devises a 'sexually differentiated' notion of citizenship in which women's bodies and motherhood are central. According to Pateman, motherhood affects women's citizenship status in two ways: it excludes women from aspects of public life yet it bestows a political role on mothers in the private sphere, because child-bearing contributes to society. She constructs motherhood as fluid; it is a private and a political act at the same time. The key benefit of this model is that it moves toward developing a notion of participation that distinguishes women's experiences and capacities and eschews the masculine image of modern citizenship.

However, Pateman's emphasis on recognising 'women *as* women' in citizenship debates is criticised by Chantal Mouffe, who argues that it universalises and essentialises women and perpetuates the public/private dichotomy. Mouffe argues a case for reducing the significance accorded to sexual difference and designs a model of citizenship that incorporates experiences and relations that break free of traditional male/female roles. In Mouffe's vision of citizenship, sexual difference should become 'effectively non-pertinent' (Mouffe 1992, p. 376) and difference in women's experiences and ambitions should instead become the key factors in the construction of new understandings of citizenship. Debates on citizenship should take into account women's shifting identities and their multiple experiences of subordination. According to Mouffe, once essential identities are challenged, the equality versus difference debate is no longer relevant because sexual difference is no longer limited to the idea of 'woman' in opposition with 'man' but occurs in diverse ways. These theories form the backbone of Mouffe's 'radical democratic project', which is built on a belief in liberty and equality for all (Mouffe 1992).

Mouffe's analysis of plurality, and multifaceted and shifting identity, makes a significant point concerning the ways in which the representation of women's diverse lifestyles and different experiences of subordination have been eclipsed in many feminist debates on citizenship. While analyses of women's means of participating in politics and the questioning of citizenship rights in public and private spheres may well advance feminist re-conceptualisations of status and equality within a society, they do not adequately address the issue of how women's varied and multiple interests can be best represented. Here I am referring to the representation of interests that may extend beyond one's own interests as a mother or a mainstream political participant. In a rapidly globalising world where multiplicity and cultural and sexual difference have been writ large, the representation of women's diverse interests surely should be paramount in feminists' consideration of citizenship. Debates about difference are no longer just about the differences between women and men. Feminist theory now acknowledges that differences also exist between women and women (Barrett and Phillips 1992; Bock and James 1992; Mouffe 1992; Gunew and Yeatman 1993). Feminists have been alerted to the differences that exist in women's experiences, such as class, race, ethnicity, sexual orientation, religion and family, which demonstrate that women's interests are not universal or static (Young 1998). An extensive range of literature details the complexities and elasticity of the category 'woman' (see for example Hartmann 1981; Hooks 1991; Huggins and Saunders 1993; Vasta 1991; Bell 1994; Jeffreys 1997).

Given that we function in such a heterogeneous world, it is pertinent to question how different voices can be represented. Feminist debates on citizenship need to take into account that a definition of citizenship based exclusively on motherhood or mainstream political participation excludes other groups of women who do not fall into these clearly demarcated categories. For example, in what ways can citizenship be extended to women with disabilities who may not be able to have children or actively participate in public life? The experiences and views of people with disabilities are rarely acknowledged in feminist literature on citizenship (Meekosha and Dowse 1997). Furthermore, would lesbian, single and black mothers receive the same citizenship rights as white, partnered, heterosexual mothers? This begs the question of whether women's diverse experiences will be counted as part of the criteria for citizenship. Would women who occupy positions of political power as mothers or within public institutions be able to represent other women's experiences in order to ensure that all women are included as full and equal citizens? The issue of representing women who do not identify as mothers presents yet another twist in the search for a new model of citizenship. The 'motherhood' model excludes a range of women who derive their emotional life from a role other than motherhood, such as women who focus on careers, women who work in voluntary positions, and women who enjoy a contented domesticity without children. For a variety of reasons the categories of women's life experience extend beyond motherhood and this needs to be recognised in citizenship debates if they are to become more inclusive.

In recent years, younger, third-wave feminists have responded to the bifurcated notion of women as mothers and women as participants in the public sphere by emphasising the diversity of women's experience. Third-wave feminism may well provide further sustenance for the citizenship debate with its emphasis on multiplicity, contradiction, embodiment and identity. A commitment to universality, sameness and unity, which has been associated with second-wave feminism, has been displaced by third-wave feminists who celebrate women's different points of view. Individuals' lives and personal experience are a central focus of this new generation. Third-wave feminists are currently expanding the definition of citizenship by blurring the distinction between public/private and nature/culture, re-introducing the body into political discourse and taking into account the voices of marginal and minority groups. Hyphenated feminisms, such as liberal-feminism and Marxist-feminism, have been abandoned, marking further efforts to dispose of dualities. The intersection of gender, class, race, ethnicity and sexual diversity are given greater prominence by third-wave feminists, providing a richer and more energised debate (Arneil 1999).

In the Australian context, third-wave feminists offer up a different perspective on participation to that of second-wave feminists. The latter continue to value the activism of the 1970s in which they engaged. They argue that younger women owe them a debt of gratitude for the achievements of the past that provide them with better opportunities than they would otherwise have had (Summers 1994). Meanwhile, younger feminists are critical of what they perceive as an abuse of power by older feminists whose actions resemble the patriarchy (Lumby 1997). However, the notion of feminist activism has changed; femocracy is ingrained in the political system and the struggle to enter the institutions of the public world does not preoccupy third-wave feminists to the extent it did second-wave feminists (Van Acker 1999, p. 65). Third-wave feminists are more concerned with DIY feminism, which puts the spotlight on the individual. This new generation of feminists emerged in the 1990s as a diverse group of women who interpret feminism from their own experiences and draw on a range of survival strategies (Bail 1996). These recent feminist contributions have changed the parameters of the debate on participation and citizenship.

Australian feminists' participation in the public sphere

Feminist debates on citizenship provide an analytical framework for understanding how women are positioned as participants within Australian society. In particular, Chantal Mouffe's model of citizenship urges the deconstruction of essentialist identities and presents Australian policy-makers with a set of challenges in the pursuit of equal citizenship. Should policy-makers view women *as* women in the ways that Pateman and maternal feminists have argued, or should the notion of democratic citizenship rest on a down-playing of the opposition between men and women, as advocated by Mouffe, in order to erase the bifurcation of public and private?

Policy agendas assembled by Australian femocrats show that, while there have been moves to abandon the sharp distinction between public and private, opposition between men and women continues to hold currency in debates that relate to citizenship. The case study of Australian feminists' involvement in policy-making, which follows below, reveals that constructing notions of citizenship in ways that make sexual difference irrelevant is a difficult task. Embracing diversity in new visions of women's citizenship has been a more manageable project for femocrats, who have made inroads into incorporating women's different life experiences into policy. However, the extent to which an emphasis on the diversity of women's experiences can inform policy outcomes is limited by governments' commitments to policies of economic rationalism that impede the development of women's full citizenship.

In many respects Australian feminists have been closely aligned with a liberal-feminist approach to participation and citizenship through their preparedness to interact with the state as femocrats since the 1970s. The key aims of femocrats are to make policy-making processes and policy outcomes women-friendly. This has involved creating specific women's policy machinery within government, such as the Office of the Status of Women, and making equal opportunity a legitimate part of governments' policy agendas.

Feminists' carefully planned foray into state structures that has enabled them to participate in the public sphere through policy-making has been a key factor in redefining citizenship for women. These reforms to the apparatus of government and legislation have been set up with the specific purpose of valuing and incorporating women's different experiences and requirements from men into policy-making. Herein lies one of the key difficulties in adapting Mouffe's model of citizenship to the Australian case. Australian feminists have increased women's life opportunities, and hence citizenship rights, precisely because they have recognised that women have different experiences from men that need to be acknowledged in public policy. Equal opportunity legislation and anti-discrimination policies are examples of how an adherence to the opposition between men and women has been central in devising revisions in policy-making that increase women's citizenship rights. Furthermore, femocrats have carved out a legitimate position for themselves in the policy process on the basis that they are different from men. Therefore, the project of achieving full and equal citizenship rights for Australian women has rested on a perpetuation of certain binaries.

However, femocrats' representation of the interests of women in the home suggests that the definition and practice of citizenship in Australia involves some blurring of the demarcation between what have been traditionally regarded as public and private spheres. While an initial reading of feminists' direct involvement in the policy process may indicate that Australian feminists have equated citizenship primarily with participation in the public sphere, it is important to note that mothers' entitlements to citizenship have been a central component of femocrats' policy initiatives. Femocrats and grassroots feminist groups have put the issues of maternity leave and access to child-care at the forefront of their agenda for policy reform. Therefore, contributions that women make to policy formulation have been a key factor in redefining citizenship for women who work in paid employment as well as in the home. On the one hand, femocrats have achieved status and a high degree of power in the policy process, enabling them to initiate policies that benefit women who participate in the public sphere, such as affirmative action and equal opportunity. On the other hand, issues concerning women that have traditionally been considered to be private and outside the realm of the state have in fact been recast as public issues by femocrats (Franzway et al 1989; Watson 1990; Sawer and Simms 1993; Eisenstein 1996; Hancock 1999; Lake 1999). The politicisation of rape in the home and domestic violence are additional examples of how femocrats have linked women's citizenship rights to activities that governments previously dismissed as belonging to the private sphere. In representing a range of women's interests, including those of women in paid work and women in the home, femocrats can down-play the division between public and private and move away from essentialising women's identity.

While femocrats' policy initiatives have reaped significant citizenship benefits for many women, they have not been without controversy. The contradictions of women working within the confines of the patriarchal and fraternal state have been well-documented (Eisenstein 1996; Yeatman 1990) and serve as a reminder of the limitations on women's participation and access to equal citizenship. The extent to which femocrats can maintain loyalty to grassroots feminists while been employed by the state continues to be a point of contention within the feminist movement. Femocrats have been subjected to criticisms from the wider feminist movement that they have 'sold out' by colluding with the state. This raises the issue of representation. Questions have been raised concerning the ability of femocrats, who are typically white, heterosexual and working in the primary labour market, to represent the interests of women of colour, ethnic-minority migrant women, lesbian women and women with disabilities (Yeatman 1990; Huggins 1994; Lucashenko 1994; Kaplan 1996). These debates have prompted femocrats to consider more carefully how they can cater for the differences that exist between women in order to increase citizenship rights for women of different backgrounds.

However, in a climate of economic rationalism, the extent to which femocrats' strategies can remain effective and representative of a range of women's interests is questionable. The public sector, which accommodates femocrats, has been downsized and the provision of many women's services has been slashed in the name of efficiency and effectiveness. Femocrats have been able to stem some of these cutbacks to state services but it has become clear that hard-won gains can be easily whittled away.

The impact of neo-liberal policies resonates loudly in the area of women's policy. Women's policy machinery and the delivery of services to women have been beleaguered by governments intent on rolling back the welfare state, emulating private sector practices, and declaring their devotion to market forces. Sawer has documented in detail the gamut of recent changes to the policy machinery that femocrats set up in the 1970s. Key changes imposed by the Howard Government have entailed: cutting the budget to the Federal Office of the Status of Women by 40 per cent in 1996; abolishing the federal Women's Budget; reducing the statistical monitoring of the status of women; and cutting in half funding from the Office of the Status of Women to non-government organisations (Sawer 1999). State governments have also moved women advisers out of powerful positions within state bureaucracies. The abolition of the Office of Commissioner for Equal Opportunity in Victoria by the Kennett Government when it came to power in 1992 was a clear indication of where government directives concerning women's policy issues were heading. The Howard Government has severely cut and withdrawn a range of services that were originally designed to benefit women, particularly in relation to the family program and child-care (Mitchell 1999). There have been shifts from community-based, non-profit child-care facilities to privatised, user-pays child-care across the country. This has had the effect of keeping women at home in the role of carers and disadvantaging women from participating equally in the workplace (Brennan 1999). Clearly, economic rationalism has affected women's ability to participate in society as equal citizens. While conservative governments have swung the sharpest axe in cutting back welfare and community services, Labor governments have also instigated economic-rationalist-inspired policies that ultimately have a negative effect on low- and middle-income women (Eisenstein 1996). Consequently, both sides of politics must be held accountable for the erosion of women's citizenship rights.

Conclusion

The theories and practice of feminist citizenship bring traditional notions of public and private spheres into focus and prompt a questioning of what constitutes participation in politics. In analysing feminist discourses on citizenship it is clear that it is difficult to circumnavigate the dualism of public and private because historically it has been entrenched in our way of thinking about participation and status in society, forming a framework for our way of defining citizenship. However, Mouffe's model (1992) provides many useful ingredients for a blueprint of democratic citizenship. For example, it is clear that discussing the notion of citizenship in the context of dualities may not serve the best interests of women. A down-playing of the division of public and private may be the key to ensuring that women do not have to compete with each other for citizenship rights nor define their citizenship status in relation to a male discourse on participation and identity. However, abandoning the opposition of men and women so that sexual difference becomes irrelevant, as recommended by Mouffe, is not a viable solution in the context of policy-making in Australia, where femocrats are employed for the purpose of representing women's interests. Addressing the specific interests of women in policy-making does not assume that men and women are suited to different tasks on which definitions of citizenship should be moulded. Rather than essentialising women, the recognition that women have different life experiences from men brings women's oppression to the surface and augurs for the need to redress imbalance and provide women with equal citizenship rights. Furthermore, the recognition of women's specific interests within policy-making does not necessarily create a homogenous and essentialist category of 'woman'. Increasingly, femocrats are recognising the multiple forms of subordination that exclude women from full citizenship and they are extending notions of citizenship to incorporate women's diverse life experiences. These new perspectives derive from recent feminist analyses of identity that celebrate and respect plurality. As Mouffe argues, it is important that particularity and difference receive full attention in order for a more refined definition of women's citizenship to emerge.

Putting these discourses on citizenship and diversity into action through policy-making is, however, not a simple procedure when governments adhere to neo-liberal agendas that have an adverse affect on women. Policies associated with the neo-liberal state overshadow arguments concerning social justice for women; consequently, there are limited opportunities for women to augment citizenship rights by cultivating diversity. It is time for governments to rethink the parochial policies that have been created to promote economic rationalism and to take into account the ways in which citizenship may be reinvigorated, particularly in relation to the diversity of women's experiences. For example, the Commonwealth's Affirmative Action policy could place greater emphasis on encouraging the employment of women from a wide range of backgrounds. Another key policy reform could entail providing more flexible working opportunities for women in the public service. There is a crossover between these suggestions for reform and other pressing policy issues that concern women, such as equal pay and accessible, quality child-care. Clearly, the potential exists for the state to play a major role in restoring public interest so that it is more inclusive of women. Moreover, the state has a responsibility to recognise that women should not be treated as one homogenous, cohesive group if democratic citizenship is to be achieved. Citizenship must be extended to accommodate the broadest range of people; this requires full consideration of women's diverse experiences.

endnotes

Chapter 1: The role of government in 21st Australia

1. See Prime Minister's speech on mandatory sentencing in the House of Representatives, Hansard on 4 July 2000 (Howard 2000b). Under the Constitution this is a prima facie area of State responsibility. Despite constitutional limitations, it would still be possible to enact effective Commonwealth measures.
2. For example, the Coalition opposed the use of the external affairs power of the Constitution by the Commonwealth in respect of the Franklin Dam case in Tasmania, the Wet Tropics of North Queensland, the Lemonthyme Forest of Tasmania, and Kakadu.
3. In March 2000 the Coalition Government announced a review of the operation of the United Nations treaty committee system as it affects Australia (Downer 2000).
4. In May 1999 unemployment among young people who left school in Years 10 and 11 exceeded 20 per cent and for those who left school before completing Year 10 it was 41.7 per cent (ABS 1999, p. 19).
5. Australian Institute of Criminology statistics indicate the incidence of breaking and entering per 100,000 of population in 1969–70 was 663 and that by 1997–98 it had risen to 2125.

Chapter 3: The contract state and the public interest

1. The author is grateful to Martin Painter and the editors for many helpful suggestions.

Chapter 4: Rethinking the public: paying attention to citizens and clients

1. For example, more than one Minister in the incoming Bracks Labor Government in Victoria has made it very clear that their departments should not refer to their publics as 'customers'.

2. In either the public or private sector, the supplier may be a monopolist.
3. This term is used without the judgemental nuances it has in various debates in the welfare sector. It refers simply to people who receive services without paying for them directly.
4. For a critical review of vouchers in education, see Le Grand, Propper and Robinson 1992, pp. 79–83.
5. For details of the Coalition Government's scheme, see the Federal Department of Employment, Workplace Relations and Small Business website at www.dewrsb.gov.au/wfd.

Chapter 7: Unchaining the ABC

1. Tanner (1999), pp. 94–102.
2. See Rees and Godley (1995).
3. Department of Communications and the Arts (1994). For one perspective on Keating's personal view of the ABC, see Dempster (2000), quoted in Ramsay (2000).
4. Semmler (2000), p. 79.
5. See Hage (1998).
6. See Wark (1999), pp. 224–229.

Chapter 8: Policy: the new 'hard' politics

1. Thanks to Andrew Leigh for discussions and comments upon an earlier draft of this essay.
2. We can define policy-making as the process by which government and political parties translate their political vision into programs and action to deliver outcomes which are desired changes in the real world (U.K. Government 1999, p. 15).
3. A comprehensive list can be found at www.policy.com.

Chapter 9: Tackling social exclusion

1. I am indebted to Rod Glover, Michael Perusco, Perri 6 and Justin Wolfers for their comments on an earlier draft. All errors are mine.
2. Federal Government spending now totals around $140 billion per year, or 23 per cent of G.D.P. The largest allocation is the $50 billion spent on social security and welfare.
3. Based on the head of the family not working, and including housing costs (Melbourne Institute of Applied Economic and Social Research 2000).
4. The gap between DSP and the Newstart Allowance (unemployment benefit) is likely to widen. Whilst DSP is indexed to average weekly earnings, the Newstart Allowance is indexed to the consumer price index — so DSP will probably grow around 1.5

per cent per annum faster than the Newstart Allowance. In addition, the income and assets tests are more generous for DSP than for the Newstart Allowance. Finally, DSP provides a Pensioner Concession Card, giving substantial savings and concessions on expenses such as municipal rates, electricity and car registration.

5. At the same time, by creating more 'churning' within the labour market, the growth in contracting out has also increased the opportunities for unemployed people to find work.

6. Research on poverty has produced similar results. One study of poverty dynamics in Canada, Germany, Britain and the United States found that around half of those who fall below the poverty line in a given year are likely to be out of poverty the following year. Yet of those who leave poverty, approximately one-quarter will be back in poverty the following year — and less likely to leave it than they were before (Oxley 1999).

7. According to figures supplied by Martin et al (2000, p. 41), the gross value of agricultural production has tended to fluctuate by between $25 billion and $30 billion over the past two decades.

8. During the 1990s, the relative importance of wool, wheat and beef declined substantially, whilst canola, wine, cotton, sugar and horticulture all grew (Chudleigh 1999).

9. Highly sophisticated production methods and a strong export orientation are two factors that have driven demand for skilled labour in the farm sector (Chudleigh 1999, pp. 96–7). See also Craik (1999).

10. Some of the industries that have provided new jobs in non-urban areas are food and beverage manufacturing, meat processing, wineries, flour milling and oilseed crushing (Garnaut et al 2000). Other areas, such as Cairns and Alice Springs, have been successful in creating substantial numbers of jobs in the tourism sector.

11. North and West Moreton, Wide Bay/Burnett and the NSW mid-North Coast are three of the seven regions in Australia that now receive more in welfare benefits than they pay in income tax.

12. On the factors that have pushed up housing and rental prices, see the various contributions to Yates and Wulff (1999).

13. Strikingly, despite the substantial overall increase in female employment, Gregory and Sheehan (1998, p. 124) point out that in a quarter of Australian urban neighbourhoods the proportion of women in the labour market had fallen since the 1970s. See also Gregory and Hunter (1994) and Gregory and Hunter (1995).

14. Examples of such programs appear in Bentley and Guru-murthy (1999, pp. 66–89); Dusseldorp (1999); and Social Exclusion Unit (1998).

15. Australian children who do not finish high school are 40 per cent more likely to be unemployed (OECD 1996). One British study found that adults with low basic skills were five times more likely to be unemployed than those with average basic skills — with poor numeracy especially important (Sparkes 1999).
16. This mirrors Australian research showing that poor children as young as three show signs of lower participation in stimulating activities such as child-care and playgroups (Gilley and Taylor 1995).
17. Australia's public investment in education is forecast to fall by 6 per cent between 1996–97 and 2001–02.
18. This differs from the situation in the United States, where 39 States prohibit (at least in part) discrimination in health insurance based on genetic tests, and 15 have some ban on discrimination in employment (Begley 2000, p. 39).
19. One of the most comprehensive reviews of early-intervention programs is the RAND study, which reviewed nine early-intervention studies and found programs that made a statistically significant improvement to employment, earnings, participation in crime, school results and IQ scores (Karoly et al 1998). Early intervention programs must be carefully designed, however, since many have been shown to fail, or to have only temporary benefits (Currie and Thomas 1995; Crane 1998).
20. For example, the December 1984 reallocation of bicentennial celebrations to PM&C (Castleman 1995).
21. Such as the 1949 movement of the Office of Education and the Universities Commission to PM&C (Walter 1992, p. 31), and the December 1972 transfer of the arts and tariffs to PM&C (Castleman 1992, p. 295).
22. For example, the decision in December 1984 to shift youth affairs to PM&C (Castleman 1995, p. 7).
23. A Women's Affairs Section was created in PM&C in 1974. It was removed in 1977. In 1983 it was returned, this time renamed the Office of the Status of Women (Sawer 1999, pp. 37–8).
24. Aboriginal and Torres Strait Islander issues were moved to PM&C in 1993 (Castleman 1995). In 1996 the unit was renamed the Office of Indigenous Policy.
25. The Office of Multicultural Affairs was created in PM&C in 1987 (Gardiner-Garden 1989, pp. 3–4) and removed in 1996.

Chapter 11: Communities on-line: a practical strategy for rebuilding rural and regional communities

1. Rhys Edwards, Office of the Premier of Tasmania. This paper represents the views and opinions of the author. It does not

necessarily represent the views or policies of the Tasmanian Government.

2. What is rural and regional Australia? Apart from its useful alliteration, 'rural and regional' as a definition lacks precision in meaning. Without a qualifier, everywhere can claim to be a region somewhere. The popular debate usually stresses the 'bush' versus 'city' divide. However, regional Australia should include cities and towns with population densities that are clearly not rural. Tasmanian governments have long considered the entire State to be part of 'regional' Australia. This chapter uses the term rather loosely to mean those parts of Australia outside of the capital cities and larger urban settlements.

3. This is not to say that money fixes all problems. One of the principles in regional development is the notion that the key to success is local communities taking charge of their own destiny and solving their own problems.

4. Leader stands for Liaisons Entre Action de Dèveloppement l'Èconomie Rurale. The aim of the program is to stimulate the development of rural areas by encouraging those who live in rural areas to find innovative ways to develop their areas.

5. Source: ABS Labour Force (WS) wage and salary earners 6291.0.40.001.

6. There is probably an important distinction to make here between government and Government. Trust in specific Governments and politicians is often found in survey evidence to be low but trust in government as an institution may nevertheless be high. For example, in results from the 1998 Federal election study, 68 per cent of respondents agreed that 'government by its nature, is the best instrument for promoting the general interests of society', while only 11 per cent of respondents agreed with the statement that 'government by its nature, threatens peoples' rights'.

7. To be fair to the current generation of Tasmanian apple-growers, the industry is undergoing a revival with total value of production of $46 million in 1998–99 helped by increased export markets, including high-value markets in Asia.

8. The authors go on to outline four definitions of globalisation in common use in both the scholarly and policy community. These are (1) globalisation as historical epoch, (2) globalisation as the confluence of economic phenomena, (3) globalisation as the triumph of American values, and (4) globalisation as sociological and technological revolution (Higgott & Reich 1998).

9. See Rural Policy Research Unit, www.rurpri.org/ for information on this subject from a U.S. perspective.

10. This is not to imply that action by nation states has become

impossible as many globalisation writers contend, merely more difficult.

11. Vertical Fiscal Imbalance (VFI) is the name given to the situation where the Commonwealth of Australia has power over most revenue-raising measures (particularly income taxation). but the States have the responsibility for service provision of public services, most notably health and education.

12. For a discussion on the role and impact of telecommunications and information economy developments on the concept of community, the implication on the high cost of 'social space' faced by those living in rural and regional areas, and the role of public policy in relation to these issues see Rural Policy Research Unit, www.rurpri.org/.

13. For a critical view of the claim that a new and normatively compelling concept of equality based on social capability will renew the social democratic agenda, see Watts (1999).

14. Social capital is one element in a wide variety of elements that make up the multidimensional nature of 'social exclusion'. For a discussion of social exclusion as a framework for social policy analysis, see Jones and Smyth (1999).

15. The financial difficulties were the result of the Commonwealth Government withdrawing funding. The Commonwealth's position was that funding was provided to give communities a 'taste' of technology and that centres were intended to be self-funding after twelve months. This position totally ignores the financial reality of these enterprises. The Commonwealth tactic of refusing to commit to recurrent funding for projects and leaving the States to pick up the funding gap is well-known to those who work in intergovernmental financial relations. In the case of OACs, the Tasmanian Government has increased its funding contribution and is waiting for the Commonwealth to do the same.

16. There are a number of democracy online interactive projects that the interested reader may like to further examine — see Minnesota E-Democracy www.e-democracy.org or United Kingdom Citizen Online Democracy www.democracy.org.uk.

17. Segell (1997) identifies four models of electronic democracy: the Electronic Bureaucracy Model, the Information Management Model, the Populist Model and the Civil Society Model.

Chapter 12: Why Australians hate politicians: exploring the new public discontent

1. The classic American work on this topic is by E. J. Dionne Jr., *Why Americans Hate Politics*, New York, Simon and Schuster, 1991.
2. Up to 66 per cent of Australians do not trust the government

(McAllister 1997, p. 248). Over 60 per cent believe that politicians make promises in election campaigns which they have no intention of keeping (D716 *Saulwick Poll,* March 1990, ssda.anu.edu.au). Social researcher Hugh Mackay finds that the level of cynicism towards politicians is 'bordering on contempt' (Mackay 1998, p. 39).

3. In a Saulwick Poll (1991) 61 per cent of Australians said they had 'not much' or 'no' confidence in the political system.

4. See Bean and McAllister (1998), McAllister and Wales (1987) and Jaensch (1995).

5. A white-collar worker seems just as likely to be dissatisfied as an unemployed person. The difference lies in the *depth* of their discontent, with the unemployed and those at the lower end of the socioeconomic spectrum seemingly the *most* discontented (Papadikis 1999, p. 88).

6. In 1993, Clive Bean found that 77 per cent of Australians surveyed agreed that the Government 'has a duty to see that everybody has a job and a decent standard of living' (Bean 1993, p. 65).

7. Papadikis (1999).

8. A 1994 Canadian survey found that most respondents saw nothing wrong with cheating on their expense accounts or evading taxes but were appalled by the suggestion that politicians might do likewise (Wilson-Smith 1995).

9. Such expectations may develop in the form of fuzzy images of the institution as a whole, arise from very partisan or ideological perspectives or from specific socialisation such as school textbooks or first-hand contact with an MP (Kimball and Patterson 1997, p. 701).

10. An objective assessment is made impartially on the basis of outward things which actually exist rather than on thoughts and feelings which can be illusory, personal or individual (subjective).

11. Starobin (1995). See also Corrigan 1992, p. 12; Cappella and Hall 1996; Owen 1996; Harwood 1996.

12. Particularly in the infamous 'xenophobia/please explain' exchange with Tracey Curro of '60 Minutes'.

13. In a 1996 survey, six out of ten people said they did not believe it made much difference who they voted for (McAllister 1998, p. 18).

Chapter 13: Education for democratic citizenship: the importance of civics education in the era of economic rationalism

1. This socialising process sees the political identity of the individual undergo a transition from being under the power of a sovereign authority (e.g. teacher, nation state, Queen, etc.) to

218   labor essays 2001

a member of a polity in which every citizen has free and equal input into determining the conditions of his or her association with fellow citizens (i.e. democratic citizenship).

2. The Wyndham Report's recommendation to further expand comprehensive schooling was described by the *Bulletin* as 'a landmark in the history of the decay of education in Australia'. The Report's proposal for greater access to secondary schooling for groups such as girls and migrants was seen as a threat to existing standards, inviting nothing less than a 'collapse [of] the whole of education'. (*Bulletin* 1961, p. 11; Wyndham 1962).

3. Between 1983 and 1995, Australian universities experienced the highest rate of increase in student enrolments compared to any other OECD country (up by 70 per cent) even though government expenditure on education was comparative low (OECD 1997).

4. See Held's discussion of Giddens (Held 1989).

bibliography

Introduction

Considine, M. (2000), 'Contract Regimes and Reflexive Governance: Comparing Employment Service Reforms in the United Kingdom, the Netherlands, New Zealand and Australia', in *Public Administration* (forthcoming).

Giddens, A. (1998), *The Third Way: The Renewal of Social Democracy*, Polity Press.

Hodge, G. (1999), *Privatisation: An International Review of Performance*, Westview Press.

Chapter 1: The role of government in 21st Australia

Access Economics (1999), *Economic Monitor*, Canberra, August.

Australian Bureau of Statistics (1999), *Transition from Education to Work*, 6227.0, Canberra.

Beazley, K. (2000a), 'Address to the Australian Industry Group National Industry Forum', Canberra, 6 March.

Beazley, K. (2000b), 'Address to the Sydney Institute', Sydney, 13 April.

Beazley, K. and McMullan, B. (2000), 'Australia's Future Compromised — "BERD" Down Again', Media Release, Canberra, 3 July.

Birrell, R. (1999), 'Residential Relocation in Sydney and the NSW Coast Over the Period 1991 to 1996', *People and Place*, Centre for Population and Urban Research, Monash University, vol. 7, no. 2, pp. 33–47.

Commonwealth Government (1998), *Agreement on Principles for the Reform of Commonwealth-State Financial Relations*, 13 November.

Commonwealth Government (1999), *Intergovernmental Agreement on the Reform of Commonwealth-State Financial Relations*, 9 April.

Costello, P. (1999a), Statement after delivering an address at the Forecasting Conference of the Economic Society of Victoria, 19 August 1999, reported in the *Australian Financial Review*, 20 August.

Costello, P. (1999b), Transcript of interview, 'Meet the Press', National Ten Network, 30 May.

Costello, P. (1999c), 'Address to Economic Society Forecasting Conference Lunch', Park Hyatt, Melbourne, 19 August.

Costello, P. (2000), Transcript of interview, on Radio 3AW, 24 January.

Department of the Parliamentary Library (2000), 'Are Incomes Becoming More Unequal? Are Real Incomes Increasing?' *Current Issues Brief*, no. 15, Canberra, 20 June.

Dixon, P. (1999), 'The GST: A Failure in Policy Formulation', Centre of Policy Studies, Monash University, Melbourne, 22 June.

Downer, A. (2000), Press Release, 30 March.

Gregory, R. G. and Hunter, B. (1995), 'The Macro Economy and the Growth of Ghettos and Urban Poverty in Australia', Discussion Paper No. 325, Centre for Economic Policy Research, The Australian National University, Canberra, April.

Hancock, K. (1930), *Australia*, Jacaranda, reprinted in 1961.

Hewson, J. (2000), 'GST: Now for the Hard Part', *Australian Financial Review*, 30 June.

Howard, J. (2000), Transcript of interview on Radio 3AW, 11 February.

Howard, J. (2000b), Hansard of Proceedings, House of Representatives, 4 July.

Murphy, C. (1999), 'Modelling a New Tax System (ANTS) — Comparing Monash and MM303', Report to the Senate Select Committee on a New Tax System, Canberra, 14 February.

NATSEM (1997), 'The Suffering Middle: Trends in Income Inequality in Australia 1982 to 1993–94', Discussion paper no. 21, Canberra.

NATSEM (2000), 'Advance Australia Where', series, *Australian*, June 17–24.

OECD (1998), *Education at a Glance*, Paris.

OECD (1999a), *Report on the Outlook for the Future of Governance*, Public Management Committee, Paris, March.

OECD (1999b), 'The Future: What Policy-makers Have to Think About', *OECD Observer*, Paris, Summer.

Vinson, A. (1999), *Unequal in Life: The Distribution of Social Disadvantage in Victoria and New South Wales*, The Ignatius Centre, August.

Widom, C. (1992), 'The Cycle of Violence', Child Protection Seminar Series no. 5, NSW Child Protection Council, Sydney.

Williams, P. (1997), *Progress of the National Drug Strategy: Key National Indicators. Evaluation of the National Drug Strategy: Statistical Supplement.*

Chapter 2: Bridging the divide between GDP and quality of life

ABS Various Publications.

ACTU (1999), *Employment Security & Working Hours — A National Survey of Current Workplace Issues*, ACTU, Melbourne, July.

Baumol, W. and Oates, W. (1988), *The Theory of Environmental Policy*, Cambridge University Press.

Campbell, I. (1999), 'Reduced Working-Time and Unemployment: European Experiences', Paper for the 6th National Conference on Unemployment, Newcastle, 23–24 September.

Crowe, M. (1996), *An Assessment of the Impacts of Restructuring Payroll Tax*, New South Wales Treasury Research and Information Paper, TRP 97–4.

Crowe, M. (1999), *The Case for Payroll Tax*, New South Wales Treasury Information Paper, TRP 99–3.

Eckersley, R. (1999), *Quality of Life in Australia: An Analysis of Public Perceptions*, The Australia Institute, Discussion Paper no. 23.

Gabbitas, O. and Eldridge, D. (1998), *Directions for State Tax Reform*, Productivity Commission Staff Research Paper, Ausinfo.

Harcourt, T. (1998), 'Working-Time Arrangements and Economic Security: Key Policy Issues for the Labour Movement', Speech at ALP Academic Forum, Parliament House, Canberra, 5 March.

Mackay, H. (1999), *The Mind and Mood of Australia '99*, The Mackay Report.

Mankiw, N. G., Gans, J. and King, S. (1999), *Principles of Microeconomics*, Harcourt Brace and Company, Australia.

Pope, J., Fayle, R. and Chen, D. L. (1993), *The Compliance Costs of Employment Related Taxation in Australia*, Australian Tax Research Foundation.

Ryan, M. (1995), *What Future for Payroll Taxes in Australia?* Commonwealth Treasury Research Paper no. 10, Australian Government Publishing Service.

Chapter 3: The contract state and the public interest

Alford, J. (1993), 'Towards a New Public Management Model: Beyond "Managerialism" and its Critics', *Australian Journal of Public Administration*, vol. 52, no. 2, pp. 135–148.

Alford, J. (1998), 'A Public Management Road Less Travelled: Clients as Co-Producers of Public Services', *Australian Journal of Public Administration*, vol. 57, no. 4, pp. 128–137.

Althaus, C. (1997), 'The Application of Agency Theory to Public Sector Management' in G. Davis, B. Sullivan and A. Yeatman (eds), *The New Contractualism?* Macmillan, pp. 137–154.

Barry, B. (1965), *Political Argument*, Routledge and Kegan Paul.

Blair, T. (1998), *The Third Way: New Politics for the New Century*, London, Fabian Society.

Boston, J. (1995), 'Inherently Governmental Functions and the Limits to Contracting Out' in Boston, J. (ed.), *The State Under Contract*, Bridget Williams Books, pp. 78–111.

Brennan, D. (1998), 'Government and Civil Society: Restructuring Community Services', in P. Smyth and B. Cass (eds.), *Contesting the Australian Way: States, Markets and Civil Society*, Cambridge University Press, pp. 124–137.

Cassinelli, C. W. (1962), 'The Public Interest in Political Ethics, in C. J. Friedrich (ed.), *Nomos V: The Public Interest*, Atherton Press, pp. 44–53.

Cox, E. (1995), *A Truly Civil Society*, ABC Books.

Davis (1997), 'Implications, Consequences and Futures', in G. Davis, B. Sullivan, and A. Yeatman (eds.), *The New Contractualism?*, Macmillan, pp. 224–238.

Davis, G. and Wood, T. (1998), 'Is There a Future for Contracting in the Australian Public Sector?', *Australian Journal of Public Administration*, vol. 57, no. 4, pp. 85–97.

Faux, J. (1999), 'Lost on the Third Way', *Dissent*, vol. 46, no. 2, pp. 67–76.

Finlayson, A. (1999), 'Third Way Theory', *The Political Quarterly*, vol. 70, no. 3, pp. 271–279.

Friedrich, C. J. (ed.), 1962. *Nomos V: The Public Interest*, Atherton Press.

Giddens, A. (1998), *The Third Way: The Renewal of Social Democracy*, Polity Press.

Goodin, R. E. (1996), 'Institutionalizing the Public Interest: The Defense of Deadlock and Beyond', *American Political Science Review*, vol. 90, no. 2, pp. 331–343.

Gregory, R. (1995), 'The Peculiar Tasks of Public Management: Towards Conceptual Discrimination', *Australian Journal of Public Administration*, vol. 54, no. 2, pp. 171–183.

Gunn, J. A. W. (1989), 'Public Interest', in T. Bal, J. Farr and R. L. Hanson (eds), *Political Innovation and Conceptual Change*, Cambridge University Press, pp. 194–210.

Held, V. (1970), *The Public Interest and Individual Interests*, Basic Books.

Hood, C. C. (1986), *Administrative Analysis*, Wheatsheaf Books.

Hood, C. C. (1997), 'Which Contract State? Four Perspectives on Over-Outsourcing for Public Services', *Australian Journal of Public Administration*, vol. 56, no. 3, pp. 120–131.

Mansbridge, J. (1998), 'On the Contested Nature of the Public Good', in W. W. Powell and E. S. Clemens (eds.), *Private Action and the Public Good*, Yale University Press, pp. 3–9.

Moore, M. (1995), *Creating Public Value: Strategic Management in Government*, Harvard University Press.

Muetzelfeldt, M. (1994), 'Contracts, Politics and Society', in J. Alford and D. O'Neill (eds.), *The Contract State: Public Management and the Kennett Government*, Deakin University, pp. 136–157.

Mulgan, R. (2000), 'Perspectives on 'the Public Interest'', *Canberra Bulletin of Public Administration*, no. 95, pp. 5–12.

OECD (Organisation for Economic Cooperation and Development) (1997), *In Search of Results: Performance Management Practices*, Paris, OECD.

Painter, C. (1999), 'Public Service Reform from Thatcher to Blair: A Third Way', *Parliamentary Affairs*, vol. 52, no. 1, pp. 94–112.

Painter, M. (1996) 'Economic Policy, Market Liberalism and the "End of Australian Politics",' *Australian Journal of Political Science*, vol. 31, no. 3, pp. 287–300.

Putnam, R. D. (1993), *Making Democracy Work: Civic Traditions in Modern Italy*, Princeton University Press.

Ryan, A. (1999), 'Britain: Recycling the Third Way', *Dissent*, vol. 46, no. 2, pp. 77–80.

Shields, J. and Evans, B. M. (1998), *Shrinking the State: Globalization and Public Administration 'Reform'*, Fernwood Publishing.

Yeatman, A. (1995) 'Interpreting Contemporary Contractualism', in J. Boston (ed.), *The State Under Contract*, Bridget Williams Books, pp. 124–139.

Yeatman, A. (1997), 'Contract, Status and Personhood', in G. Davis, B. Sullivan and A. Yeatman (eds.), *The New Contractualism?*, Macmillan, pp. 39–56.

Chapter 4: Rethinking the public: paying attention to citizens and clients

Ayres, I, and Braithwaite, J. (1992), *Responsive Regulation: Transcending the Deregulation Debate*, Oxford University Press.

Bardach, E. and Kagan, R. (1982), *Going by the Book: The Problem of Regulatory Unreasonableness*, Temple University Press.

Blau, P. (1964), *Exchange and Power in Social Life*, Wiley.

Ekeh, P. (1974), *Social Exchange Theory: The Two Traditions*, Heinemann.

Diver, C. (1980), 'A Theory of Regulatory Enforcement', *Public Policy*, vol. 28, no. 3, pp. 257–299.

Goodin, R. (1998), 'More Than Anyone Bargained For: Beyond the Welfare Contract', *Ethics and International Affairs*, vol. 12, pp. 141–158.

Grabosky, P. (1995), 'Counterproductive Regulation', *International Journal of the Sociology of Law*, vol. 23, pp. 347–369.

Hayes, J. and Nutman, P. (1981), *Understanding the Unemployed: The Psychological Effects of Unemployment*, Tavistock.

Hughes, O. (1994), *Public Management and Administration: An Introduction*, MacMillan.

Jahoda, M. (1981), 'Work, Employment and Unemployment: Values, Theories and Approaches in Social Research,' *American Psychologist*, vol. 36, pp. 184–191.

Kelvin, P. and Jarrett, J. (1985), *Unemployment: its Social Psychological Effects*, Cambridge University Press.

Layard, R., Nickell, S. and Jackman, R. (1991), *Unemployment: Macroeconomic Performance and the Labour Market*, Oxford University Press.

Le Grand, J., Propper, C. and Robinson, R. (1992), *The Economics of Social Problems*, 3rd edition, MacMillan.

Levi-Strauss, C. (1949/1969), *The Elementary Structures of Kinship*, Beacon Press.

Lipsky, M. (1980), *Street-Level Bureaucracy: Dilemmas of the Individual in Public Services*, Russell Sage Foundation.

Major, J. (1991), *The Citizen's Charter: Raising the Standard*, HMSO.

Marshall, T. H. (1950/1992), *Citizenship and Social Class and Other Essays*, Cambridge University Press.

Moore, M. (1994), 'Public Value as the Focus of Strategy', *Australian Journal of Public Administration*, vol. 53, no. 3, pp. 296–303.

OECD (Organisation for Economic Co-operation and Development) (1987), *Administration as Service: The Public as Client*, Paris, OECD.

Office of Corrections (1994), *Unit Operational Plan 1994–5*, Melbourne, Office of Corrections.

Osborne, D. and Gaebler, T. (1992), *Reinventing Government: How the Entrepreneurial Spirit is Transforming the Public Sector*, Plume.

Patterson, P. (1998), 'Market Metaphors and Political Vocabularies', *Public Productivity and Management Review*, vol. 22, no. 2, pp. 220–231.

Pegnato, J. (1997), 'Is a Citizen a Customer?', *Public Productivity and Management Review*, vol. 20, no. 4, pp. 387–394.

Pollitt, C. (1990), *Managerialism and the Public Services: The Anglo-American Experience*, Basil Blackwell.

Savas, E. (1987), *Privatization: The Key to Better Government*, Chatham House.

Schachter, H. L. (1997), *Reinventing Government or Reinventing Ourselves: The Role of Citizen Owners in Making a Better Government*, State University of New York Press.

Scrivens, E. (1991), 'Is there a Role for Marketing in the Public Sector?', *Public Money and Management*, Summer, pp. 17–23.

Self, P. (1993), *Government by the Market?: The Politics of Public Choice*, Macmillan.

Sparrow, M. (1994), *Imposing Duties: Government's Changing Approach to Compliance*, Praeger.

Tyler, T. (1990), *Why People Obey the Law*, Yale University Press.

Wanna, J., O'Faircheallaigh, C. and Weller, P. (1992), *Public Sector Management in Australia*, Macmillan.

Wilson, J. Q. (1989), *Bureaucracy: What Government Agencies Do and How They Do It*, Basic Books.

Wittmer, D. (1991), 'Serving the People or Serving for Pay: Reward Preferences Among Government, Hybrid Sector and Business Managers', *Public Productivity and Management Review*, vol. 14, no. 4, pp. 369–383.

Chapter 5: Governing diversity: prospects for putting the public back into public service

Capling, A., Considine, M. and Crozier, M. (1998), *Australian Politics in the Global Era*, Longman.

Considine, M. (1996), 'Market Bureaucracy: the Changing Form of Social Administration in Australia', in A. Farrar and J. Inglis (eds), *Keeping It Together: State and Civil Society in Australia*, Pluto Press, pp. 76–91.

Craig, J. (1955), *A History of Red Tape: An Account of the Origin and Development of the Civil Service*, MacDonald and Evans.

Donahue, J. (1989), *The Privatisation Decision: Public Ends, Private Means*, Basic Books.

Ernst, J., Glanville, L. and Murfitt, P. (1997), *Breaking the Contract?* Victoria University of Technology.

Foster C. and Plowden, F. (1996), *The State Under Stress*, Open University Press.

Handler, J. (1996), *Down from Bureaucracy: The Ambiguity of Privatisation and Empowerment*, Princeton University Press.

King, S. and Maddock, R. (1996) *Unlocking the Infrastructure: The Reform of Public Utilities in Australia*, Allen & Unwin.

Pack, J. (1991), 'The Opportunities and Constraints of Privatisation', in W. Gormley (ed.), *Privatisation and its Alternatives*, University of Wisconsin Press.

Reeves, W. P. (1902), *State Experiments in Australia and New Zealand*, Grant Richards.

Spann, R. N. (1973), *Public Administration in Australia*, NSW Government Printer.

Van Horn, C. (1991), 'The Myths and Realities of Privatisation', in W. Gormley, (ed.), *Privatisation and its Alternatives*, University of Wisconsin Press.

Chapter 6: Putting the social back into socialism...

Bowden, P. (1997), *Caring: Gender-Sensitive Ethics*, Routledge.

Cox, E. (1995), *A Truly Civil Society*, ABC Books.

Cox, E. (2000), 'Feminism and Citizenship', in W. Hudson and J. Kane (eds.), *Rethinking Australian Citizenship*, Cambridge University Press, pp. 56–65.

Durkheim, E. (1982), *The Rules of Sociological Method*, Macmillan.

Hobbes, T. (1968), *Leviathan*, Penguin.

Mansbridge, J. (1990), 'On the Relation of Altruism and Self-Interest', in J. Mansbridge *Beyond Self-Interest*, The University of Chicago Press.

Mauss, M. (1996), *The Gift — Forms and Functions of Exchange in Archaic Societies*, Routledge and Kegan Paul.

Offe, C. (1998a), 'Personal Communication', paper presented at a Sydney seminar.

Offe, C. (1998b), 'Present Historical Transitions and Some Basic Design Options for Societal Institutions', paper based on lecture to the Congress on Society and the Reform of the State, Sao Paulo, March 26–29.

Putnam, R. (1993), *Work: Civic Traditions Making Democracy in Modern Italy*, Princeton University Press.

Rousseau, J. J. (1947), *The Social Contract*, Oxford University Press.

The Russell Sage Foundation (1997–99), Series of research papers on the game theory aspects of trust, offered by the Working Group on the construction and maintenance of trust.

Toennies, F. (1974), *Community and Association*, Routledge and Kegan Paul.

Chapter 7: Unchaining the ABC

ABC National Advisory Council, ABC Corporate Affairs (1997) *Attracting a Youth Audience.*

ABC Youth Symposium (1996) *Report.*

Cole, G. D. H. (1928), *The Payment of Wages: A Study in Payment by Results under the Wage-system*, G. Allen & Unwin.

Cole, G. D. H. (1935), *The Simple Case For Socialism*, Gollancz.

Department of Communications and the Arts (1994), *Creative Nation: Commonwealth Cultural Policy, October 1994*, Department of Communications and the Arts.

Davies, A. (2000), 'Axe falls on news and TV as Shier unveils vision', *Sydney Morning Herald*, 25 October, p. 3.

Dempster, Q. (2000), *Death Struggle*, Allen & Unwin.

Hage, G. (1998), *White Nation: Fantasies of White Supremacy in a Multicultural Society*, Pluto Press.

Heyward, M. (1993), *The Ern Malley Affair*, University of Queensland Press.

Mansfield, B. (1997) *The Challenge of a Better ABC*, AGPS.

Morris, W. and Bax, E. B. (1896), *Socialism: Its Growth & Outcome*, Longman.

Moore, Tony (1997), 'These Babies Stopped Booming in 1975', *Australian*, February 20, Opinion page.

Ramsay, A. (2000), 'Revealed: Colourful Language Behind 8c a Day ABC', *Sydney Morning Herald*, 28 October, p. 26.

Rees, S. and Rodley, G. (eds) (1995), *The Human Costs of Managerialism: Advocating the Recovery of Humanity*, Pluto Press.

Semmler, C. (2000), 'In the Belly of the Whale', review of G. Stone *Compulsive Viewing: The Inside Story of Packer's Nine Network*, in *Quadrant*, October, p. 79.

Tanner, L. (1999), *Open Australia*, Pluto Press.

Wark, M. (19??), *Celebrities, Culture and Cyberspace: the Light on the Hill in a Postmodern World*, Pluto Press.

Webb, B. and S. (1897), *Industrial Democracy*, Longman.

Chapter 8: Policy: the new 'hard' politics

Baer, K. (2000), *Reinventing Democrats: The Politics of Liberalism from Reagan to Clinton*, Kansas University Press.

Cain, J. (1995), *John Cain's Years*, Melbourne University Press.

Denham, A. and Garnett, M. (1998), *British Think Tanks and the Climate of Opinion*, UCL Press.

Demos (website at www.demos.co.uk).

Economist (1997), 'New Labour Gurus: The Apostles of Modernity', 25 October.

Economist (1999), 'The Cafitiere Theory of Government', 21 August.

Giddens, A.(19??), *The Third Way: The Renewal of Social Democracy*, Polity Press.

Glover, D. (2000), 'Machiavelli for a New Millennium', *Fabian Newsletter*, vol.40, no.1, March, pp. 4–5.

Lloyd, J. (1999), 'Falling Out', *Prospect*, October, www.prospect-magazine.co.uk/

McAuley (2000a), 'Dumbing Down in Canberra: A Guide to the Public Service Reform Industry', *Dissent*, vol. 2, Autumn/Winter, pp. 31–7.

McAuley (2000b), 'Dumbing Down in Canberra: A Guide to the Public Service Reform Industry', part 2, *Dissent*, forthcoming.

McKew, J. (2000), Interview with John Hay, *Bulletin*, 11 April.

Menadue, J. L. (1999), *Things You Learn Along the Way*, David Lovell Publishing.

Morris, D. (1999), *The New Prince: Machiavelli Updated for the Twenty-First Century*, Renaissance Books.

New Democrat (online magazine at www.dicppi.org).

Patmore, G. and Glover, D. (1999), *New Voices for Social Democracy: Labor Essays 1999–2000*, Pluto Press.

Policy.com (at www.policy.com).

Reich, R. B.(19??), *The Work of Nations: preparing ourselves for 21st century capitalism*, Knopf.

Scott, A. (2000), *Running on Empty: 'Modernising' the British and Australian Labour Parties*, Pluto Press.

Stiglitz, J. (2000), Debate: 'Boosting the Net Economy', (at www.netecon2000.com).

U.K. Government (1999), *Modernising Government White Paper*, March (at www.citu.gov.uk/moderngov/whitepaper/moderngov.pdf.

Chapter 9: Tackling social exclusion

Adams, P. and Meagher, G. (1999), *Australia's Workforce Trends to 2010: Forecasts from the Monash Model*, Centre of Policy Studies, Monash University.

Ainley, J., Malley, J. and Lamb, S. (1997), *Thematic Review of the Transition from Initial Education to Working Life*, Australian Council for Educational Research, Canberra.

Australian Bureau of Statistics (1999a), *Use of the Internet by Householders*, 8147.0, ABS, Canberra.

Australian Bureau of Statistics (1999b), *Job Quality and Churning*, 6293.0, ABS, Canberra.

Australian Bureau of Statistics (1997), *Labour Force, Australia*, 6203.0, ABS, Canberra.

Begley, S. (2000), 'Decoding the Human Body', *Newsweek*, 10 April, pp. 32–39.

Bentley, T. (1998), *Learning Beyond the Classroom: Education for a Changing World*, Routledge.

Bentley, T. and Gurumurthy, R (1999), *Destination Unknown: Engaging with the Problems of Marginalised Youth*, Demos.

Berry, M., Jackson, J., Johnson, L., Kerkin, K. and Winter, I. (1996), 'The Production of Outer Suburbia: Report to the Australian Housing and Research Council', Report no. 198.

Birch, D. (1997), 'Do You Take Cash?' in I. Christie and H. Perry, (eds.), *The Wealth and Poverty of Networks: Tackling Social Exclusion*, Demos Collection 12, Demos, pp. 22–4.

Blair, T. (1997), 'Bringing Britain Together', Speech delivered at Stockwell Park School, Lambeth, on 8 December 1997.

Budge, T. (1996), 'Population Decline in Victoria and Tasmania' in P. Newton and M. Bell (eds), *Population Shift: Mobility and Change in Australia*, AGPS, pp. 192–204.

Bynner, J. (1998), 'Use of Longitudinal Data in the Study of Social Exclusion', Paper prepared for an OECD expert seminar held on 22–23 January 1998, OECD Centre for Educational Research and Innovation, Paris.

Castleman, B. (1992), 'Changes in the Australian Commonwealth Departmental Machinery of Government 1928–1982', Ph.D Thesis, Faculty of Social Sciences, Deakin University.

Castleman, B. (1995), 'The Hawke and Keating Departmental Machinery of Government Changes: Patterns and Prospects', Parliamentary Research Paper 18 1994/95, Department of the Parliamentary Library, Canberra.

Chudleigh, J. (1999), 'Leadership Challenges: The Changing Structure and Operating Environment of Agriculture', in *ABARE, Outlook 99: Agriculture*, vol. 2, ABARE, Canberra.

Combes, J. (1998), 'Social Exclusion', Paper prepared for an

OECD expert seminar held on 22–23 January 1998, OECD Centre for Educational Research and Innovation, Paris.

Commission of Inquiry Into Poverty (1975), *Poverty in Australia, First Main Report*, AGPS, vol. 1.

Craik, W. (1999), 'Regional Australia Under Stress', Australia Unlimited: Proceedings, the *Australian*.

Crane, J. (ed.), (1998) *Social Programs that Work*, Russell Sage Foundation.

Currie, J. and Thomas, D. (1995), 'Does Head Start Make a Difference?', *American Economic Review*, vol. 85, no. 3, pp. 341–364.

Danziger, S. and Waldfogel, J. (2000), *Investing in Children: What Do We Know? What Should We Do?*, CASE Paper 34, Centre for the Analysis of Social Exclusion, London School of Economics.

Department of Family and Community Services (2000), *The Future of Welfare in the 21st Century — People with Disabilities*, FACS, Canberra.

Dusseldorp, J. (1999), *Australia's Youth: From Risk to Opportunity. Practices and Potential of Community Partnerships*, Victorian Industry Education Partnership Forum, Melbourne, 27 October 1999.

Etzioni, A. (1993), *The Spirit of Community: Rights, Responsibilities and the Communitarian Agenda*, Crown Publishers.

Fincher, R. and Wulff, M. (1998), 'The Locations of Poverty and Disadvantage', in R. Fincher and J. Nieuwenhuysen (eds), *Australian Poverty: Then and Now*, Melbourne University Press, pp. 144–164.

Foster, L. and Hawthorne, L. (1998), 'Poverty, Education and Training', in R. Fincher and J. Nieuwenhuysen (eds) *Australian Poverty: Then and Now*, Melbourne University Press, pp. 203–219.

Fukuyama, F. (1996), *Trust: The Social Virtues and the Creation of Prosperity*, Penguin Books.

Gardiner-Garden, J. (1989), 'Multiculturalism', Parliamentary Research Paper, Department of the Parliamentary Library, Canberra.

Garnaut, J., Lindsay, R., Connell, P. and Curren, B. (2000), 'Country Australia: Influences on Population and Employment', in ABARE, *Outlook 2000: Agriculture and Regional Australia, Vol 2*, ABARE, Canberra.

Geyer, R. (1999), 'Can EU Social Policy Save the Social Exclusion Unit and Vice Versa?' *Politics*, vol. 19, no. 3, pp. 159–164.

Gilley, T. and Taylor, J. (1995), *Unequal Lives? Low Income and the Life Chances of Children*, Brotherhood of St Laurence.

Granovetter, M. (1973), 'The strength of weak ties', *American Journal of Sociology*, vol. 78, pp. 1360–80.

Gregg, P. (1999), 'The Impact of Unemployment and Job Loss on

Future Earnings', in *Persistent Poverty and Lifetime Inequality: The Evidence: Report of a Seminar Organised by HM Treasury and CASE,* CASE Report 5, Centre for Analysis of Social Exclusion, London.

Gregory, B. and Hunter, B. (1994), 'The Spatial Structure of the Labour Market', Paper presented to the Metropolitan Roundtable, 17–18 March 1994, Canberra.

Gregory, B. and Hunter, B. (1995), 'The Macro Economy and the Growth of Ghettos and Urban Poverty in Australia', Discussion Paper 325, Centre for Economic Policy Research, Australian National University.

Gregory, B. and Sheehan, P. (1998), 'Poverty and the Collapse of Full Employment' in R. Fincher and J. Nieuwenhuysen (eds) *Australian Poverty: Then and Now,* Melbourne University Press, Melbourne, pp. 103–126.

Hall, P. (1997), *Social Capital in Britain,* Centre for European Studies, Harvard University.

Hawke, R. and Howe, B. (1990), *Towards a Fairer Australia: Social Justice Strategy Statement 1990–92,* Australian Government Publishing Service.

Hawker, D. (1999), *Regional Banking Services: Money Too Far Away,* House of Representatives Standing Committee on Economics, Finance and Public Administration, Canberra.

IBIS (2000), *K7321 Banks,* vol 7, February 2000.

Istance, D. (1997), 'Education and Social Exclusion', *OECD Observer,* no. 208.

Jencks, C. (1992), *Rethinking Social Policy: Race, Poverty, and the Underclass,* Harvard University Press.

Jones, A. and Smyth, P. (1999), 'Social Exclusion: A New Framework for Australian Social Policy Analysis?', Paper presented at the 26th AASW National Conference, September 1999.

Karoly, L., Greenwood, P., Everingham, S., Hoube, J., Kilburn, M., Rydall, C., Sanders, M. and Chiesa, J. (1998), *Investing in Our Children: What we Know and Don't Know About the Costs and Benefits of Early Childhood Interventions,* RAND.

Keays, D. (1999), 'The Legal Implications of Genetic Testing: Insurance, Employment and Privacy', *Journal of Law and Medicine,* vol. 6, pp. 357–372.

King, A. (1999), *The Cost to Australia of Early School Leaving,* National Centre for Social and Economic Modelling and Dusseldorp Skills Forum.

KPMG (1999), *Review of the Social Exclusion Unit,* KPMG Consultants, London.

Kruger, D. (1997), 'Access Denied', in I. Christie and H. Perry (eds) *The Wealth and Poverty of Networks: Tackling Social Exclusion,* Demos Collection 12, Demos, pp. 20–1.

Latham, M. (1998), *Civilising Global Capital: New Thinking for Australian Labor,* Allen and Unwin.

Maher, C. (1999), 'Locational Disadvantage and Concentrations: A Review and Evaluation of the Findings', in K. O'Connor (ed), *Houses and Jobs in Cities and Regions: Research in Honour of Chris Maher,* University of Queensland Press, pp. 17–58.

Maher, C. and Stimson, R. (1994), *Regional Population Growth in Australia,* AGPS.

Martin, P., Lubulwa, M., Riley, C. and Sepideh, H. (2000), 'Farm Performance: Managing Risks', in ABARE, *Outlook 2000: Agriculture and Regional Australia, Vol. 2,* ABARE.

Melbourne Institute of Applied Economic and Social Research (2000), *Poverty Lines: Australia, September Quarter 1999.*

Meredyth, D. et al (1999), *Real Time: Computers, Change and Schooling,* Australian Key Centre for Cultural and Media Policy, Canberra.

Mingione, E. (1997), 'Enterprise and Exclusion', in I. Christie and H. Perry, (eds) *The Wealth and Poverty of Networks: Tackling Social Exclusion,* Demos Collection 12, Demos, pp. 10–12.

Organisation for Economic Co-operation and Development (OECD) (1988), *The Long-term Unemployed and Measures to Assist Them,* Labour Market and Social Policy Occasional Papers No 7, OECD, Paris.

Organisation for Economic Co-operation and Development (OECD) (1996), *Lifelong Learning for All,* OECD, Paris.

Organisation for Economic Co-operation and Development (OECD) (1997), *Labour Market Policies: New Challenges. Policies for Low-paid Workers and Unskilled Job Seekers,* OECD, Paris.

Oxley, H. (1999), 'Poverty Dynamics in Four OECD Countries', in *Persistent Poverty and Lifetime Inequality: The Evidence. Report of a Seminar Organised by HM Treasury and CASE,* CASE Report 5, Centre for Analysis of Social Exclusion, London, pp. 22–27.

Perri 6, P (1997), 'Social Exclusion: Time to be Optimistic', in I. Christie and H. Perry (eds), *The Wealth and Poverty of Networks: Tackling Social Exclusion,* Demos Collection 12, Demos, pp. 3–9.

Perri 6, P (1998), *The Future of Privacy, Vol 1: Private Life and Public Policy,* Demos.

Perri 6, P, Leat, D., Seltzer, K. and Stoker, G. (1999), *Governing in the Round: Strategies for Holistic Government,* Demos.

People Together Project (1996), *'And Then My Dad Got the Sack': The Report of the People Together Project, Moe Community Audit,* Moe, Victoria.

Price Waterhouse (1997), *Mapping Local Authority Estates Using the Index of Local Conditions,* Department of the Environment, London.

Probert, B. (1999), 'Fast Capitalism, New Kinds of Jobs and Appropriate Education', Australia Unlimited: Proceedings, the *Australian.*

Putnam, R. (1993), *Making Democracy Work: Civic Traditions in Modern Italy*, Princeton University Press.

Putnam, R. (1995), 'Bowling Alone: America's Declining Social Capital', *Journal of Democracy*, vol. 6, no. 1, Jan., pp. 65–78.

Putnam, R. (1996), 'Who Killed Civic America?', *Prospect*, March, www.prospect-magazine.co.uk/

Raskall, P. (1995), *Who Gets What Where? Spatial Inequality Between and Within Australian Cities*, Department of Housing and Regional Development, Canberra.

St John-Brooks, C. (1997), 'Involving In', *OECD Observer*, no. 208.

Sawer, M. (1999), 'The Watchers Within: Women and the Australian State', in L. Hancock (ed) *Women, Public Policy and the State*, Macmillan, pp. 36–53.

Schneider, J. (1997), 'Welfare-to-network' in I. Christie and H. Perry (eds), *The Wealth and Poverty of Networks: Tackling Social Exclusion*, Demos Collection 12, Demos, pp. 30–2.

Sen, A. (1985), 'A Sociological Approach to the Measurement of Poverty: A Reply to Professor Peter Townsend', *Oxford Economic Papers*.

Seligman, A. (1997), *The Problem of Trust*, Princeton University Press.

Social Exclusion Unit (1998), *Bringing Britain Together: A National Strategy for Neighbourhood Renewal*, Cm 4045, SEU, London.

Smith, G. (1999), *Area-based Initiatives: The Rationale and Options for Area-targeting*, CASE Paper 25, Centre for the Analysis of Social Exclusion, London School of Economics.

Sparkes, J. (1999), *Schools, Education and Social Exclusion*, CASE Paper 29, Centre for the Analysis of Social Exclusion, London School of Economics.

Walter, J. (1992), 'Prime Ministers and Their Staff', in P. Weller, (ed.), *Menzies to Keating: The Development of the Australian Prime Ministership*, Melbourne University Press, Melbourne, pp. 28–65.

Wilson, W. (1996), *When Work Disappears: The World of the New Urban Poor*, Alfred A Knopf.

Yates, J. and Wulff, M. (1999), *Australia's Housing Choices*, Australian Housing and Urban Research Institute, Melbourne.

Chapter 10: Connecting government

ALP National Platform (2000), Canberra.

Australian Bureau of Statistics (2000), *Use of the Internet by Householders*, 8147.0.

Australian National Audit Office (1999), *Electronic Service Delivery, Including Internet Use, by Commonwealth Government Agencies*, AGPS.

Birdsell, D. and Muzzio, D. (1999), 'Government Programs Involving Citizen Access to Internet Services', Baruch College School of Public Affairs.

Budde, P. (1999), 'Australia — High-speed access networks — x DSL'.

Clark, D. (1999) 'High Speed Data Races Home' and associated articles, *Scientific American*, October.

Communications, Electrical and Plumbing Union (1999), *Issues in Telecommunications Policy*, September 1999.

Department of Communications, Information Technology and the Arts (2000), *Commonwealth Government Support for IT & T in Australia*, AGPS.

Department of Communications, Information Technology and the Arts (1999), *Annual Report 1998–99*, AGPS.

Forman, D. (1999), 'Gilder's Law Stretches New Economy's Rubber Bandwidth', *Australian*, 15 November 1999.

Mid-Year Economic and Fiscal Outlook (1999), AGPS.

Morrison, K. (1999), 'Telstra's Ultra-Fast Access on Trial', *Sydney Morning Herald*, 21 September 1999.

National Bandwidth Inquiry Discussion Paper (1999).

National Health Information Management Advisory Council (1999), *Health Online: A Health Information Action Plan for Australia*, AGPS.

Nicholas, K. (1999), 'Telstra Gets Hip on Cable', *Sydney Morning Herald*, 15 November 1999.

Office of Government Information Technology (1998), *Annual Report*, 1997–98, AGPS

Office of Government Online (2000*)*, *Government Online — The Commonwealth Government's Strategy*.

Patrick, A. (1999), 'Telstra, the Big Spender with Strong Connections', *Financial Review*, 30 June 1999.

Stockdale, A. (n.d.), 'Government Online Implementation — Progress Reporting System and Target Adjustment', Victorian Government, unpublished Cabinet submission.

Victorian Government (2000), 'Government Logs On: Victorian Government Agency Case Studies'.

Chapter 11: Communities on-line: a practical strategy for rebuilding rural and regional communities

Beazley, K. (2000), 'Address to the Lawson Institute', Link 2000, Perth, 25 January.

Clift, S. (1998), 'Democracy is Online', www.e-democracy.org/do.

Clift, S. (1999), 'A Wired Agora: Minneapolis, Citizen Participation, the Internet and Squirrels' www.publicus.net/present/agora.html.

Davies, A. (1995), *Local Economies and Globalisation*, LEED Note Book No. 20, OECD.

Department of Transport and Regional Services (1999), *Regional Australia Summit: Proposed Strategies*, Commonwealth of Australia.

Friedman, T. (1999), *The Lexus and the Olive Tree*, Harper-CollinsPublishers, London.

Flittner, N. (1999), 'Meander Online', www.meander.tco.asn.au.

Gillard, J. (1999), 'An Australian Way: A Federal Agenda for the ALP', in G. Patmore and D. Glover (eds.), *New Voices for Social Democracy*, Pluto Press, pp. 21–34.

Haley, M. (2000), 'Poll snub for MPs', *Mercury*, 3 January, p. 1.

Hewson, J. (2000), 'Good Times Roll in the Bush', *Australian Financial Review*, 4 February, p. 25.

Higgott, S. and Reich, S. (1998), 'Globalisation and Sites of Conflict: Towards a Definition and Taxonomy', Centre for Study of Globalisation and Regionalisation, Working Paper No 01/98, University of Warwick.

Jacobs, M. (1999), 'The Third Way', www.netnexus.org/library/papers/jacobs.htm.

Jones, A. and Smyth, P. (1999), 'Social Exclusion: A New Framework for Social Policy Analysis', *Just Policy*, vol. 17, pp. 11–20.

Moisi, D. (1999), 'Globalisation: Challenges and Discontents', Paper presented at 21st Century Trust Conference, Ifrane, Morocco, 11 September.

O'Connor, K., Stimson, R., Baum, S. and Mullins, P. (1999), 'Australia's Regional Cities and Towns: Modelling Community Opportunity and Vulnerability', Paper presented at ANZRSAI Conference, Newcastle, Australia.

Puttnam D. (1999), 'Is Globalisation Americanisation?', Paper presented at 21st Century Trust Conference, Ifrane, Morocco, 11 September.

Putnam, R. (1995), 'Bowling Alone: America's Declining Social Capital', *Journal of Democracy*, vol. 6, pp. 65–78.

Reinicke, W. (1997), 'Global Public Policy', *Foreign Affairs*, vol. 76, pp. 127–137.

Scobbie, M. (1999), in 'The Third Way: Summary of the NEXUS On-line Discussion', in D. Halpern and D. Mikosz (eds), www.netnexus.org/library/papers/3way.html

Segell, G. (1997) 'The Role of the Internet in an Establishment System of Government: the United Kingdom', netnexus.org/library/papers/segell.htm.

Sen, A. (1992), *Inequality Re-Examined*, Oxford University Press, London.

Shearman, C. (1999), 'Local Connections: Making the Net Work for Neighbourhood Renewal', www.communities.org.uk/.

Sheil, H. (1999), 'Transformation: From Despair to Optimism', Centre for Rural Communities Inc, Submission to Regional Australia Summit.

Tanner, L. (1999), *Open Australia*, Pluto Press, Melbourne.

Tapscott, D. (1999), 'Growing up Digital', www.growingupdigital.com/flecho.html.

United States Department of Commerce (1999), *Falling Through the Net: Defining the Digital Divide*, A Report on the Telecommunications and Information Technology Gap in America.

Wagner, R. (1999), 'A Report on the European Union Rural Development Policy — the Leader Program', Unpublished Churchill Fellowship report.

Watts, R. (1999), 'Australia's Welfare Policy and Latham's Third Way: A Critical Commentary', *Just Policy*, vol. 17, pp. 21–31.

Chapter 12: Why Australians hate politicians: exploring the new public discontent

Abbott, T. (1998), 'The Feral Right' in R. Manne (ed.), *Two Nations: The Causes and Effects of the Rise of the One Nation Party in Australia*, Bookman Press, pp. 10–19.

Adams, P. and Burton, L., (1997), *Talkback: Emperors of the Air*, Allen & Unwin.

Anasolabehere, S. and Iyengar, S. (1995), *Going Negative: How Negative Political Advertisments Shrink and Polarize the Electorate*, The Free Press.

Bean, C., Gow, D. and McAllister, I. (1998), *D1001 Australian Election Study 1998*, Social Science Data Archives Study no.1001, ssda.anu.edu.au/perl/studies?fn=d&ss=Australian+Election+Study+1987&hn=5

Bean, C. (1993), 'Conservative Cynicism: Political Culture in Australia', *International Journal of Public Opinion Research*, vol. 5, no. 1, pp. 58–77.

Bessant, J. and Watts, R. (1999), *Sociology Australia*, Allen & Unwin.

Brown, T. (1999), 'Can't Trust Anyone These Days', *Herald-Sun*, 22 June.

Cappella, J. N. and Hall J. K. (1996), 'News Frames, Political Cynicism and Media Cynicism', *The Annals of the American Academy of Political and Social Science*, vol. 546, pp. 71–85.

Corrigan, D. (1992), 'The Media Thrives on Conflict — and Politicians Pay the Price', *St. Louis Journalism Review*, vol. 22, p. 145.

Donovan, B. (1999), 'Chooks and Politicians', *Melbourne Times*, 23 June, p. 13.

Edwards, B. and Foley, M. W. (1997), 'Social Capital and the Political Economy of Our Discontent', *American Behavioural Scientist*, vol. 40, pp. 669–79.

Evans, G. (1998), 'Politics and the Media Circus: Sideshow Alley', *Australian Quarterly*, vol. 70, p. 16.

Finsberg, B. and Shefter, M. (1999), *Politics By Other Means: Politicians, Prosecutors and the Press From Watergate to Whitewater*, W. W. Norton and Co.

Forrest, J. and Marks, G. N. (1999), 'The Mass Media, Election Campaigning and Voter Response: The Australian Experience', *Party Politics*, vol. 5, p. 99.

Gore, A. (1994), 'Cynicism or Faith: The Future of a Democratic Society', Speech delivered at Harvard University, 9 June.

Grattan, M. (1998), 'Pauline Hanson's Hijack of John Howard', in Manne, R. (ed), *Two Nations: The Causes and Effects of the Rise of the One Nation Party in Australia*, Bookman Press, pp. 75–88.

Ingelhart, R. (1997), 'Postmaterialist Values and the Erosion of Institutional Authority', in J. S. Nye Jr., P. D. Zelikow and D. C. King (eds), *Why People Don't Trust Government*, Harvard University Press, pp. 217–236.

Jaensch, D. (1995), *Election: How and Why Australia Votes*, Allen & Unwin.

Kelly, P. (1998), 'Players, Pollies and Party Games', *Australian Quarterly*, vol. 70, p. 19.

Kimball, D. C. and Patterson, S. C. (1997), 'Living Up to Expectations: Public Attitudes Toward Congress', *Journal of Politics*, vol. 59, no. 3, pp. 701–27.

Kingmann, H. and Fuchs, D. (eds) (1995), *Citizens and the State*, Oxford University Press.

Lawe Davies, C. (1997), 'Media Publics', *Culture and Policy, vol. 8, pp.* 3–9.

Lawrence, R. Z., (1997), 'Is It Really the Economy, Stupid?' in J. S. Nye Jr., P. D. Zelikow and D. C. King (eds), *Why People Don't Trust Government*, Harvard University Press, pp. 111–133.

McAllister, I. (1998), 'Civic Education and Political Knowledge in Australia', *Australian Journal of Political Science*, vol. 33, no. 1, pp. 7–34.

McAllister, I. and Wales, M. A. (1987), *D445 Australian Election Study 1987*, Social Science Data Archives Study Number D445, ssda.anu.edu.au/perl/studies?fn=d&ss=Australian+Election+Study+1987&hn=11.

McGregor, C. (1997), *Class in Australia*, Penguin Books.

McGuinness, P. P. (1998), 'The Political Elites' Contribution to Hansonism', in R. Manne (ed.), *Two Nations: The Causes and Effects of the Rise of the One Nation Party in Australia*, Bookman Press, pp. 131–40.

Mackay, H. (1993), *Reinventing Australia: The Mind and Mood of Australia in the 1990s*, Angus and Robertson.

Mackay, H. (1998), *Mind and Mood*, Mackay Research.

Manne, R. (ed.) (1998), *Two Nations: The Causes and Effects of the Rise of the One Nation Party in Australia*, Bookman Press.

Nye, J. S. Jr., Zelikow, P. D. and King, D. C. (eds.) (1997), *Why People Don't Trust Government*, Harvard University Press.

Owen, D. (1996), 'Remote and Controlled: Media Politics in a Cynical Age', *Political Science Quarterly*, vol. 111, no. 1, pp. 178–80.

Papadakis, E. (1999), 'Constituents of Confidence and Mistrust in Australian Insititutions', *Australian Journal of Political Science*, vol. 34, no. 1, pp. 75–93.

Patterson, T. E. (1996), 'Bad News, Period: Negative Political Coverage', *PS: Political Science and Politics*, vol. 29, pp. 97–109.

Pilger, J. (1996), 'End of the Keating Myth', *New Statesman and Society*, vol. 9, p. 14.

Reider, R. (1996), 'A Skeptical View of the Cynicism Epidemic', *American Journalism Review, vol. 18, no. 5, p. 6.*

Saulwick Research (1991), D744 Saulwick Poll (June), ssda.anu.edu.au

Simons, M. (1999), *Fit to Print: Inside the Canberra Press Gallery*, UNSW Press.

Starobin, P. (1995), 'A Generation of Vipers: Journalists and the New Cyncism', *Columbia Journalism Review*, vol. 33, no. 6, pp. 25–33.

Suter, K. (1999), 'Australia: Wealth and Despair', *Contemporary Review*, vol. 274, no. 1598, pp. 137–43.

Walter, J. (1998), 'Australian Democracy and the American Century', in H. Bolitho and C. Wallace-Crabbe (eds), *Approaching Australia: Papers from the Harvard Australian Studies Symposium*, Harvard University Press, pp. 199–216.

Weaver, D. H. (1996), 'What Voters Learn from the Media', *The Annals of the American Academy of Political and Social Science*, vol. 546, pp. 34–48.

Wilson-Smith, A. (1995), 'The Moral High Ground: Do As We Say, Voters Seem to be Telling their Elected Officials', *Maclean's*, vol. 108, no. 4, pp. 18–20.

Wooldridge, M. (1998), 'A Pathology in the Political Process', in R. Manne (ed.), *Two Nations: The Causes and Effects of the Rise of the One Nation Party in Australia*, Bookman Press, pp. 178–92.

Woodward, D., Parkin, A. and Summers, J. (1997), *Government, Politics, Power and Policy in Australia* (6th ed.), Longman Cheshire Pty Ltd.

Chapter 13: Education for democratic citizenship: the importance of civics education in the era of economic rationalism

Australian Education Council Review Committee (Brian Finn, Chair) (1991), *Young People's Participation in Post-Compulsory Education and Training (Finn Review)*, AGPS.

Australian Vice Chancellor's Committee (1997), *Submission to the Review of Higher Education Financing and Policy: Australia's Future: Investing in Higher Education (West Review)*, AV-CC.

Back, K., Davis, D. and Olsen, A. (1996), 'Internationalisation and Higher Education: Goals and Strategies', IDP Education Australia, Evaluations and Investigations Program Higher Education Division, DEETYA.

Baker, C. and Baker, J. (1997), 'What does Australian Citizenship Mean Today? A Review of Recent Research and Scholarly Literature', Monash University AOL Democracy www.arts.monash.edu.au/ncas/abctest/rn/civics/abc/citizen-meaning.html

Bauman, Z. (1988), *Freedom*, Open University Press.

Bauman, Z. (1993), *Postmodern Ethics*, Blackwell.

Beck, U., Giddens, A. and Lasch, S. (1994), *Reflexive Modernisation: Politics, Tradition and Aesthetics in the Modern Social Order*, Polity Press.

Blake, L. J. (ed.) (1973), *Vision and Realisation — A Centenary History of State Education in Victoria*, Education Department of Victoria.

Bobbio, N. (1987), *The Future of Democracy: A Defence of the Rules of the Game*, Polity Press.

Bourdieu, P. (1977), *Outline of a Theory of Practice*, Cambridge University Press.

Bourdieu, P. (1993), 'The Field of Cultural Production', in R. Johnson, *The Field of Cultural Production: Essays on Art and Literature*, Columbia University Press, pp. 29–73.

Bruce, D. (1993), 'Inequities Continue in NZ Schools Despite Significant Education Reforms', *Age*, 3 August, pp. 13–14.

Bulletin (1961), 'Plain English', July 29, p. 11.

Carey, A. (1995), *Taking the Risk Out of Democracy*, UNSW Press.

Civics Expert Group (CEG) (1994), *Whereas the People... Civics and Citizenship Education, Report of the Civics Expert Group*, AGPS.

Coombs, P. H. (1968), *The World Educational Crisis; A Systems Analysis*, Oxford University Press.

Curriculum Corporation (1998), 'Discovering Democracy', Carlton South, Victoria, Curriculum Corporation (Australia).

Cunningham, S., Tapsall, S., Ryan, Y., Stedman, L., Bagdon, K. and Flew, T. (1998), *New Media and Borderless Education, A Review of the Convergence between Global Media Networks and Higher Education Provision Evaluations and Investigations Program*, Higher Education Division, DEETYA.

Dawkins, J. (1988), *Higher Education: A Policy Statement* (White Paper), AGPS.

Dawkins, J. (1992), 'Post-Compulsory Education and Training: The National Challenge', *Unicorn, Journal of the Australian College of Advanced Education*, vol. 18, no. 1, pp. 7–12.

Department of Employment Education Training and Youth Affairs (DEETYA) (1998), *Literacy for All: The Challenge for Australian Schools: Commonwealth Literacy Policies for Australian Schools*, Australian Schooling Monograph Series; no. 1, 48, Canberra.

Ellmore, D., Olson, S. and Smith, P. (1998), 'Reinventing Education The Technology Is Now!' (Paper presented at the *Reinventing Education The Technology Is Now!* conference, USA, 10–12 May 1993).

Employment and Skills Formation Council (Laurie Carmichael,

Chair) (1992), *The Australian Vocational Certificate Training System: Report of the Employment and Skills Formation Council*, AGPS.

Held, D. (1989), 'Citizenship and Autonomy', in *Political Theory And The Modern State*, Polity Press, pp. 190–197.

Hughes, P. (1995), 'Internationalisation of Education and Curricula for the Twenty-first Century,' *Education, Research and Perspectives*, vol. 22, no. 2 (December), pp. 1–16.

IMF (1997), 'World Economic Outlook', World Economic and Financial Surveys, International Monetary Fund, www.imf.organ/external/pubs/wcomay/010VERV.htm.

Kymlicka, W. and Norman, W. (1994), 'Return of the Citizen: A Survey of Recent Work on Citizenship Theory', *Ethics*, vol. 104, no. 2, pp. 352–381.

Marginson, S. (1997), 'To Market, to Market in Learning', the *Age* Education Magazine, www.theage.com.au/daily/971117/education_mag/mag5.html.

Mayer Committee (Eric Mayer, Chair) (1992), *Employment-related Key Competencies: A Proposal for Consultation*, Australian Education Council.

Ministerial Council on Education Employment Training and Youth Affairs (MCEETYA) (1998), *Australia's Common and Agreed Goals for Schooling the Twenty-First Century: A Review of the 1989 Common and Agreed Goals for Schooling in Australia (the Hobart Declaration)*, A Discussion Paper, Melbourne, MCEETYA, 7.

McGaw, B. (1996), *Their Future: Options for Reform of the Higher School Certificate*, Sydney, DETC (Summary).

Murphy, D. (1998), *CHED Flexible Learning Guide*, Monash Centre for Higher Education Development, www.adm.monash.edu.au/ched/index.html.

Open Learning Technology Corporation (OLTC) (1996), 'Teachers, Educational Learning and Professional Development', netspot.com.au/oltc/crt/intro1.htm.

Organisation for Economic Co-operation and Development (OECD) (1997), *Thematic Review of the First Years of Tertiary Education Australia*, Directorate for Education, Employment, Labour and Social Affairs, OECD.

Patrick, K. (1997) 'Internationalising Curriculum', Paper presented at the HERDSA Conference, RMIT, Australia, 1997.

Print, M. (1996), 'Pedagogical Strategies for Civics and Citizenship Education', Curriculum Corporation, www.curriculum.edu.au/civprint.htm.

Pusey, M. (1987), *Jürgen Habermas*, Ellis Horwood.

Ralston Saul, J. (1995), *The Unconscious Civilisation*, Penguin Books.

Senate Select Committee on Employment Education and Training (SCEET) (1989), *Education for Active Citizenship in Australian Schools and Youth Organisations*, AGPS.

Vught, F. A. van (1997), 'Information Technology: the Next Step in the Development of Academic Institutions', Paper delivered at the NUFFIC Seminar on Virtual Mobility: New Technologies and Internationalisation, 12 May.

Walsh, L. and Salvaris, M. (1998), 'What Qualities of Citizenship Should Schools Emphasise?' in R. Hattam, W. J. Smyth and M. Lawson, *Schooling For A Fair Go*, Leichhardt, NSW, Federation Press, pp. 27–48.

West, R., Banks, G., Baume, P., Chipman, L., Clark, D., Doherty, C., and Dow, K. L. (1997), *Learning for Life: Review of Higher Education Financing and Policy — A Policy Discussion Paper*, DEETYA.

West, R., Banks, Gary B., Peter, C., Lauchlan, C., Doreen, D., Doherty, C. and Dow, K. L. (1998) — Executive Summary www.deetya.gov.au/highered/hereview/toc.htm.

West, R., Banks, Gary B., Peter, C., Lauchlan, C., Doreen, D., Doherty, C. and Dow, K. L. (1998a), *Learning for Life: Review of Higher Education Financing and Policy Affairs — Final Report*, DEETYA.

Wyndham Committee (H. S. Wyndham, Chair) (1957), *Report of the Committee Appointed to Survey Secondary Education in New South Wales*, NSW Minister for Education.

Chapter 14: Redefining citizenship and public interest: feminist perspectives

Arneil (1999), *Politics & Feminism*, Blackwell.

Bail, K. (ed.) (1996), *DIY Feminism*, Allen & Unwin.

Barrett, M. and Phillips, A. (eds) (1992), *Destabilizing Theory: Contemporary Feminist Debates*, Polity Press.

Bell, S. (1994), *Reading, Writing and Rewriting the Prostitute Body*, Indiana University Press.

Bock, G. and James, S. (eds) (1992), *Beyond Equality and Difference: Citizenship, Feminist Politics and Female Subjectivity*, Routledge.

Brennan, D. (1999), 'Child Care: Choice or Charade?' in L. Hancock (ed.), *Women, Public Policy and the State*, Macmillan, pp. 85–98.

Dietz, M. (1985), 'Citizenship with a Feminist Face: The Problem with Maternal Thinking', *Political Theory*, vol. 13, pp. 19–37.

Dietz, M. (1998), 'Context is All: Feminism and Theories of Citizenship', in A. Phillips (ed.), *Feminism and Politics*, Oxford University Press, pp. 378–400.

Eisenstein, H. (1996), *Inside Agitators: Australian Femocrats and the State*, Allen & Unwin.

Elshtain, J. B. (1981), *Public Man, Private Woman: Women in Social and Political Thought*, Princeton University Press.

Elshtain, J. B. (1998), 'Antigone's Daughters', in A. Phillips (ed.), *Feminism and Politics*, Oxford University Press, pp. 363–77.

Franzway, S., Court, D. and Connell, R. (1989), *Staking a Claim: Feminism, Bureaucracy and the State*, Allen & Unwin.

Gunew, S. and Yeatman, A. (eds) (1993), *Feminism and the Politics of Difference*, Allen & Unwin.

Hancock, Linda (ed.), *Women, Public Policy and the State* (1999), Macmillan Education, South Yarra.

Hartmann, H. I. (1981), 'The Unhappy Marriage of Marxism and Feminism: Towards a More Progressive Union', in L. Sargent (ed.), *Women and Revolution: A Discussion of the Unhappy Marriage of Marxism and Feminism*, South End Press, pp. 1–41.

Hooks, B. (1981), *Ain't I a Woman: Black Women and Feminism*, South End Press.

Huggins, J. (1994), 'A Contemporary View of Aboriginal Women's Relationship to the White Women's Movement', in N. Grieve and A. Burns (eds), *Australian Women: Contemporary Feminist Thought*, Oxford University Press, pp. 70–9.

Huggins, J. and Saunders, K. (1993), 'Defying the Ethnographic Ventriloquists: Race, Gender and the Legacies of Colonialism', in 'Dealing with Difference: Feminism and Ethnicity', Conference Papers, *Lilith: A Feminist History Journal*, no. 8, pp. 60–70.

Jeffreys, S. (1997), *The Idea of Prostitution*, Spinifex Press.

Kaplan, G. (1996), *The Meagre Harvest: the Australian Women's Movement 1950s-1990s*, Allen & Unwin.

Lake, M. (1995), 'The Constitution of Australian Women Citizens', *Voices*, Summer.

Lake, M. (1999), *Getting Equal: The History of Australian Feminism*, Allen & Unwin.

Lumby, C. (1997), *Bad Girls: The Media, Sex and Feminism in the 1990s*, Allen & Unwin.

Lucashenko, M. (1994), 'No Other Truth: Aboriginal Women and Australian Feminism', *Social Alternatives*, vol. 12, no. 4, pp. 21–4.

Meekosha, H. and Dowse, L. (1997), 'Enabling Citizenship: Gender, Disability and Citizenship in Australia', *Feminist Review*, no. 57, pp. 49–72.

Mitchell, D. (1999), 'Family Policy and the State', in L. Hancock (ed.), *Women, Public Policy and the State*, Macmillan, pp. 73–84.

Mouffe, C. (1992), 'Feminism, Citizenship and Radical Democratic Politics', in J. Butler and J. Scott (eds) *Feminists Theorize the Political*, Routledge, pp. 369–84.

Okin, S. M. (1978), *Women in Western Political Thought*, Princeton University Press.

Pateman, C. (1988), *The Sexual Contract*, Stanford University Press.

Pateman, C. (1989), *The Disorder of Women*, Polity Press.

Pateman, C. (1992), 'Citizen Male', *Australian Left Review*, no. 137, pp. 30–3.

Phillips, A. (1991), *Engendering Democracy*, Polity Press.

Phillips, A. (1993), *Democracy and Difference*, Policy Press.

Phillips, A. (1995), *The Politics of Presence*, Clarendon Press.

Phillips, A. (1998), 'Democracy and Representation: Or, Why Should it Matter Who our Representatives Are?', in A. Phillips (ed.), *Feminism and Politics*, Oxford University Press, pp. 224–40.

Ruddick, S. (1990), *Maternal Thinking: Towards a Politics of Peace*, The Women's Press.

Sawer, M. (1990), *Sisters in Suits: Women in Public Policy in Australia*, Allen & Unwin.

Sawer, M. (1999), 'The Watchers Within: Women and the Australian State' in L. Hancock (ed.), *Women, Public Policy and the State*, Macmillan, pp. 36–53.

Sawer, M. and Simms, M. (1993), *A Woman's Place: Women and Politics in Australia*, Allen & Unwin.

Sullivan, B. and Whitehouse, G. (eds) (1996), *Gender, Politics and Citizenship in the 1990s*, University of New South Wales Press.

Summers, A. (1994), *Damned Whores and God's Police* (2nd ed.), Penguin.

Trioli, V. (1996), *Generation f: Sex, Power & the Young Feminist*, Reed Books.

Van Acker, E. (1999), *Different Voices: Gender and Politics in Australia*, Macmillan.

Vasta, E. (1991), 'Gender, Class and Ethnic Relations: The Domestic and Work Experience of Italian Migrant Women in Australia', in G. Bottomley, M. deLepervanche and J. Martin (eds), *Intersexions: Gender/Class/Culture/Ethnicity*, Allen & Unwin, pp. 159–77.

Watson, S. (ed.) (1990), *Playing the State: Australian Feminist Interventions*, Allen & Unwin, Sydney.

Yeatman, A. (1990), *Bureaucrats, Technocrats and Femocrats: Essays on the Contemporary Australian State*, Allen & Unwin.

Young, I. (1998), 'Polity and Group Difference: A Critique of the Ideal of Universal Citizenship' in A. Phillips (ed.), *Feminism and Politics*, Oxford University Press, pp. 401–29.

index